The Reluctant Pillar

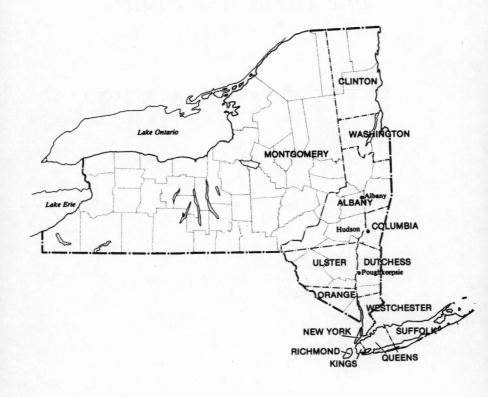

New York State, 1788

Courtesy of the University of North Carolina Press and KTO Press

THE RELUCTANT PILLAR

*New York
and the Adoption of the
Federal Constitution*

STEPHEN L. SCHECHTER

Editor

Russell Sage College
Troy, New York

The Reluctant Pillar:
New York and the Adoption of the Federal Constitution

This publication was made possible, in part, by grants
from the National Endowment for the Humanities
and the Center for the Study of Federalism,
Russell Sage College, Troy, NY 12180

Map of New York State, 1788, adapted from Boyd, Stephen R.,
The Politics of Opposition: Antifederalists and the Acceptance of the Constitution.
Millwood, New York: KTO Press, 1979.
Reproduced with permission of the publisher,
and courtesy University of North Carolina Press.

Library of Congress Cataloging in Publication Data

Main entry under title:
The reluctant pillar.
    Includes index.
    1. New York (State)—Politics and government—1775–1865—
Addresses, essays, lectures. 2. United States—Constitutional history—
Addresses, essays, lectures.
I. Schechter, Stephen L., 1945–
JK161.N7R45   1985   974.1'03   84–22266
ISBN 0-930309-00-6

Contents

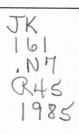

PEOPLE AND PLACES

CHRONOLOGIES

Introduction

New York was the eleventh state to ratify the federal Constitution; hardly a memorable distinction in a process that required only nine states to bring the new Constitution into effect. What distinguishes the role of New York in the debate over the Constitution is not when the state ratified but why it waited so long.

The most straightforward explanation of New York's reluctance is that both sides had an interest in the strategy of delay. As the state's minority party, Federalists were in favor of late elections and a late convention in the hopes of swaying the electorate or the delegates to their side; and, if those efforts failed, there would be no early negative vote by New York to embarrass or thwart their efforts elsewhere. Antifederalists had their own reasons for delay, as John P. Kaminski explains in his essay. Though astute observers were placing their bets on an Antifederalist majority, no good politician (and Governor George Clinton was among the best) feels sanguine about a sure bet in the world of politics. Clinton's forces needed time to assess their statewide strength and to organize the diversity of interests required to form a majority in a state like New York. There was also the hope that, with time, Antifederalists could build an interstate movement for a second constitutional convention and wait for another large state to become the first to say no.

In its barest form, then, New York was a reluctant pillar because its leaders on both sides were unwilling to risk an early decision. Delay was a purely political yet perfectly honorable choice and so too were the tactics of vocal debate and quiet organization. Alexander Hamilton was neither moralizing nor improvising when he wrote: "It has been frequently remarked, that it seems to have been reserved to the people of this country, by their conduct and

example, to decide the important question, whether societies of
men are really capable or not, of establishing good government
from reflection and choice, or whether they are forever destined
to depend, for their political constitutions, on accident and force."
This was the opening salvo of *The Federalist* No. 1, published on
27 October 1787, and its message to the voters of New York was
an appeal for time, cast in the language of republican enlighten-
ment.

About this Publication

This collection of essays is intended for both the general reader
and the specialist. The collection is organized into five sections:
theory; history; materials; people and places; and events. Each
section is designed to pave the way for the one that follows, with
the overall aim of providing the reader with the basic elements
needed for an introductory survey and reference aid to the role
of New York in the adoption of the federal Constitution. With
the exception of Martin Diamond's essay, all of the contributions
were prepared for this collection.

In his introductory essay in the first section, Daniel J. Elazar
sets out the traditions of American constitution-making and explains how those traditions helped shape the federal Constitution
and the process of ratification. Elazar begins with a discussion of
constitution-making as an eminently political act and proceeds to
unravel the dimensions of modern constitutions, the features of
American constitution-making, and the contributions of the federal Constitution to the modern principle of representation. Drawing on *The Federalist* No. 1, he then identifies three models of
constitution-making and distinguishes the American model and its
compact-covenant traditions of choice and consent.

Martin Diamond's contribution, reprinted from one of his
earlier works, offers a perspective of political thought often missing from standard histories of the ratification debate. He believes
that the most important difference between Federalists and Antifederalists concerns their expectations of what ends a republic
should serve and how those ends could best be achieved. In the
elegant prose of a philosopher, Diamond argues that Antifederalists operated on the basis of a classic "small republic" conception
of society, in which citizen virtue and freedom from despotic rule
were maintained by the very smallness of the country and pro-

tected by a federal alliance much like that envisioned in the Articles of Confederation. By contrast, Federalists sought an extended and compound republic as the best safeguard of republican freedom and virtue, and, in breaking with the past, they forever changed the meaning of federalism (then understood as an alliance) by directing it toward the ends of modern nation-building.

The contributions by political scientists on the theory of the Constitution are followed in the second section by two essays on the adoption of the Constitution and the role of New York in it. In his background essay, Richard Leffler succinctly surveys the period 1775 to 1788 as an age of constitution-making, initiated in the opening months of the American Revolution and concluded with the adoption of the federal Constitution over a decade later. He begins with a review of early state constitutions and proceeds to examine the adoption of the Articles of Confederation (America's first Constitution), the efforts to strengthen the Articles, the movement for a new Constitution, the proceedings of the Constitutional Convention in Philadelphia, and the struggle for the ratification of the new federal Constitution.

With this background in mind, we turn to the involvement of New York and its leaders in the struggle for a new Constitution. John P. Kaminski presents a most sensible and carefully researched interpretation of New York as a reluctant pillar. Drawing on the extensive files of The Documentary History of the Ratification of the Constitution Project, Kaminski provides an unbroken account of constitutional politics in New York from the adoption of the state's first constitution in 1777 through the years of consolidation by Governor George Clinton to the debate over the new federal Constitution and its final ratification in 1788. Of particular interest is the analysis of Clinton's role in state politics, the extensive treatment of county politics in the election campaigns for the state ratifying convention, the interpretation of convention politics, and the reasons for Melancton Smith's "conversion" at the convention.

The third section brings together the basic reference aids needed for the independent study of the ratification debate in New York in 1787–88. No one is better equipped to lead this task than Gaspare J. Saladino, co-editor with John Kaminski of *The Documentary History of the Ratification of the Constitution*. The first part of Saladino's essay is a guide to primary sources, including: sources for the Constitutional Convention; legislative and executive records for New York; personal papers; newspapers; pamphlets and broadsides; printed primary sources; editions of *The Federalist*; and sources for the state ratifying convention. The second part of his essay is a thoroughgoing bibliographic review of the published studies and dissertations on the ratification of the Constitution by New York. He also offers an evaluation of local histories and genealogies and concludes with suggestions for further study.

Another source is fiction in novel form, and this is the subject of Jack VanDerhoof's essay. As VanDerhoof explains, any novel is a historical novel either because it deals with some aspect of past or imagined reality or because it is itself of the past. VanDerhoof distinguishes the novel's two functions—of insight and perspective—for the historian. He reviews Howard Breslin's *Shad Run*, a novel set in Poughkeepsie, New York, during the spring of 1788 when the shad were running, the politicians were politicking, and Lancey and Dirck (the novel's principal characters) were courting. VanDerhoof concludes with a reading list of nineteen novels set at the time of the ratification debate, supplemented by works on history and fiction.

The fourth section contains reference aids that can be used to locate the people and places of the debate in New York in 1787–88. The first aid is a biographical gazetteer, compiled by this writer, presenting entries for 255 New Yorkers involved in the debate. Organized by county, each entry contains the participant's name, party affiliation, offices held and sought, town or ward of residence, and its present-day place name designation. The second aid is an inventory of the surviving homes of New York Federalists and Antifederalists. Compiled by this writer, the inventory identifies seventy-five homes still standing. The next contribution of this writer is a regional guide to the historic sites of the debate in New York. Included in this guide are inventoried homes now maintained as historic sites, supplemented by a review of related historic sites, districts, and museum collections.

The last section consists of two chronologies. The first chronology, compiled by Richard Leffler, lists the key events in the constitutional history of the United States from the meeting of the First Continental Congress in 1774 to the adoption of the U.S. Bill of Rights in 1792. The second, compiled by John Kaminski, is concerned with the principal events in New York State from the adoption of the state constitution in 1777 to the ratification of the U.S. Constitution in 1788.

Acknowledgments

This project is a labor of love, owing in no small part to the professionalism and good cheer of all those involved. First and foremost, this publication is a product of its contributors; and a special note of appreciation goes to each of them. I am particularly grateful to John P. Kaminski and Gaspare J. Saladino for their additional assistance and advice on various aspects of the publication; and to Jack VanDerhoof for his collegial support throughout this two-year undertaking.

This publication was made possible, in part, by grants from the National Endowment for the Humanities and the Center for the Study of Federalism. A special note of thanks goes to these institutions for their support. I also take this opportunity to thank Dean Robert F. Pennock of Russell Sage College who shepherded this project through its various expansions. However, the views expressed in this publication are those of the authors and do not necessarily reflect the views of the grantors.

Particular notes of appreciation have been accumulated by this writer in preparing the biographical gazetteer, inventory of homes, and guide to sites. I am especially grateful for the meticulous care and extra effort of my two research assistants, Bethann Gordon and Gail Filippini, who assisted at every step. I am also particularly grateful for the continuing advice and research assistance of James Corsaro of the New York State Library who served as a project consultant; Kathleen Roe of the New York State Archives for her advice on how to organize the entries to the gazetteer and accompanying inventory; and Kristin Gibbons and Paul Huey, Bureau of Historic Sites, New York State Office of Parks, Recreation and Historic Preservation, for reviewing the final manuscript.

As a compiler, I am indebted to the scores of local experts, including librarians, site specialists, municipal historians, and other local historians, who helped identify and confirm the various pieces of information that were finally put together to form the gazetteer, inventory, and guide.

For their countywide assistance, I am especially grateful to Michele Figliomeni, President of the Orange County Historical Society; Ruth Piwonka of the Columbia County Historical Society; Barbara Van Liew and Carol Traynor of the Society for the Preservation of Long Island Antiquities; Kenneth Hasbrouck, Ulster

County historian; and Norman Rice and the staff of the Albany Institute of History and Art. And for their boroughwide assistance, I express my thanks to Steven Barto of the Staten Island Historical Society; Professor Arthur Konop, Director of the Kelly Institute for Local Historical Studies, St. Francis College, Brooklyn; and Laura Tosi, Associate Librarian, Bronx County Historical Society.

For their assistance in completing various pieces of the puzzle in New York City, I wish to thank Joseph Bresnan, Director of Historic Parks of the City of New York; Kenneth Cobb of the Municipal Archives, New York City Department of Records and Information Services; Anne Gordon, Director of the Municipal Reference Library, also in the city department of records; Marjorie Pearson of the Landmarks Preservation Commission of the City of New York; William Butler of the Museum of the City of New York; the reference staff of the New-York Historical Society; the reference staff of the New York Public Library; and, on Staten Island, Loring McMillen, Richmond County historian.

For Long Island entries, a special appreciation to Nicholas Falco of the Queens Borough Public Library; Richard Foster, Southhampton town historian; George H. Furman of the Manor of St. George; Peggy Gerry, Roslyn Historic District Board; Jay Graybeal of the East Hampton Historical Society; Louise Green, Shelter Island town historian; Louise Hall of the Smithtown Historical Society; Margaret Joyce of the Shelter Island Historical Society; Dorothy King of the East Hampton Free Library; Rufus Langhans, Huntington town historian; David Overton, Brookhaven town historian; Vincent Seyfried, Newtown historian; Edward Smits, Director, and Richard Winsche, Nassau County Museum; Donald Wyckoff of the Wyckoff Family Foundation; the staff of the Queens County Historical Society; and the staff of the Suffolk County Historical Society.

For Westchester County entries, I am indebted to that county's town historians, particularly to Doris Auser of Yorktown; Edythe Quinn Caro of Harrison; Edmund Halsey Cox of Mount Pleasant; Alvin Jordan (retired) of Salem; Donald Marshall of Bedford; Ethel Scofield of Poundridge; and Susan Swanson of Pelham. I also wish to thank Linda McLean Connelly of the John Jay Homestead and Kathleen Johnson of Sleepy Hollow Restorations, Inc. Across the Hudson River, assistance in locating Rockland County entries was provided by Ralph Braden and Peter Talman of Spring

Valley and by Wilfred Talman of Upper Saddle River, New Jersey, Trustee Emeritus of the Holland Society.

For Dutchess County entries, I wish to thank Elizabeth Carter, Poughkeepsie city historian; Rosemary Coons, Red Hook village historian; Joyce Ghee, Dutchess County historian; DeWitt Gurnell, Rhinebeck town historian; Melodye Kaltz, Director of the Dutchess County Historical Society; Neil Larson, Historic Preservation Field Services, New York State Office of Parks, Recreation and Historic Preservation; and Willa Skinner, Fishkill town historian. Additional assistance in Ulster County was provided by Herbert Cutler, President of the Ulster County Historical Society, and by Clare McDonald of the Senate House Museum.

For Upper Hudson entries, additional assistance was provided by Elizabeth Abel, Stillwater town historian; Stefan Bielinski, Division of Historical and Anthropological Services, New York State Museum; Shirley Dunn of the Esquatak Historical Society; Charles Gehring of the New York State Library; Mary Hart of the Knickerbocker Society; Mable Hewitt, Hoosick town historian; Ruth Houghtaling, Catskill town historian; Paul Huey, Bureau of Historic Sites, New York State Office of Parks, Recreation and Historic Preservation; Doris McEachron, Argyle town historian; and Mildred Southard, Washington County historian. Finally, a special word of thanks for Mohawk Valley entries goes to Mary Antoine de Julio, Director of the Montgomery County Historical Society; Mildred Rathburn of the Heritage and Genealogical Society of Montgomery County; Volkert Veeder, Fonda village historian; and the staff of the Schenectady County Historical Society.

REDEUNT SATURNIA REGNA.

On the erection of the Eleventh PILLAR of the great National DOME, we beg leave most sincerely to felicitate "OUR DEAR COUNTRY."

Rise it will.

The foundation good—it may yet be SAVED.

The FEDERAL EDIFICE.

The metaphor of the federal structure supported by the state pillars was used elsewhere, but the *Massachusetts Centinel* was the first newspaper to print an illustration bringing the metaphor to life. On 16 January 1788 a cartoon was printed under the heading "THE FEDERAL PILLARS," showing five pillars erected with a sixth pillar labelled "Mass." in the process of being raised. The cartoon was updated as each state ratified the Constitution. This version, showing New York raised, appeared on 2 August 1788.

The Reluctant Pillar

THEORY

The U.S. Constitution and the American Tradition of Constitution-Making

DANIEL J. ELAZAR
Temple University

It may appear to be a truism to state that constitution-making is an eminently political act. Nevertheless, after a generation of withdrawal on the part of many scholars from considerations of all that is labelled "constitutional" in the world of government and politics, on the grounds that such matters are merely "formal" and hence not "real," it is a truism that needs restating. The essays in this collection fully demonstrate its validity.

Constitution-making, properly considered, brings us back to the essence of the political. However much extra-political forces may influence particular constitution-making situations or constitutional acts, ultimately both involve directly political expressions, involvements, and choices. In that sense, the dynamics of constitution-making have to do with questions of constitutional choice. A proper study of the subject, then, involves not only what is chosen but who does the choosing, and how.

Constitutional choice is more art than science. There are scientific principles involved in the making of constitutions, as the framers of the United States Constitution of 1787 demonstrated in their reliance on the "new science of politics," which had discovered such vital principles of republican regimes as separation of powers, federalism, and the institution of the presidency. But the combination of those elements and their adaptation to the constituency to be served is an art. Thus a constitution is a political artifact; making one combines science, art and craft, including the identification of basic scientific principles of constitutional design and the technologies which are derived from them by a constitutional artisan or group of artisans.

It is an even greater art to bring the constituency to endow the constitution with legitimacy. Constitutional legitimacy involves consent. It is not a commitment which can be coerced—however much people can be coerced into obedience to a particular regime. Consensual legitimacy is utterly necessary for a constitution to have real meaning and to last. The very fact that, while rule can be imposed by force, constitutions can only exist as meaningful instruments by consent, is another demonstration that constitution-making is the preeminent political act.

Dimensions of Modern Constitutions

While the idea of constitutionalism is quite ancient in the Western world and actual constitutions can be found as many as 3,000 years ago, constitution-making as we know it is a modern invention. Indeed, for all intents and purposes, it is an American invention. The essence of modern constitution-making involves the making of positive law by popular act. That is, modern constitutions are not handed down from Heaven nor simply inherited from the traditions of the past. Rather, they involve positive legislative acts on the part of the constitution-makers, according to a design which they develop as representatives of those upon whom the constitution is to be binding, and with the latter's consent to the final product. It is true that constitutions represent special or extraordinary legislation and presumably serve as bridges between eternal principles of natural justice and right and the immediate needs and circumstances of the population to be served. It can even be said that each of the elements in modern constitution-making can be found even in ancient times, but their coming together into a single comprehensive package based upon modern premises of government is what makes the difference.

There are various constitutional models in the modern world. American constitutions follow the frame of government model, delineating the basic governing structure, institutions, and procedures of the *polity* (i.e., the organized political system or political society). Hence they are not designed to be highly specific and are only explicit in connection with those elements which must be made explicit in order for the constitution to frame a government. American constitutions frame governments and not the state because what is characteristic of the American system is the absence of any sense of "the State" as a pre-existing phenomenon, a reified entity like the French *État* or German *Staat* which continues to exist regardless of how it is constitutionalized (or not constitutionalized) at any particular moment.

Frame-of-government constitutions establish polities as often as they establish governments. Indeed, in many cases the two are inseparable. In fact, written constitutions of this model often are designed to be devices for organizing new societies founded in new territories, such as the United States, Canada, Australia, New Zealand, and South Africa.

But constitutions are not only frames of government. They are also "power maps"; that is to say, they reflect the socio-economic realities of the distribution of political power in the polity served. They also reflect the moral principles underlying polities as regimes, explicitly or implicitly. These are, in fact, the three dimensions of constitutionalism, recognized as such by Aristotle and by students of the subject ever since. They can be visualized as being in a triangular relationship, as portrayed in Figure 1.

Every modern constitution must directly provide for a frame of government. Different constitutions more or less reflect the other two dimensions as well, sometimes directly and sometimes by implication. A constitution which does not sufficiently reflect and accommodate socio-economic power realities remains a dead letter. Revolutionary constitutions actually specify the new power arrangements being instituted by the revolutionary regime. While the moral underpinnings of most constitutions may be confined to codewords or phrases, in the preamble or declaration of rights, and are virtually unenforceable, they have a reality and power of their own, nonetheless. The moral dimension of the constitution serves to limit, undergird, and direct ordinary political behavior within constitutional systems. At the very least, it embraces the rules of the game; often it expresses far more. In every case, the moral basis of a constitution is an expression of the political culture of the political society it serves.

FIGURE 1
Three Dimensions of the Constitution

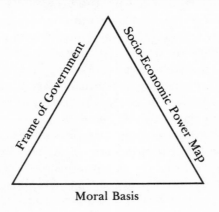

Moral Basis

Features of American
Constitution-Making

A major feature of modern constitution-making is that modern constitutions generally serve polities so large in population and extensive in territory as to require the institutions of representative government. This means that direct public involvement in the constitution-making process, as in the other processes of government, is limited to voting and various group processes. Yet at the same time, it must be real enough to be deemed consent by those who must live according to the constitution which binds them. As Martin Diamond explains in his essay, experiments in democracy prior to the American Revolution were based on the assumption that in order to allow all the citizens to participate, democratic polities had to be small enough to allow face-to-face contact among the citizenry. Unfortunately, such small polities were open to various political problems, particularly the exacerbation of the division between the rich and the poor, which generated the instability of bipolar conflict.

The American founders saw representative government as a positive good on democratic grounds. They argued that representative government is a democratic good in that it allows every citizen to participate in the choosing of his representatives, thereby giving all a meaningful role in the political process, while transferring the routine exercise of power to elected representatives. If the public was large enough, the citizenry would reflect a multiplicity of interests and so would their representatives. Bipolar instability would be avoided while the possibilities for deliberation would be maintained among the representatives, who, as a smaller group, working on a face-to-face basis, would be less prone to demagoguery. In this respect, not only did the American founders provide for the drafting of the federal Constitution by delegates from the several states but they also made provisions for a representative decision-making process in the states to achieve adoption of the constitutional instrument itself.

It is this feature which is of particular significance in the development of modern democratic republics. Constitution-making American style was taken from the hands of a single lawgiver or an ordinary legislature and given first to a special convention whose representatives were chosen expressly to write a constitution, then to the people themselves to choose other representatives who would deliberate on the work of the first set. This American invention of a constitutional convention, followed by popular ratification, revolutionized constitutionalism and the constitution-making process by making the constitution-makers representatives of popularly elected bodies, whose work was then submitted to another set of popularly elected representatives. In each case, the representatives' task was to deliberate first over the writing of the constitution, then over its appropriateness. In both cases, the people took a direct hand in the process through the election of their representatives and indirectly participated in the public discussions surrounding their deliberations during the ratification process.

By the time of the writing of the federal Constitution in 1787, Americans had more than 150 years of experience with representative government, going back to 1619, so that the principle of representation only had to be adapted to a greatly extended republic by the founders to make it work for the new United States of America. As Richard Leffler suggests in his essay, the great constitutional invention of the American revolutionary generation did not spring full-grown from the brows of the founders. The first state constitutions were adopted by the state legislatures; and the Articles of Confederation, the first constitution of the United States, was written by the Continental Congress.

The Massachusetts Constitution adopted in 1780 was the first to involve the two-step process of a convention chosen expressly to write a constitution that was then submitted to the people for ratification. In this instance, ratification occurred not by special convention but by town vote, leading to an extraordinarily vital and important set of deliberations. In 1784 New Hampshire became the first state to *require* both steps in its constitution. The federal Constitution brought the process to a new plane. The delegates to the Constitutional Convention were chosen by their respective state legislatures, all popularly elected. The Convention submitted its product to the Congress which then sent it to the states so that the voters of each state could elect delegates to a state convention to deliberate on the product of the Constitutional Convention and decide whether or not to ratify it. In this way, the constitution-making process involved not only the work of the Constitutional Convention in Philadelphia but also the campaigns for and deliberations by state ratifying conventions which significantly widened the debate to include some 1,720 delegates representing nearly 670 local constituencies.

The role of the states in this process leads to another feature of American constitution-making. The United States is a democratic republic based on representative government, but it is also a federal republic, or federal democracy. In strictly governmental terms, federalism is a form of political organization that unites separate polities within an overarching political system so that all maintain their fundamental political integrity. It distributes power among general (e.g., national) and constituent (e.g., state) governments so that they all share in the system's decision making and executing processes. In a larger sense, federalism represents the linking of a free people and their communities through lasting but limited political arrangements to protect certain rights and achieve specific common ends while preserving the respective integrities of the participants.

Federal democracy is an authentic American contribution to democratic thought and republican government. It represents a synthesis of the Puritan idea of the covenant relationship as the foundation of all proper human society and the constitutional ideas of the English "natural rights" schools of the seventeenth and early eighteenth centuries. The covenant idea (*foedus*, the Latin root of the word "federal," means covenant or compact), which the Puritans took from the Bible, demands a different kind of political relationship (and perhaps, in the long run, a different kind of human relationship) than theories of mass democracy that have attracted many adherents since the French Revolution. It emphasizes partnership between individuals, groups, and governments in the pursuit of justice; cooperative relationships that make the partnership real; and negotiation among the partners as the basis for sharing power. The Lockean understanding of the social compact as the basis for civil society represents a secularized version of the covenant principle. The synthesis of the two undergirds the original American political vision.

Contractual noncentralization—the structured dispersion of power among many centers whose legitimate authority is constitutionally guaranteed—is the key to the widespread and entrenched diffusion of power that remains the principle characteristic of federal democracy. Noncentralization is not the same as decentralization, though the latter term is frequently—and erroneously—used in its place to describe the American system. Decentralization implies the existence of a central authority, a central government. The government that can decentralize can recentralize if it so desires. Hence, in decentralized systems the diffusion of power is actually a matter of grace, not right, and as history reveals, in the long run it is usually treated as such.

In a noncentralized political system, power is so diffused that it cannot legitimately be centralized or concentrated without breaking the structure and spirit of the constitution. The United States has such a noncentralized system. We have a national—or general—government that functions powerfully in many areas for many general or nationwide purposes, but it is not a central government controlling all the lines of political communication and decision making. Our states are not creatures of the federal government but, like the latter, derive their authority directly from the people. Structurally, they are substantially immune from federal interference. Functionally, they share many activities with the federal government but without necessarily forfeiting their policy-making roles and decision-making powers. In short, they are constituent yet complete polities in their own right, not administrative subdivisions or agents of the national government.

The founders of our federal republic, taking due cognizance of what they understood to be a "new science of politics," created a political system that was unique in its time and remains a source of marvel to this day. That system was not a power pyramid, with channels for giving orders from the top to the bottom, but a matrix of authoritative governmental units located within a framework provided by the Constitution. This matrix, termed a "compound republic" by the framers, combined a national or general government—which could make authoritative decisions, especially on so-called "boundary" questions—with state governments equally authoritative within their areas of constitutional competence. The whole system was based upon the federal ("fail-safe") principle of redundancy, of more than one authoritative body responsible for the conduct of the government and capable of exercising its responsibilities; a principle, by the way, upon which much of today's cybernetic and communications systems are based.

The matrix of American government was written into the Constitution and reflected in the two-step convention method by which the Constitution was made. It was so much a part of American political culture that Washington, D.C., was consciously laid out in its image, with the executive, legislative, and judicial branches of government at different points in the matrix and the administrative offices originally placed between the first two. Despite later efforts to replace or reshape it, the matrix survives as the fundamental reality of American government, albeit in an increasingly battered (and embattled) way.

While the American matrix or compound republic is composed of multiple centers, these centers are not separated unto themselves. They are bound together within a network of distributed powers with lines of communication and decision making that force them to interact. It is not the need for interaction or common action that is special here, but the form and character of that interaction—sharing through bargaining, or negotiated cooperation rather than directive.

The noncentralized communications network itself has two rigidly rooted anchors, as it must if the matrix is to exist. The general government (that term of the eighteenth and nineteenth centuries still has great merit for the precision and clarity it brings to the subject) sets the framework for the matrix as a whole by defining and delineating the largest arena. The states, whose boundaries are constitutionally fixed, provide the basic decision-making arenas within the matrix. Both together provide the constitutional basis for the diffusion of powers necessary to prevent hierarchical domination.

The American Model
of Constitution-Making

Alexander Hamilton had three models of constitution-making in mind when he wrote: "It has been frequently remarked, that it seems to have been reserved to the people of this country, by their conduct and example, to decide the important question, whether societies of men are really capable or not, of establishing good government from reflection and choice [republican consent], or whether they are forever destined to depend, for their political constitutions, on accident [organic development] and force [conquest]." (*The Federalist* No. 1.)

The basic processes for constitutional change are shaped by the fundamental form or character of the polity. Let us refer for a moment to the question of how polities are founded. Throughout the ages, from ancient times to the present, political scientists have identified three basic models of political founding and organization: (1) polities founded by conquest which generate power pyramids in which political organization is hierarchical; (2) polities which evolved organically out of more limited forms of human organization and which over time concretize power centers which govern their peripheries; and (3) polities founded by design through covenant or compact in which power is shared through a matrix of centers framed by the government of the whole, on the basis of federal principles broadly understood. These three models are portrayed in Figure 2.

FIGURE 2
Forms of Polity and Constitutional Design

Form	*Process*	*Mechanism*	*Means of Consenting*
Hierarchical	Handed down from top	Charter	Fealty
Organic	Ordinary acts through existing institutions	Legislative acts	Informal agreement
Covenantal	Convention of partners or their representatives	Comprehensive constitution	Formal consent

In hierarchical polities, constitution-making is essentially a process of handing down a constitution from the top, the way medieval kings granted charters. Indeed, the principal constitutional mechanism in hierarchical systems is the charter. The basic means of consenting to such a constitution is through pledges of fealty up and down the hierarchy. Constitutions are changed only when there is a necessity to do so to restore fealty ties or to alter the lines of fealty. Constitutions established by contemporary authoritarian and dictatorial regimes are of this kind, whatever trappings the regime's rulers or ruler may give them to make them seem as if they were something else.

In organic polities, constitution-making occurs through the regular process of lawmaking, consisting of a series of acts negotiated among the established bodies that share in the governance of the polity, whether medieval estates, territorially-based groupings, or other mediating social and political institutions. These bodies speak for the various segments of society represented in the center, reflect their interests, and can negotiate among themselves to resolve constitutional questions as they arise. Constitutional change in such polities is relatively infrequent since it only occurs when custom and tacit understandings are no longer sufficient to determine the rules of the game. Ordinary processes of lawmaking often serve as the mechanisms for establishing such constitutional acts but those processes are involved only after consensus has been reached through negotiation.

The means of consenting to such constitutions is informal or at best quasi-formal. In organic polities, whole constitutions are rarely written and are even more rarely replaced. Rather, constitution-making and constitutional change come in bits and pieces. The United Kingdom is perhaps the prime example of an organic polity with an organic constitution. Each step in the constitution-making process from Magna Carta to the present follows this pattern.

In polities founded by covenant or compact, the process of constitution-making involves a convention of the partners to the pact, or their representatives. Constitutional change is instituted through similar conventions or through referral of the issue to all partners to the polity, that is to say, all citizens, in a referendum. The reasons for this are clear. As a pact among equals, or the political expression of such a pact, the constitution can only be changed through the consent of either all of the partners or a majority thereof if it has been so agreed. The result produced by such polities is what we commonly refer to as a written constitution, that is to say, a comprehensive document deliberately given the status of fundamental law, written, adopted, and preserved through extraordinary rather than ordinary legislative procedures.

The means of consenting to such constitutions, the way in which consent is given, and the kind of consent involved, are all formal. Constitutions as covenants, compacts, or extensions thereof can either be changed in their entirety or can involve frequent amendment, because issues of constitutional choice become part of the coin of the realm, as it were, and publics constituted as partnerships see themselves as empowered to participate in constitutional design in a relatively direct way.

This constitutional model is characteristic of the federal Constitution and, in varying degrees, of the first state constitutions. In fact, the Massachusetts Constitution of 1780 and the U.S. Constitution of 1787 are the first modern constitutions to have employed this constitutional model and its elements of covenant, comprehensive constitution, convention, consent, and federalism.

The federal Constitution does not include a covenant within its text but implicitly refers in its Preamble to the fact that such a covenant was made earlier. The beginning of that Preamble—"We the People of the United States, in Order to form a more perfect Union . . ."—refers back to the covenant contained in the Declaration of Independence which established that "people of the United States" and their perfectable union. In fact, the linkage between the two documents is often recognized so much that the two are often confused.

The Constitution, then, does not include a covenant, but it does extend the covenant struck by the Declaration of Independence. As a frame of government, the Constitution delineates the basic governing structure, institutions, and procedures of the polity; and as a protector of citizens, it declares certain rights to be basic (even before the Bill of Rights) and provides the means for their protection in civil society. In these respects, the Constitution and the Declaration of Independence are connected in a telic (or means-ends) relationship in which the Constitution establishes and frames the institutions and procedures needed to actualize and protect the first principles set out in its Preamble and in the Declaration of Independence.

Some constitutions are treated as basic, fundamental laws of the land while others are more like extraordinary statutory codes. The federal Constitution is of the former type and hence a comprehensive constitution, not a code. It is not designed to be highly specific (in fact, it is noted for its purposeful ambiguity) and is only explicit in connection with those elements essential to the two tasks of framing governing institutions and protecting citizens. The federal Constitution is not comprehensive in the sense that it can replace state constitutions. Rather, it is comprehensive as a complete statement of all those fundamentals essential to its two tasks and the larger purpose behind them; namely, of actualizing the first principles set out in its Preamble and in the Declaration of Independence.

Both in its writing and adoption, the Constitution utilized the covenantal device of conventions as a means of bringing together the partners to the pact in a setting that was both formal and extraordinary. As noted earlier, the use of conventions to write and ratify the Constitution revolutionized the constitution-making process by making the drafters of the Constitution representatives of popularly elected bodies, whose work was then submitted to another set of popularly elected representatives. The Constitution even provided for the possibility of amendment by convention, though recourse to it has been used only once to ratify an amendment (the repeal of Prohibition), but never as yet to propose an amendment.

One other point deserves to be made in this connection. The Constitution was written and ratified by committees. Despite the adage that a camel is a horse designed by a committee, these were committees that worked. Today we have theories about team behavior which can help us explain why those particular committees worked and not others. For those who live within a world of committees that might be worth exploring further as part of the commemoration of the Constitution and its ratification.

In all these respects, the federal Constitution provided a basis for formal consent that was both republican in nature and federalist in form. The constitutional process provided an important way of building consensus and hence citizen participation in determining the basic aims and procedures of government, and in providing a popular check on representative institutions. In the case of New York, for example, the election of delegates to the ratifying convention was the first election in the history of the colony and state to be based on universal manhood suffrage. At the same time, the process was federalist in form by virtue of the multiplicity of arenas in which it occurred and the consequent opportunities it provided for formal participation and representation on both state and national planes.

Conclusion

The theory that government is instituted by covenant or compact leads us to the principle that governments are only legitimate if they have been instituted by the consent of the governed. Such consent must be both informed and freely given. Consent cannot legitimately be extracted by force.

Consent is a continuing process. It is not a one-time act of the founders to be simply accepted by their descendants, but involves a continuing process of participation by which citizens constantly give or withhold their consent. This idea of consent, that "the people shall judge," is the heart of democracy. Although it is based, in part, on the idea that "the opinions of mankind" deserve "decent respect," a continuing problem for democracy is that the people be able to judge well rather than poorly. Hence, the idea of covenant also implies a certain responsibility on the part of the citizen to be informed, and of the government to be informative rather than secretive. One of the great achievements of the federal Constitution has been to harness political power and direct it toward those ends.

THEORY

The Ends of Federalism

Martin Diamond

The specific questions regarding the future of American federalism, which have come to concern contemporary Americans point us to two related underlying questions. Namely: What is federalism? What do we want from federalism?

To preserve federalism or to modify it or to make it effective and equitable are considerations that obviously raise the question of what precisely federalism is. But to ask what federalism is should raise instantly also the question of what human purposes or ends we seek to have it serve. Indeed it is only in the light of the ends of federalism that the nature of federalism becomes visible. All political institutions and processes are intelligible only in the light of the purposes or ends for which men devise them or which, unintentionally, they come to serve. They have no nature or meaningful pattern, nothing worth human attention, save with regard to such purposes or ends. So to speak, political things *are* the way they serve or fail to serve the ends sought from them.

Serve or fail to serve—there's the rub. Institutions are subtle and recalcitrant things. They are not neutral with respect to human purposes; rather each institution and process has its peculiar propensity to produce certain outcomes and not others. But it is

From Martin Diamond, "The Ends of Federalism," *Publius: The Journal of Federalism* 3, no. 2 (Fall 1973): 129–152. Copyright © 1973 Center for the Study of Federalism, Philadelphia. Excerpt reprinted by permission.

Acknowledgement is hereby gratefully made by the author to the Atlanta Foundation and, especially, to its leading spirit, Mr. Oscar van Leer, for early, generous, and understanding support. The present article is but a partial and belated recompense for the kindness.

not easy to know these propensities, to know which institutions and processes are best suited for what ends. Accordingly, human beings often do not do their political work well. They seek more than a given institution can supply, or they seek from it contradictory ends, or they blend processes which work at cross-purposes, etc. Thus deliberate purposes often give way to or become blended with unintended purposes, which institutions generate from their natures. What men want and, as it were, what their institutions want, blend and blur in the practical unfolding of affairs. From this mixture of human intention and institutional nature arises much of the frustration of political life, its confusions, tensions, failures, and partial successes.

This is the perspective within which federalism must be understood—as a political arrangement made intelligible only by the ends men seek to make it serve, and by the amenability or recalcitrance of federalism to those ends. At various times, men have sought varying ends from federalism, and the variety of federal systems has resulted from that variety of ends; each actual federal system differs from all others, as we shall see, by the peculiar blend of ends sought from the particular federal system. But the nature of federalism as such reveals itself in the ways federalism has served and failed to serve those varying ends.

I

The distinguishing characteristic of federalism is the peculiar ambivalence of the ends men seek to make it serve. Quite literally an ambivalence: Federalism is always an arrangement pointed in two contrary directions or aimed at securing two contrary ends. One end is always found in the reason why the member units do not simply consolidate themselves into one large unitary country; the other end is always found in the reason why the member units do not choose to remain simply small wholly autonomous countries. The natural tendency of any political community, whether large or small, is to completeness, to the perfection of its autonomy. Federalism is the effort deliberately to modify that tendency. Hence any given federal structure is always the institutional expression of the contradiction or tension between the particular reasons the member units have for remaining small and autonomous but not wholly, and large and consolidated but not quite.

The differences among federal systems result from the differences of these pairs of reasons for wanting federalism.

This view of federalism is fully borne out in the first federalism of which we have any knowledge. Unfortunately, a proper understanding of ancient Greek federalism, and hence of federalism as such, has been hindered by the parochial tendency of contemporary observers who take American federalism as the very model of federalism as such. From this parochial perspective, they regard Greek federalism as so peculiarly the inept and dated product of Greek political incapacity as hardly to be worthy of notice. The classic and profound expression of this condemnatory view is to be found in the first paragraph of Hamilton's *Federalist 9.* The "petty republics" of Greece, glorious as they were in other respects, were politically contemptible. They were wracked by "domestic faction and insurrection" and perpetually vibrated "between the extremes of tyranny and anarchy." The reason for this political imbecility, according to Hamilton, was their failure to achieve "a firm Union," that is, their failure to develop a satisfactory form of federalism.

But this seems unjust to the Greeks and does not see the problem of federalism with sufficient regard for their perspective. The ancient reasoning regarding federalism gave rise to what I have termed *polis*-federalism.[1] This term conveys of itself everything necessary to explain why the Greeks did not move forward to "a firm Union." Their approach to federalism rested upon the Greek view that the worthwhile life could be lived only in very small political communities. The term for these communities— polis—is usually translated as city-state; but, as Professor Leo Strauss has made clear in other connections, this translation blurs an essential point. These were not cities in our modern sense, that is, subdivisions of some larger whole, and hence readily capable of absorption or partial absorption into that whole. Rather, they were autonomous (literally: self-lawgiving) small countries. The Greeks believed that only in such an autonomous polis—no larger, say,

---

[1]The first two parts of this paper draw heavily on some work I have previously published. See "On the Relationship of Federalism and Decentralization," in D. J. Elazar *et al.*, eds., *Cooperation and Conflict* (F. E. Peacock Publishers, 1969); with W. M. Fisk and H. Garfinkel, *The Democratic Republic* (Rand McNally, 1970), pp. 133 *ff.*; "*The Federalist's* View of Federalism," in G. C. S. Benson *et al.*, *Essays on Federalism* (Institute for Studies in Federalism, 1961). (In the last named essay Hamilton's contemptuous treatment of Greek federalism, mentioned above, is considered more thoroughly.)

than Athens—could men come to know each other, truly govern themselves, share a vision of a good life, and create the conditions in which the highest human potential could be actualized. This was their deepest political "value." Thus the Greeks had a profoundly important reason to preserve the autonomy of each small country; that preservation was *the* precondition of the good life.

It followed then that any effort truly to enlarge the political community—to create government on a larger scale—necessarily made life less worthwhile. Nonetheless, they recognized the utility of union and invented federalism as a way of achieving some of the advantages of consolidation. But they could not agree with the familiar modern federal idea that the governing power of a people should be divided between a central government and a group of local governments. Because of the profound importance they attached to the polis as the complete political community, the Greeks could not agree that *any* of the governing power of the polis should be shared with a larger federal government. Typically, then, they saw in federalism only a way to have certain minimal common functions performed among a group of otherwise quite autonomous small countries, especially functions related to problems of war and common defense. That is, they saw federalism chiefly as an aspect of the foreign policy of the polis, an exercise of what Locke and Burke two thousand years later could still call the "federative power" or the foreign policy function of government.

This minimal view of federalism explains why federalism figures so little in Greek political writing (e.g., there is no serious reference to it in all of Aristotle's *Politics*) and, for that matter, in all political writing until quite modern times. Classical or pre-modern federalism was not conceived as an essential aspect of government; it had nothing to do with the nature of the polis or polity, but was only something that polities did to protect themselves or to participate in certain religious observances.

The very word federalism—"Federal . . . from foedus [faith] . . . Relating to a league or contract"[2]—suggests its essential characteristics as they were understood by perhaps all writers up until the modern era. Instead of the modern federal principle of dividing power over the same population between member states and a national government, the pre-modern theory of federalism developed three operating principles for federal systems:

[2]Samuel Johnson, *Dictionary of the English Language.*

1. The central federal body does not govern individual citizens; it deals only with the member governments. Indeed, it does not *govern* anyone, citizens or member states, but operates rather by the voluntary consent of the member states to central decision.

2. The central federal body does not deal with the fundamental political problems of the population; these are considered internal matters and remain with the member governments. The central authority (if authority is not indeed too strong a term) is confined narrowly to certain external tasks of mutual interest to the member states.

3. Each member government has an equal vote in the central federal body. This equality of suffrage derives from the equality of sovereignty possessed by the individual governments. With respect to their individual citizenries, each was equally an autonomous polis or, in later times, a sovereign government. Hence, no matter what their differing sizes or strengths, the individual governments are the equal citizens of the federal system, the equal parties to its federal compact.

The voluntary association of equal political communities for minimal central purposes—this is what federalism typically meant for more than two thousand years, from the Greek experience to the framing of the Constitution in 1787.[3] Indeed, federalism had this traditional meaning in the framing period as well. As can be seen, this list of three characteristics is precisely what the Antifederalists contended was required for a system to be federal. Now, interestingly, most of the leading Federalists held the identical view of the characteristics requisite to federalism. But what, then, of the fact that the Constitution manifestly went beyond or violated these operating principles of federalism? The Constitution created a government which governed citizens directly, dealt with important "internal" domestic problems, and which did not rest wholly or even primarily on the equal suffrage of the states. Is this not proof that the meaning of federalism was undergoing a change at the time and that a new, a modern, form of federalism was being created? Not at all. The simple fact is that no one during the framing period seriously held that the Constitution created a purely federal form of government, or that the proposed government

[3]But see Patrick Riley, *Historical Development of the Theory of Federalism, 16th-19th Centuries* (unpublished doctoral dissertation, Harvard University, 1968) for a serious examination of important federal developments in the period preceding the American Founding.

would be merely a new variety of federalism. The most accurate, and at the same time most widely held, view was that expressed by James Madison at the end of *Federalist 39*: "The proposed Constitution . . . is, in strictness, neither a national nor a federal Constitution, but a composition of both." This is, of course, also precisely the view of Tocqueville. "Evidently this is no longer a federal government, but an incomplete national government, which is neither exactly national nor exactly federal."[4]

Now this "composition," or compoundly federal and national government, emerged from the compromises of the Convention. But to understand those compromises and the kind of "federalism" that was created, it is necessary to consider briefly an important development in the history of federalism that anteceded the American Constitution. The great formulator of this new stage in federalism was Montesquieu and the federalism he discussed may be termed *small republic*-federalism. This new small republic-federalism is similar in many respects to polis-federalism, but a vital change occurs in the end or purpose of federalism. The smallness of the country is no longer conceived as the precondition to living the good life, but only as the precondition of republicanism and republican liberty; the small and intimate character of a country is no longer the precondition of all the virtues, but now only of republican citizenliness. The reason for preserving the autonomy of the small country is thus somewhat diminished, and hence the argument against enlarging the federal authority or even against complete consolidation with others into a single large country is somewhat less formidable.

To acquiesce to substantial consolidation, the Greeks would have had to revise their thinking on the entire question of politics and human existence. But now to accept such consolidation, the small republic-federalist, as taught by Montesquieu, would have to be convinced only that the republican form of government could somehow be made secure in a large country. And that is precisely what came to pass in America in 1787. Madison developed a theory in which republican government was shown to be not only compatible with a large extent of territory and quantity of population but indeed to require them. Persuaded by Madison's argument that his republicanism was safe, the small republic-federalist was now prepared to abandon or at least qualify his fed-

---

[4]*Democracy in America* (Vintage Books, n.d.), I, 164.

eralism. Thus the shift in reasoning regarding the ends of federalism—from an emphasis on the good life to an emphasis on republicanism—was a decisive step in the development of what is called modern or American federalism.

Now Montesquieu's argument reducing the end of federalism to the preservation of republicanism influenced American thinking on federalism; but in the American understanding the argument for federalism was reduced further and made even less stringent. Montesquieu's reason why republics had to be small, and hence could unite only federally and not nationally, had two strands—so to speak, a positive and a negative argument. On the positive side, republics had to be small because only in a small country (which was also egalitarian and frugal) could patriotic virtue, the "spring" or "principle" of republicanism, be engendered in the citizenry. The negative argument was based on the conviction that "a large empire supposes despotic authority in the person who governs," that is, a degree of authority incompatible with the preservation of republican liberty. This latter became the American truncated version of Montesquieu. The concern with citizenly virtue, although it obviously entered American thought and mores, received far less attention than the fear of inevitable "despotic authority" in the central government of a large country. In this truncated or attenuated small republic-federalism argument, then, the reasons for preserving the autonomy of the small member republics became still less profound than those Montesquieu gave, and far less profound than the polis-federalism reasons for preserving the autonomy of the polis. Consequently, the reasons became much less profound for limiting the functions of the central authority or for not forming a consolidated large republic under an authentic government. Antifederalists and others who maintained this attenuated small republic argument still thought in terms of federalism, but it was now a devitalized federalism, a transformed federalism, no longer fully insistent on the priority of the member republics, but one now capable of treating them merely as parts of a larger political whole.

This transformation in the reason for federalism merely to a defense against despotism in a large republic made possible the compromises from which the Constitution resulted; it explains both the great victory of the nationalists at Philadelphia in 1787 and also their partial defeat. The continued belief in federalism, although thus attenuated, obliged the leading Framers, all nationalists, to consent to the grafting on to the Constitution of some authentically federal features. And their opponents, seeing in federalism, no longer the full-blown traditional reasons for autonomous republics, but only one among many possible means for securing liberty, were contented with the modest degree of federalism they achieved. The compromise over federalism created "an incomplete national government, which is neither exactly national nor exactly federal."

The Constitution of
the United States:
The End of the Revolution

RICHARD LEFFLER

University of Wisconsin–Madison

The period 1775 to 1789 was an age of constitution-making, but the United States Constitution was hardly an innovating force for that period. It came at the end of the era, borrowed heavily from the state constitutions that came before it, and was actually a reaction to the tumult of the post-revolutionary period, an attempt to restore order and national discipline. The United States declared itself independent in 1776, but it was not until 1789 that the Constitution became the supreme law of the land. Prior to the adoption of the Constitution, all of the states had adopted their own constitutional forms, and there were two earlier forms of federal government: from 1776 until 1781 the powers of the general government were lodged in the Continental Congress, which operated under no formal constitution; from 1781 until 1789 the constitution of the United States was the Articles of Confederation. The United States Constitution was derivative in its reliance on republican and federal principles, as those terms were then understood. Where it innovated was in the joining of national and federal elements to establish an extended and compound republic.

The State Constitutions

The colonies had been pushing the Continental Congress for advice on how to reform their governments at least since June 1775. Finally, in May 1776 Congress responded by recommending to the colonies "where no government sufficient to the exigencies of their affairs have been hitherto established[,] to adopt such Government as shall, in the opinion of the Representatives of the People, best conduce to the Happiness and Safety of their Constituents in particular and America in general." Congress shortly after added a preamble that instructed the colonies to suppress all authority derived from the British Crown. Congress made no suggestions as to what features of republican government should be adopted, nor the procedures for consulting the people. Each state was free to choose its own path to legitimate government within the bounds of republicanism.

Two states, Connecticut and Rhode Island, decided to retain their colonial charters. Connecticut's General Assembly declared that the Charter of 1662 was still in effect. Rhode Island's legislature simply removed the name of the king in all official documents and replaced it with "The Governour and Company of the English colony of Rhode Island and Providence Plantations." The Charter of 1663 was otherwise still valid.

New Hampshire had begun the process of forming a new government even before Congress' actions in May. Its "charter" was simply a royal commission. Acting on a recommendation of Congress, New Hampshire elected a provincial congress to write a new constitution and to legislate for the colony as well. This congress adopted its own proposals for constitutional reform on 5 January 1776, declared itself the house of representatives, and chose the second house (the council). New Hampshire had its new form of government, one that would stand until 1784.

This pattern, in which the provincial congress wrote the constitution and transformed itself into the new government, with no consultation with the people, was followed in most of the states. Some of the congresses bowed in the direction of public consent by proposing elections for a new congress, with the specific understanding that this new congress would write a constitution. Delaware and Pennsylvania went a little further: they provided for the election of conventions that would write constitutions; but even here, the products of the conventions were not submitted to the people for their consent.

Massachusetts was different. On 1 May 1776 the General Court (the state's legislature) renounced the Charter of 1691 and consulted with the towns about the procedure to follow for adopting a constitution. Although a minority of towns called for the election of a special constitutional convention, the General Court recommended that the towns give newly elected legislators the power to write a constitution; the towns would then vote on the constitution. A constitution was proposed by the General Court in February 1778, but was defeated 9,972 to 2,083 (the individual votes were recorded because a two-thirds majority of votes cast was needed for adoption). The General Court then agreed to a constitutional convention, which met in Cambridge on 1 September 1779. On 2 March 1780 the convention adopted a final text (largely the work of John Adams), which was submitted to the towns. The towns offered many amendments and voted down many provisions, creating havoc in deciding whether the proposed constitution had been adopted by a two-thirds majority. The convention reconvened and declared that the draft had been adopted by the required majority. The constitution went into effect on 25 October 1780. Massachusetts, then, had created a new procedure for assuring the legitimacy of government: a convention was chosen with the single purpose of writing a constitution that was then ratified by the people.

These state constitutions were widely different in form. Pennsylvania and Georgia had unicameral legislatures, the rest had bicameral legislatures; in New Hampshire and South Carolina the lower house of the legislature elected the upper house; in Maryland the upper house was elected by an electoral college, and in the other states the upper house was directly elected by the people. Some of the state executives were elected by the people, others were chosen by the legislatures; most of the governors were virtually powerless, but in Massachusetts and New York the governor had strong veto powers (in New York he shared this power). The terms of officeholders varied: in some states governors could not succeed themselves, nor could legislators serve more than a few years consecutively; in other states there were no such restrictions. There were, therefore, many models of government in this period, though all were firmly rooted in the still novel republican principles of consent by the governed and popular representation.

Congress Adopts a Constitution

When Richard Henry Lee of Virginia first proposed on 7 June 1776 that "these United Colonies are, and of right ought to be, free and independent States," he also proposed that "a plan of confederation be prepared and transmitted to the respective Colonies for their consideration and approbation." On 12 June Congress appointed a committee to draft the plan of confederation. Lee's first resolution was adopted on 2 July. On 4 July Congress adopted the Declaration of Independence, and eight days later Congress was presented with a draft of "Articles of Confederation and perpetual union." The plan was debated sporadically from 22 July 1776 until 15 November 1777. The draft proposed the creation of a strong general government in which Congress would be denied only the power to tax. The states were guaranteed control over their internal affairs, but only insofar as it did not interfere with the powers of Congress.

This proposal to create a powerful Congress aroused the opposition of those who believed power should reside principally in the states and who, like Thomas Burke of North Carolina, feared "that unlimited Power can not be safely Trusted to any man or set of men on Earth." Burke warned that the unrestrained power the draft Articles gave to Congress would enable Congress to "explain away every right belonging to the States and to make their own power as unlimited as they please." Burke therefore proposed an amendment to the draft that eventually became Article II of the Articles of Confederation: "Each state retains its sovereignty, freedom and independence, and every Power, Jurisdiction and right, which is not by this confederation expressly delegated to the United States, in Congress assembled."[1]

Article II profoundly altered the nature of the Articles. The states retained their equal and sovereign status with relatively few restrictions on their powers. Congress, on the other hand, had only those powers that were specifically delegated to it. The Ar-

---

[1]Quoted in Merrill Jensen, *The Articles of Confederation: An Interpretation of the Social-Constitutional History of the American Revolution 1774–1781* (1940; reprint ed., Madison, Wis., 1976), 174. Citations are provided for quotations from letters and speeches. Quotations from official sources are not cited, but citations to these can be found in Merrill Jensen, ed., *Constitutional Documents and Records, 1776–1787* (Madison, Wis., 1976) and John P. Kaminski and Gaspare J. Saladino, eds., *Commentaries on the Constitution: Public and Private,* 5 vols. (Madison, Wis., 1981–), 1:3–43; both volumes are part of Merrill Jensen et al., eds., *The Documentary History of the Ratification of the Constitution* (Madison, Wis., 1976–).

ticles, however, gave Congress considerable power in domestic, foreign, and military affairs. Congress could declare war and peace, enter into treaties and alliances, receive and send ambassadors, and resolve interstate disputes. Congress could borrow money and emit bills of credit; it had power to maintain an army and navy. But Congress was denied some essential powers: Congress could not (1) regulate foreign and domestic commerce; (2) raise a revenue independently of the states; (3) exercise coercive power against the states to enforce its laws or collect its revenues; (4) control the western lands; or (5) act directly on the people without the interposition of the states.

Other important issues were decided during the debates in Congress on the draft Articles. The draft Articles provided that each state had one vote in Congress. The small states wanted this equality to prevent domination by the large states. The large states wanted voting to be in proportion to population. This argument took on larger ramifications: Was Congress a representative body of the states or of the people? The small states won this argument.

The draft proposed that the expenses of the general government be apportioned among the states according to population. But a serious argument developed over whether slaves should be included in the apportionment. The northern states thought they should be; the southern states disagreed. The Articles provided that expenses were to be apportioned according to the value of land granted or surveyed.

Several of the states had large land claims (some extending west to the Mississippi River and beyond) dating back to their colonial charters. The draft Articles sought to limit these claims by giving the land to the United States. The landed states naturally objected. The Articles provided that "no state shall be deprived of territory for the benefit of the United States."

Congress formally adopted the Articles on 15 November 1777 and sent them to the states for ratification. Unanimous ratification by the thirteen states was required. By 22 February 1779 twelve states had ratified. Only Maryland remained. Maryland demanded that Congress be given the power to limit the western boundaries of the states with large land claims. Virginia, which had huge claims, opposed this, but on 2 January 1781 it ceded its lands northwest of the Ohio River to Congress. Virginia's cession, the threat of British invasion, and the financial distress of the country convinced Maryland to adopt the Articles on 2 February 1781.

The state's delegates signed the Articles in Congress on 1 March 1781. The Articles were in effect. The years of the Confederation had begun.

The Efforts to Strengthen the Articles

Even before the Articles were adopted, a movement had arisen to increase the revenue going to the general government. The steady depreciation of the Continental currency during the war had rendered it useless and Congress became heavily dependent upon the requisitions it levied on the states. This was considered an inadequate method to finance the government and the war effort. In August 1780 delegates from New Hampshire, Massachusetts, Connecticut, and New York met in Boston to consider war-related problems. Among other actions, the meeting issued invitations to the New England states and New York to attend a convention in Hartford in November. New York Governor George Clinton sent the proceedings of the Boston meeting to the legislature which, in September, appointed three delegates to go to Hartford. A month later the legislature urged that Congress be given sufficient power to conduct the war effectually, including the power to use military force to require recalcitrant states to comply with congressional requisitions. The New York delegates were instructed to put such a proposal before the Hartford Convention.

In November 1780 the Hartford Convention adopted resolutions that recommended giving the commander in chief broad powers to require the states to comply with requisitions and that urged the states to give Congress power to levy import duties to provide enough revenue to pay the interest on the public debt. The convention also declared that the "implied contract" among the states certainly gave Congress "every power essential to the common defense and which had the prosecution of the war, and the establishment of our General Liberties for its immediate object."

On 1 February 1781 Thomas Burke made a motion in Congress that would have given Congress the power to levy duties, but the proposal failed on a tie vote. John Witherspoon of New Jersey then moved to give Congress the right to regulate the commercial regulations of the states so as to assure that none was contrary to the common interest, and to give Congress the power to lay import duties. Burke seconded this motion, but it too failed. Burke then renewed his own impost proposal and this time it passed.

The proposed impost measure of 1781 declared that it was "indispensibly necessary" that the states give Congress the power to levy a 5 percent duty on imports. The impost was to be used to pay the principal and interest on the war debts of the United States and was to remain in force until the debts were paid. The impost was not intended to make Congress completely independent of the states, but it was hoped that this independent source of revenue, together with revenue from the sale of the land ceded to Congress, from the post office, and from the loan office would give Congress additional stature and, as Thomas McKean of Delaware said, "give new confidence and importance [to] the United States."[2] The president of Congress, when he sent the impost proposal to the states, described it as "a permanent Fund to support the national Credit and cement more effectually the common Interest of the United States."

The proposed impost of 1781 was the first of several attempts to increase the power of Congress. None of these proposals was adopted. The impost was not adopted despite the fact that every state in the Union accepted it—except one. Just as the Articles had to be adopted by every state before they could go into effect, so too amendments had to be adopted by every state. By late summer of 1782 every state but Rhode Island had adopted the impost. Rhode Island's delegates to Congress expressed the fear that if Congress had an independent and perpetual revenue it could coerce the states economically and militarily, and they foresaw a future of unwanted and innumerable customs officials and financial officers. In November 1782 the Rhode Island legislature rejected the impost as unfair to the commercial states upon whom the greatest burden would fall and as a violation of the state's constitution, because it would allow Congress to appoint officers in the state who were not accountable to the state. The impost, by providing a permanent revenue, would make Congress "independent of their constituents; and so the proposed impost is repugnant to the liberty of the United States."

Congress defended the impost against the charges made by Rhode Island and appointed a deputation to go to Rhode Island

---

[2]Thomas McKean to the Speaker of the Delaware Council, 3 February 1781, Edmund C. Burnett, ed., *Letters of Members of the Continental Congress*, 8 vols. (Washington, D.C., 1921–1936), V:557.

to try to change its vote. But the deputation returned when it heard the news that Virginia had repealed its ratification of the impost on 6 December 1782. Virginia's act of repeal declared that the levying of taxes and duties on the people of Virginia wounded the "Sovereignty" of the state and "may prove destructive of the rights and liberty of the people."

On 6 March 1781, five days after the Articles had been ratified, Congress appointed a committee of three "to prepare a plan to invest the United States in Congress assembled with full and explicit powers" to allow the general government to execute the laws. The committee report, in the handwriting of James Madison, was presented to Congress on 16 March. The report said that Congress under the Articles had an implied power to enforce its laws against recalcitrant states. Therefore, the report recommended that the Articles be amended to allow Congress to use force to compel states to abide by their obligations. Congress did not consider the amendment until 2 May and then referred it to a grand committee of all the states. On 20 July the grand committee rejected the amendment and submitted it to another committee. This latter committee recommended a long list of reforms to make the Confederation effective. There is no record that this report was ever considered by Congress.

In July 1782 the New York legislature met in a special session and adopted resolutions calling for a congressional power to tax and a general convention to revise the Articles. These resolutions, in the handwriting of Alexander Hamilton, called the situation of America "critical," and placed most of the blame on the inability of Congress to impose discipline on the states or to raise a revenue. The legislature asked Congress to propose a constitutional convention of the states to revise the Articles, "reserving a Right to the respective Legislatures, to ratify their Determinations." The resolutions were sent to Congress and considered by several committees until September 1783, when it was recommended that action be postponed indefinitely.

On 21 February 1783 a special committee of five was appointed by Congress to consider the means of providing Congress with a revenue-raising power. This committee, two of whose members were James Madison and Alexander Hamilton, made two reports to Congress which were debated and led to the next proposal to amend the Articles—the impost of 1783.

Congress submitted the impost of 1783 to the states on 18 April 1783. The impost was a part of a thorough economic program. The states were asked to give Congress the power to lay duties on imports for twenty-five years in order to pay the principal and interest on the federal debt; the states would appoint the collectors, but Congress could remove them. In addition, the states were asked to provide supplemental funds of $1,500,000 (approximately $30,000,000 in 1984 dollars) annually for twenty-five years, also to pay the debt, the state quotas to be apportioned "according to the rule which is or may be prescribed by the articles of confederation." Both revenue proposals had to be adopted by all the states before they could take effect, and once adopted could not be revoked except by the unanimous consent of the states or by a majority of the states in Congress. Finally, the states were urged to make cessions of western lands they claimed, the revenue from the sale of which also would be used to pay the debt. This package was intended to convince different interests to work together to achieve adoption. The land cessions were described by Stephen Higginson, a Massachusetts delegate to Congress, as "sweeteners to those who oppose the impost; the impost is intended to make the quotas more palatable to some States; and the receiving it in whole is made necessary to secure the adoption of the whole, by working on the fears of those States who wish to reject a part of it only."[3] Another amendment was agreed to on the same day. This amendment would have changed the way the quotas were to be apportioned. Article VIII of the Articles provided that quotas were to be based on land valuation; the amendment proposed that the basis be changed to population, counting slaves as three-fifths of a person and not including Indians not paying taxes. A census was to be taken every three years.

Congress in 1783 was also confronted with a hostile British commercial policy. In May, June, and July the British adopted orders-in-council that placed restrictions on American trade with Great Britain and closed the British West Indies to American shipping, though allowing enumerated goods to be shipped in British vessels. John Adams, minister to Britain, viewed British commercial policy as a challenge, based on British confidence that America was too disunited to respond. Adams feared that "if there is not an authority sufficiently decisive to draw together the minds, af-

[3]Stephen Higginson to Theophilus Parsons, [7?] April 1783, *ibid.*, VII:123.

fections, and forces of the States, in their common, foreign concerns, it appears to me, we shall be the sport of transatlantic politicians of all denominations, who hate liberty in every shape, and every man who loves it, and every country that enjoys it."[4] A committee of Congress reported that British policy was "highly injurious to the welfare and Commerce of these United States. . . ."[5] In December 1783 Virginia and Pennsylvania urged that Congress be given the power to respond to the orders-in-council. Congress had to have the power to regulate commerce to respond to foreign actions.

On 30 April 1784 Congress proposed that the states grant it the power to regulate commerce for fifteen years. With this power, Congress could retaliate against any nation that did not have commercial treaties with the United States by banning imports and exports in the ships of that nation. A year later Congress considered another plan that would have vested it with power to regulate interstate and foreign commerce and to levy duties on imports and exports under certain restrictions. But Congress could not ban any imports or exports outright. This proposal badly divided Congress. James Monroe, a member of the committee that prepared the amendment, wrote to James Madison that opposition arose from those who believed that it was dangerous to concentrate too much power; that the interests of the different regions of the Union were in conflict; that any single policy would hurt one section while helping another; and that these attacks on the Confederation were intended to weaken it. The proposal was considered on 28 March, and again on 13 and 14 July, but the opposition to it was so intense that it never was sent to the states.

By 1785 the United States was deep in postwar economic depression. Groups from many sections of the country called upon Congress to do something. The New York Chamber of Commerce and a group of New York artisans both urged that Congress be given the power necessary to meet the crisis. A Philadelphia town meeting in June 1785 argued that a grant of "full constitutional powers" to regulate commerce had to be given to Congress. In Boston a boycott of British goods was organized and the merchants petitioned Congress to do whatever it could. Massachusetts Gov-

[4]John Adams to Robert R. Livingston, 18 July 1783, Charles Francis Adams, ed., *The Works of John Adams . . .* , 10 vols. (Boston, 1850–1856), VIII:108.
[5]Worthington C. Ford et al., eds., *Journals of the Continental Congress, 1774–1789 . . .* , 34 vols. (Washington, D.C., 1904–1937), XXV:628–30.

ernor James Bowdoin urged that Congress be given greater powers over commerce. The legislature responded by declaring that the powers of Congress were inadequate and urging Congress to call a convention to revise the Articles.

In November 1785 the Virginia House of Delegates considered the commercial situation of the Union. Resolutions were offered supporting a permanent grant of power to Congress to regulate foreign and domestic commerce if approved by two-thirds of the states in Congress and a power to levy a 5 percent impost. These resolutions, however, were tabled by the House. As a substitute, both houses of the Virginia legislature passed a resolution on 21 January 1786 calling for the appointment of eight delegates to meet with delegates from the other states in a commercial convention "to consider how far a uniform system in their commercial regulations may be necessary to their common interest and their permanent harmony; and to report to the several States such an act relative to this great object, as, when unanimously ratified by them, will enable the United States in Congress effectually to provide for the same." The convention was to meet in Annapolis, Maryland, on the first Monday in September 1786.

In early 1786 Congress took an inventory of how things stood. Nine states had agreed to the impost of 1783, but only three had agreed to the supplemental funds. The grant of commercial power of 1784 had been adopted by ten states. Nine states had adopted the 1783 amendment on population. The states were so far in arrears paying the requisitions that the general government was unable to pay even the interest on the public debt. There was little confidence that the Annapolis Convention would do much good either. Though Madison expected it to fail, he thought it was "better than nothing."[6] George Washington also expected little from Annapolis, but he believed "something must be done, or the fabrick must fall, for it certainly is tottering."[7] John Jay of New York, Confederation Secretary for Foreign Affairs, thought there was some chance the convention might achieve something worthwhile; he was not convinced, however, that "the people are yet

---

[6]James Madison to James Monroe, 22 January 1786, William T. Hutchinson and Robert A. Rutland et al., eds., *The Papers of James Madison* (Chicago and Charlottesville, 1962–), VIII:483.

[7]George Washington to John Jay, 18 May 1786, John C. Fitzpatrick, ed., *The Writings of George Washington . . .* , 39 vols. (Washington, D.C., 1931–1944), XXVIII:431.

ripe for such a measure."[8] He much preferred a general constitutional convention that would consider far more than commercial
matters.

Before the Annapolis Convention met, one final attempt was
made to amend the Articles. On 7 August 1786 a grand committee
of Congress proposed seven amendments to the Articles. These
amendments would have given Congress power to regulate foreign
and domestic trade, establish duties, and force the payment of
requisitions; they would have required only eleven state legislatures to approve new revenue proposals; and they would have
created a court that could hear appeals from state courts in cases
involving treaties, congressional regulations on trade and commerce, federal revenue, and important questions to which the
United States was a party. The adoption of these amendments
would have gone a long way toward the needed reform of the
Articles. There is no record that Congress ever considered the
amendments.

The Movement for a New Constitution

The Annapolis Convention met on 11 September 1786. Nine states
had appointed delegates, but only twelve delegates from New York,
New Jersey, Pennsylvania, Delaware, and Virginia attended. The
convention adopted a report that was sent to Congress and the
states, and it adjourned on 14 September.

The report, in the handwriting of Alexander Hamilton, noted
that the convention had been intended to consider only commercial matters. New Jersey, however, had authorized its delegates to
consider not only commercial matters but also *"other important
matters."* New Jersey had instructed its delegates to report an act
that, when ratified by the states, "would enable the United States
in Congress-Assembled, effectually to provide for the exigencies
of the Union." The convention stated that this mandate "was an
improvement on the original plan, and will deserve to be incorporated into that of a future Convention." The report recommended the calling of such a general convention of the states, to
consider not merely commercial affairs but all the defects of the
Union. The delegates recommended unanimously that a conven-

[8]John Jay to George Washington, 16 May 1786, Henry P. Johnston, ed., *The
Correspondence and Public Papers of John Jay . . .* , 4 vols. (New York, 1890–1893),
III:186–187.

tion meet in Philadelphia on the second Monday in May 1787 "to take into consideration the situation of the United States, to devise such further provisions as shall appear to them necessary to render the constitution of the Foederal Government adequate to the exigencies of the Union; and to report such an Act for that purpose to the United States in Congress Assembled, as when agreed to, by them, and afterwards confirmed by the Legislatures of every State will effectually provide for the same." The report was sent to the states and to Congress. Congress received the report on 20 September 1786 and on 11 October appointed a grand committee to consider it.

This was not the first proposal to call a constitutional convention to enlarge the powers of Congress. The New York legislature had made such a proposal in July 1782, and the Massachusetts legislature did so in July 1785. Thomas Paine had called for such a convention as early as 1776 in *Common Sense* and again in 1780. In 1779 Henry Laurens of South Carolina advocated a "grand council" to consider "the state of the nation."[9] In 1780 Nathanael Greene of the Continental Army reported efforts in Congress to call a convention in an effort to give Congress "powers of general jurisdiction and controul over the individual states, to bind them in all cases, where the general interest is concerned."[10] John Sullivan, a New Hampshire delegate to Congress, advocated such a convention. Alexander Hamilton, in a letter to James Duane, dated 3 September 1780, urged the calling of a convention.

In 1781, while Congress was considering the 16 March committee report to give Congress coercive power, James M. Varnum of Rhode Island suggested a convention to revise the Articles of Confederation. This convention would not be composed of members of Congress, who, according to Varnum, were so afraid of the abuse of power by government that they hesitated to grant even necessary power. In 1783 the idea of a convention was espoused by General Henry Knox and Stephen Higginson of Massachusetts, Alexander Hamilton (in pursuance of the New York legislature's call), and George Washington. James Madison, however, preferred increasing the power of Congress by amendments such as the impost. In 1784 John Francis Mercer of Virginia saw

[9]Henry Laurens to William Livingston, 5 July 1779, Burnett, *Letters*, IV:298–99.
[10]Nathanael Greene to Jeremiah Wadsworth, 8 May 1780, Knollenberg Collection, Archives and Manuscripts, Yale University.

no other way to increase the powers of Congress but by "a convocation of the states."[11] Richard Henry Lee asked Madison's opinion of a convention to revise the Articles in the same year. Madison still was unenthusiastic.

In March 1786 Congress sent a delegation to New Jersey to ask its legislature to reconsider its refusal to pay its quota of the requisition until New York ratified the impost. Charles Pinckney of South Carolina told the legislature that this was not the way to achieve reform. Instead he suggested that New Jersey ask Congress to call a convention of the states to revise the Articles, "the only true and radical remedy for our public defects."[12] Pinckney repeated this proposal in Congress in May.

All of these prior attempts at calling a general convention had failed to achieve results, and even now there was substantial opposition to the Annapolis Convention proposal because it was feared that such a convention was designed to replace the Confederation with another system of government. But the political and economic conditions in the country and the inability to reform the Articles by amendment or grants of power were strong inducements to calling a general convention, whatever the dangers. Nine days after Congress appointed a grand committee to consider the Annapolis Convention report, it voted to raise 1,300 troops in response to the agrarian revolt in Massachusetts known as Shays's Rebellion.

Shays's Rebellion is only the best known of many episodes in the agrarian reaction to the depression of the 1780s. This depression, a common postwar occurrence, caused widespread hardship for farmers and other debtors. Because of falling commodity and land prices, a shortage of specie, and high taxes, debtors could not obtain money sufficient to pay their creditors. Seven states emitted paper money which often depreciated severely in value. Stay laws were passed to give debtors protection from their creditors. A nationally distributed report alleged that the "radical" Rhode Island legislature was planning to require the redistribution of property every thirteen years. In New Hampshire, farmers surrounded the legislature and demanded the abolition of debts and taxes, and called for the equal distribution of property. The at-

[11]John Francis Mercer to James Madison, 26 November 1784, Rutland, *Madison Papers*, VIII:151.
[12]Speech of 13 March 1786 before New Jersey legislature, Burnett, *Letters*, VIII:321–30.

tempts to force the collection of debts or to foreclose mortgages led to violent incidents in most of the states.

In the spring of 1786 many Massachusetts towns petitioned the legislature for relief from taxes and debts. The legislature made only minor reforms. County conventions met in July and August and called for additional reforms and constitutional revisions. In August and September farmers closed the courts in five counties. In January 1787 the state moved to crush the rebellion by mobilizing the militia. A confrontation took place near Springfield and the rebels were routed.

On 23 November Virginia and New Jersey became the first states to pass acts authorizing the election of delegates to a general convention. Virginia declared that "the crisis is arrived" and, paraphrasing the Annapolis Convention report, proposed that its delegates meet with delegates from the other states to devise "all such alterations and further provisions, as may be necessary to render the Federal constitution adequate to the exigencies of the Union." These alterations were to be submitted to Congress and, once agreed to by Congress, were to be sent to the states for their approval. This eloquent political statement was sent to each of the states. On 4 December the Virginia legislature appointed seven delegates, including George Mason, Governor Edmund Randolph, James Madison, and George Washington.

By 10 February 1787 seven states had chosen delegates to a general convention. But Congress had not yet acted on the Annapolis Convention report, which created a constitutional problem: could the states act to revise the Articles without authority from Congress? John Jay, who had played an important role in writing New York's constitution and who had served as the state's first chief justice, thought that "the policy of *such* a convention appears questionable; their authority is to be derived from acts of State legislatures. Are the State legislatures authorized, either by themselves or others, to alter constitutions? I think not."[13] New Hampshire, in its act appointing delegates, provided that they could attend only if Congress sanctioned the convention.

Congress convened for the new federal year on 12 February. On the same day it renewed the grand committee appointed to report on the Annapolis Convention. On 19 February the committee voted to approve the Annapolis Convention report and

[13]John Jay to George Washington, Johnston, *Jay Papers*, III:228–29.

recommended that the states send delegates to a general convention to devise such proposals as would make the general government "adequate to the exigencies of the Union." This vote in the committee passed by one vote. It was by no means clear that the convention proposal would pass Congress.

At the same time Congress was considering the Annapolis Convention report, New York was taking decisive action on the impost of 1783. In May 1786 New York passed the impost, but attached conditions that Congress rejected. Congress asked New York to reconsider. On 9 February 1787 a bill came before the legislature that would have satisfied the objections of Congress. Alexander Hamilton spoke for the bill at length on 15 February, urging the necessity of increasing the powers of Congress for the benefit of the Union. After Hamilton spoke, the bill was defeated. Madison called it "a definitive veto."

On 21 February Congress took up the report of the grand committee. New York's delegates moved to consider instead a motion based on instructions from the New York legislature. These instructions, adopted the day before, ignored the report of the Annapolis Convention and the acts of the seven states that had already appointed delegates. New York's proposal, by essentially disallowing the appointments already made, might have delayed or frustrated the effort to call a convention. New York's proposal was defeated four states to three.

Congress next considered a motion from the Massachusetts delegation. The preamble of the Massachusetts motion made reference to the provisions in the Articles for amendments with the assent of Congress and the states, and it tacitly recognized the delegates that had already been appointed. The motion placed definite restrictions on the powers of the convention when it recommended that a convention be called to meet in Philadelphia on the second Monday in May "for the sole and express purpose of revising the Articles of Confederation and reporting to Congress and the several legislatures such alterations and provisions therein as shall when agreed to in Congress and confirmed by the states render the federal constitution adequate to the exigencies of government and the preservation of the Union." This motion was adopted eight states to one (Connecticut).

This vote should not obscure the fact that Congress was, as Madison put it, "much divided and embarrassed" on the question of the convention. The proposal had passed the grand committtee by one vote. The New York substitute motion had been defeated four states to three. Serious doubts existed about the constitutionality of the convention and Madison reported that suspicions existed that the convention was "a deadly blow to the existing Confederation. . . . Others viewed it in the same light, but were pleased with it as the harbinger of a better Confederation."[14]

The Constitutional Convention

Seventy-four delegates were appointed by twelve states to sit in the Constitutional Convention and fifty-five attended. Rhode Island was the lone state to refuse to be represented in the Convention. On 15 September 1787 the General Assembly of Rhode Island wrote to the president of Congress to explain the state's refusal to send a delegation. The Assembly pointed out that their delegates to Congress were elected directly by the people, "and for the Legislative body to have appointed Delegates to represent them in Convention, when they cannot appoint Delegates in Congress . . . must be absurd; as that Delegation in Convention is for the express purpose of altering a Constitution, which the people at large are only capable of appointing the Members." The legislature also cited Article XIII of the Confederation, which provided that the Articles were to be perpetual and that any alterations were to be made only after having been agreed to in Congress and ratified by the legislatures of all the states. The legislature did not feel, therefore, that it could "appoint Delegates in a Convention, which might be the means of dissolving the Congress of the Union and having a Congress without a Confederation."

The Convention was scheduled to convene on 14 May, but no quorum was achieved until 25 May. In the meantime, the delegates from Virginia, who had arrived early, were meeting together daily for several hours. When finally a quorum was present, the Convention chose George Washington to be its president and appointed a committee to prepare the rules. The committee reported on Monday, 28 May. The rules adopted for voting were similar to those that governed Congress: each state had one vote. One other rule was notable and was to be controversial—the delegates were to discuss the proceedings of the Convention with no one outside. On the next day, Governor Randolph of Virginia,

---

[14]Notes on Debates, 21 February 1787, Rutland, *Madison Papers*, IX:291.

speaking for the state's delegation, presented fifteen resolutions to the Convention. These resolutions, known as the Virginia Plan, amounted to a revolution of government.

The first resolution provided "that the articles of Confederation ought to be so corrected & enlarged as to accomplish the objects proposed by their institution; namely, 'common defence, security of liberty and general welfare.' " This first resolution was somewhat disingenuous, for the subsequent resolutions provided not for an amendment of the Articles but their total replacement. The Virginia Plan proposed a two-house legislature, with representation in both houses based on the size of the states' "Quotas of contribution" or population. This legislature was to have power to "legislate in all cases to which the separate States are incompetent"; to veto "all laws passed by the several States contravening in the opinion of the National Legislature the articles of Union; and to call forth the force of the Union agst. any member of the Union failing to fulfill its duty under the articles thereof." An executive was proposed to carry out the laws and, together with the judiciary, to veto any act of the national legislature, subject to being overridden. A national judiciary was proposed with broad jurisdiction in national issues, the judges to hold their offices during good behavior. Resolution 14 provided that the "Legislative Executive & Judiciary powers within the several States ought to be bound by oath to support the articles of Union." Resolution 15 provided that the new form of government was to be approved by Congress and then "submitted to an assembly or assemblies of Representatives, recommended by the several Legislatures to be expressly chosen by the people, to consider & decide thereon."

When Randolph presented these resolutions, he admitted that they "were not intended for a federal government—he meant a strong *consolidated* union in which the idea of states should be nearly annihilated."[15] And when, on the following day, it was pointed out that the first resolution was an inadequate description of the plan, Randolph withdrew the resolution and proposed three new ones, including one that was adopted: that "a *national* government ought to be established consisting of a *supreme* legislative, executive and judiciary." The Convention was formally voting to abandon the Confederation in favor of something dramatically

[15]Max Farrand, ed., *The Records of the Federal Convention*, 3 vols. (New Haven, 1911), I:24.

different—a national government defined by a constitution that was to be adopted not by the state legislatures, but by state conventions chosen by the people directly. Later, the Convention decided that only nine states would be needed for ratification.

The major opposition to the Virginia Plan came from a group of small-states delegates who were afraid of domination by the larger, and from other delegates who opposed the national government envisioned in the Virginia Plan. This latter group wanted to retain the Confederation. Their alternative was presented to the Convention on 15 June by William Paterson of New Jersey. Known as the New Jersey Plan, it was submitted in the form of amendments to the Articles. The first resolution provided that "the articles of Confederation ought to be so revised, corrected & enlarged, as to render the federal Constitution adequate to the exigencies of Government, & the preservation of the Union." This essentially was the 21 February resolution of Congress. The eight following resolutions would have granted Congress power to raise revenue by impost and taxation, regulate trade, apportion requisitions according to population (including three-fifths of the slaves), and enforce collection of the requisition. The New Jersey Plan also provided for an executive branch consisting of several persons chosen and removable by Congress on application by the governors of a majority of the states. A judiciary was proposed with jurisdiction to hear on appeal from the state courts cases affecting national matters. Laws of Congress and treaties were made the supreme law, enforceable by the executive. Many of these provisions had been sought for years by advocates of a stronger central government. But now a majority of the Convention felt they were inadequate, and on 19 June, after three days' debate, the Convention rejected the New Jersey Plan and accepted the amended Virginia resolutions as the basis for further debate. The vote was seven states to three.

The remainder of the Convention consisted of an effort to complete the form of the new general government: to decide precisely how much power was to be given to it and how much was to be retained by the states; to distribute power among the branches of the new government; and to resolve representational and other issues between the large and the small states, the North and the South.

The amended Virginia resolutions were debated and revised until 24 July, when they were given to a Committee of Detail which was charged with preparing a draft constitution. The committee reported on 6 August, and the draft constitution was debated until 8 September, when a Committee of Style was appointed "to revise the style of and arrange the articles agreed to by the house." Some additional resolutions were submitted to the Committee of Style on 10 September, and on the same day the Convention instructed the committee "to prepare an address to the people to accompany the present constitution, and to be laid with the same before the United States in Congress." The work of the committee was essentially to reduce the work of the Convention to order. It transformed twenty-three articles and forty sections into seven articles and twenty-one sections. Its most important act was to change the words of the preamble from "We the People of the States of New-Hampshire, Massachusetts," etc., to "We, the People of the United States. . . ."

The Committee of Style reported on 12 September. The report was read to the Convention and a four-page broadside was printed and presented to each of the delegates the next day. The Convention made some alterations and it rejected others, including proposals to require a two-thirds majority to pass commercial regulations and to give Congress the power to grant charters of incorporation or to establish a nonsectarian university. The Convention also refused, on a unanimous vote of the states, to appoint a committee to prepare a bill of rights.

On 15 September the Convention voted unanimously "to agree to the Constitution as amended." The Constitution was then ordered engrossed and printed. The engrossed Constitution was signed on 17 September by all of the delegates present, except for Elbridge Gerry of Massachusetts (who had proposed the committee to prepare a bill of rights), George Mason of Virginia (who had seconded Gerry's motion), and, ironically, Edmund Randolph, who, on 15 September, "animadverting on the indefinite and dangerous power given by the Constitution to Congress, expressing the pain he felt at differing from the body of the Convention," proposed unsuccessfully "that amendments to the plan might be offered by the State Conventions, which should be submitted to and finally decided on by another general Convention."[16] That proposal failing, he declined to sign the Constitution derived from the proposals he had introduced on 29 May.

[16]*Ibid.*, II:631.

The Constitutional Convention adjourned on 17 September at 4:00 P.M. On the following morning, the secretary of the Convention left for New York to present the Constitution to Congress along with a letter from George Washington to the president of Congress and the resolutions of the Convention concerning procedures for the ratification and implementation of the Constitution. The Constitution was read in Congress on 20 September and was assigned for its consideration on 26 September.

On 26 and 27 September a critical debate took place in Congress. The opponents of the Constitution wanted Congress to send the Constitution to the states, but they also wanted it noted that the Constitutional Convention had exceeded the authority given to it by Congress. Supporters of the Constitution wanted Congress to express its approval of the Convention's work. Richard Henry Lee, who in 1776 had first moved in Congress for independence and the preparation of a plan of government, now opposed having Congress approve the Constitution. He proposed a motion that would have taken notice of the fact that the Articles gave Congress power only to amend the Articles, not to create an entirely new system of government with the assent of only nine states. He would have sent the Constitution to the states only out of respect for the Convention. James Madison objected to Lee's motion as disrespectful to the Convention, and he declared that if Congress failed to approve the work of the Convention, it would imply a disapproval.

The supporters of the Constitution, who took the name Federalists, then proposed a resolution approving the Constitution. Lee responded with a set of amendments to the Constitution, some structural and some forming a bill of rights, including protections for freedom of religion, a free press, trial by jury, and most of the other rights now to be found in the Bill of Rights.

On the next day, 28 September, Congress reached a compromise. Federalists agreed to send the Constitution to the states without approval, only suggesting that the states submit the Constitution to conventions as recommended by the Convention. In turn, Lee's proposed amendments were removed from the manuscript Journals of Congress. The secretary of Congress sent copies of the Constitution and the resolution of Congress to each of the states.

The Struggle for Ratification

The Federalist-controlled Pennsylvania Assembly (the state's unicameral legislature) was nearing the end of its session, while Congress was debating the Constitution. Even before Congress could send the Constitution to the states, Federalists in the Assembly began the process of calling a state convention. The minority tried to prevent this by remaining away from the session, thus depriving the Assembly of the required two-thirds quorum. A mob brought in two of the minority assemblymen, who were forced to remain until the business of calling a convention was completed.

The Pennsylvania Convention met on 20 November and was the first to consider the Constitution, though Delaware was the first state to ratify on 7 December. Pennsylvania, the state with the largest city in the Union—Philadelphia—and with probably the most widely distributed newspapers, took up the debate with ferocity: partisans on both sides wrote countless newspaper items attacking and defending the Constitution. The state convention provided a forum in which James Wilson, a member of the Constitutional Convention and a prominent lawyer, and Thomas McKean, chief justice of the state supreme court, could defend and analyze the Constitution. Wilson's defenses of the Constitution, before and during the state convention, became a standard Federalist interpretation throughout the country. The minority of the Pennsylvania Convention presented a vigorous attack on the Constitution, but most of their speeches went unreported. The convention voted to ratify the Constitution on 12 December, 46 to 23. Federalists refused to allow the minority's dissent to be placed on the journals, but the dissent was published independently. This "Dissent of the Minority of the Pennsylvania Convention" offered criticisms of the Constitution that were to be repeated by Antifederalists throughout the country.

By 9 January 1788 Delaware, Pennsylvania, New Jersey, Georgia, and Connecticut had ratified the Constitution. In all but Connecticut and Pennsylvania the conventions were unanimous. But in Massachusetts, the next state, the sides were more nearly even; in fact, Antifederalists were thought to have a majority. The Massachusetts Convention contained some of the rebels of the prior winter. John Hancock, who had considerable sympathy for them, had been elected governor and was now chosen president of the state's convention. Samuel Adams, the great patriot of the Revolution, was known to harbor serious doubts about the Constitution. Elbridge Gerry, who had refused to sign the Constitution, and whose objections to it in the form of a letter to the legislature had been widely published in the newspapers, was not a member of the convention, but he was invited to attend and to answer any questions that might be put to him. The tense divisions in the convention were revealed when this arrangement led to bitter objections and nearly resulted in a fist fight between Gerry and Francis Dana, a delegate from Gerry's home district.

After three weeks of debate, it was still not clear which side would predominate. A defeat in Massachusetts would have had devastating effects in the other undecided states. Federalists, therefore, presented a set of amendments that would be recommended by the convention for adoption by the first U.S. Congress once the Constitution went into effect. Hancock was persuaded to present these amendments to the convention as his own. On 6 February the Constitution was ratified, 187 to 168. This technique of proposing recommendatory amendments was to be crucial in achieving ratification in other states.

The New Hampshire Convention assembled on 13 February. It was generally believed that ratification was assured. But Federalists were shocked to discover that many of the delegates had been instructed by their constituents not to vote for ratification. Rather than risk defeat, Federalists maneuvered an adjournment. On 24 March Rhode Island held a referendum on the Constitution. Federalists in Providence and Newport boycotted the referendum, but the results were still dramatic: 2,711 to 239 against the Constitution.

When Maryland ratified on 26 April and South Carolina followed on 23 May, eight states had ratified, one less than needed to put the Constitution into effect. Virginia had chosen its delegates in March and the returns indicated that ratification would not be achieved easily. In New York, elections for convention delegates were held from 29 April to 3 May, and here too it seemed that there was an overwhelming majority against ratification.

The Virginia Convention convened on 2 June and was marked by the brilliant opposition of the great orator and patriot Patrick Henry. His major adversary in defense of the Constitution was James Madison, who received important support, in yet another twist, from Edmund Randolph. Henry wanted amendments to be adopted before he would agree to ratification. Madison and Randolph argued that ratification should come first. On 25 June the Virginia Convention ratified the Constitution by a vote of 89 to 79 and proposed a bill of rights and other, substantive, amendments.

The New York Convention convened on 17 June. Alexander Hamilton asked Madison to send riders immediately with news of Virginia's ratification to help his effort in Poughkeepsie, and made similar arrangements for news of New Hampshire's ratification. On 21 June the second session of the New Hampshire Convention ratified the Constitution and New Hampshire became the ninth and decisive state. News of New Hampshire's ratification reached New York on 24 June and news of Virginia's ratification arrived on 2 July. The issue in New York then became whether New York would refuse to join the Union with those states who had ratified the new government. Melancton Smith, an Antifederalist, was a major architect of a compromise that allowed unconditional ratification, but called for a second constitutional convention to amend the Constitution. On 26 July New York ratified the Constitution 30 to 27, proposed amendments, and adopted a circular letter to be sent to the other states that called for a second constitutional convention. Federalists elsewhere would almost have preferred no ratification by New York to this, but it was the price that had to be paid.

On 2 August North Carolina became the last state to act in 1788 when it declined to ratify the Constitution until a bill of rights had been adopted along with substantive amendments. But it was too late for the opposition. The ratification by New Hampshire had been read to Congress in July and Congress appointed a committee to prepare an act for putting the new Constitution into effect. On 13 September Congress adopted an ordinance for the election of electors for president of the United States and the meeting of the new government under the new Constitution. The long struggle initiated at the beginning of the Revolution to create a system of effective governance was over.

New York:
The Reluctant Pillar

JOHN P. KAMINSKI
University of Wisconsin–Madison

On 20 April 1777 the state of New York adopted its first constitution. It was, beyond a doubt, one of the most conservative Whig statements of government established by any of the thirteen rebellious colonies. The governor was elected by the people for a three-year term, while state senators were elected by the people for four-year terms. Property and residence requirements were established to vote for these officials, as well as for assemblymen, who were elected annually by the people. The state chancellor, judges of the state supreme court, and county judges were appointed for life terms during good behavior by a council of appointment consisting of the governor and four senators elected by the Assembly. A council of revision composed of the governor, the chancellor, and the judges of the supreme court had the power to revise or veto all bills passed by the legislature. The veto or changes remained in effect unless overridden by two-thirds of both houses of the legislature.

Aristocratic politicians were pleased with their newly created government, and they looked forward to electing one of their own as governor in June 1777. Much to their chagrin, however, the aristocratic Philip Schuyler of Albany was defeated by George Clinton. In a letter dated 14 July to John Jay, Schuyler lamented his loss to Clinton, a man who was by "family and connections" not entitled to "so distinguished a predominance." The election of Clinton heralded the onset of a new duality in New York politics that must be recognized to comprehend New York's history during the Confederation Period in general, and to understand how the state reacted to the proposed federal Constitution of 1787 in particular.

Prior to the Revolution, politics in New York was usually a battleground for the Livingstons and the DeLanceys. These aristocratic, manorial families each had its adherents and they strove to curry the favor of the colony's freemen. With the Revolution, the Loyalist DeLancey family was removed from political contention. The field, however, was not left solely to the Livingstons. The election of George Clinton epitomized the Revolution, and, just as the Revolution repudiated the Loyalist DeLanceys, so too the election of Clinton was a repudiation of aristocratic dominance in state government.

George Clinton of Ulster County was a modest, Loyalist-hating, lawyer-general-farmer. The idol of the country yeomen, Clinton exemplified the new era of opportunity. As such, a host of rising young lawyers, merchants, militia officers, and men from the lesser branches of aristocratic manorial families flocked to his side. But Clinton's primary electoral support came from yeoman and tenant farmers in the northern counties of Orange, Ulster, Albany, Washington, and Montgomery.

Clinton's opponents were concentrated in New York City, the cities of Albany and Hudson (the latter established in 1785), other commercial settlements along the Hudson River, and the lower counties of Kings, Queens, Richmond, and Westchester. Anti-Clintonian leaders were generally the wealthiest manor lords, lawyers, bankers, and merchants.

When George Clinton was first elected governor, the aristocracy thought him unqualified for the position. They believed that he would be unseated at the next election in 1780. Military exigencies, however, worked in Clinton's favor and he was reelected for a second term. In 1783 peace brought added prestige for the chief executive and he was easily reelected. Three years later, the governor maintained the support of most New York farmers and state public creditors with his endorsement of an antidepression paper money program. Aristocrats, merchants, and lawyers in New York and other states feared the "radical" demands of debtor-farmers and the relief programs initiated by popularly elected state legislatures. Anti-Clintonians realized that the governor was unbeatable within the state, and consequently did not run a candidate against Clinton in 1786. Instead, they worked with like-minded men in other states to strengthen the general government, in part at least to limit the radical policies of the state legislatures. Thus, the original aristocratic-middle class division of 1777 broadened into a continual political confrontation within New York between the northern and southern counties, the rural and commercial interests, and finally between the supporters of a confederation of sovereign states and advocates for a strengthened general government with coercive powers over the states and their citizens. Political skirmishes were fought throughout the Confederation years; the battle over the Constitution in 1787–88 was the most intense, but not the final, engagement.

The Revolution
and the Necessity of Union

New York probably suffered more than any other state during the war. Throughout these years, New York was often the theater for military activity, and for much of this time New York City and the six lower counties were occupied by British forces. Because of its military situation, New York constantly sought assistance from Congress; but because of its lack of power over the states, Congress was unable to offer New York much aid.

New Yorkers realized the weakness of Congress and sought to correct the problem. On this point, Clintonians and Anti-Clintonians agreed. In early September of 1780 Alexander Hamilton called for a national convention to meet and grant Congress additional powers. On 7 September Governor Clinton addressed the state legislature and echoed Hamilton's appeal for a stronger Congress. The governor proposed "that in all Matters which relate to the war, their Requisitions may be peremptory." Toward this end, the New York legislature on 25–26 September appointed three delegates to a convention scheduled to meet in November in Hartford, Connecticut. The convention was "to propose and agree to . . . all such Measures as shall appear calculated to give a Vigor to the governing powers, equal to the present Crisis." On 10 October the legislature instructed its congressional delegates and its commissioners to the Hartford Convention that Congress should "exercise every Power which they may deem necessary for an effectual Prosecution of the war." If any state failed to pay its share of the expenses apportioned by Congress, the army should be marched into that state and by "a Military Force, compel it to furnish its deficiency."

The Hartford Convention, composed of delegates from New England and New York (John Sloss Hobart and Egbert Benson), met from 8 to 22 November 1780 and proposed that the army be empowered to collect revenue and that Congress be given the power to levy import duties. Within three months Congress itself asked the states to grant it the power to levy a 5 percent import duty, the revenue of which was earmarked to pay the principal and interest of the federal debt. New York acted swiftly and on 19 March approved this impost of 1781. Eleven other states followed New York's example. Only Rhode Island refused its assent; but, because unanimous approval of the states was required to amend the Articles of Confederation, the impost was lost.

As 1781 drew to a close, the military prospects had brightened for the United States as a whole. But New York City was still occupied by British troops, and financially the entire country was in desperate straits. The army had not been paid, public creditors were not being paid the interest due on their securities, and the public debt had skyrocketed. In this atmosphere, a special session of the New York legislature met in early July 1782 and on 21 July resolved that Congress be given the power to tax and that a general convention be called to amend the Articles of Confederation accordingly. These resolutions were forwarded to Congress, but no action was ever taken.

Peace and the New Policy

On 30 November 1782 the preliminary articles of peace were signed in Europe and hostilities ceased in America in mid-March 1783. With the cessation of hostilities, the military justification for a strong Union came to an end, and the Clintonians reassessed their state's position within the Union.

Most New Yorkers agreed with the bleak picture painted by James Duane, who in mid-February 1783 wrote Alexander Hamilton that "There is such Confusion in the present Administration of our State Finances, and the Weight of our Debts is so burthensome, that a Remedy must be provided." But, at the same time, Congress faced a national financial disaster, which it appeared incapable of averting unless it was given greater power to collect revenue. There was, therefore, both a state and a national financial crisis, and it seemed impossible that both emergencies could be addressed simultaneously. Moreover, wrote Alexander Hamilton, "There are two classes of men . . . one attached to state the other to Continental politics," and in his view "the seeds of disunion [were] much more numerous than those of union."[1]

The Clintonians believed that throughout the war New York had contributed more than its rightful share of men and money, while other states had not done their fair share. Since it was not possible to solve both the state and the federal financial crises, and since the other states were not likely to assist Congress, the Clintonians decided that all their efforts would be directed at making New York as strong as possible within the loose federal alliance of the Articles of Confederation. Toward this end, the Clintonians devised a new system of revenue composed of three parts: (1) a state impost, (2) the sale of Loyalist estates and unsettled state lands, and (3) a moderate real estate and personal property tax. This new system exacerbated the dualism of New York by pitting the Clintonians against those individuals who wanted to solve the country's economic morass by strengthening Congress.

The first and most revealing step in this new policy was taken on 15 March 1783 when the Clintonians repealed New York's earlier approval of the federal impost of 1781. The state impost was to be the cornerstone of the Clintonian financial system, and as such, it could not be given up for federal use. Annual income from the state impost during the Confederation years ranged between $100,000 and $225,000, and represented one-third to over one-half of the state's annual income.[2]

The importance of the impost to the Clintonians was accentuated because much of it was paid by non-New Yorkers. About half of all foreign goods imported by Connecticut and New Jersey came through the port of New York. These two states, along with Vermont, Massachusetts and the southern states to a lesser degree, contributed to New York's impost revenues. Thus, out-of-staters helped reduce New York's economic woes. The impost was also

---

[1]To George Washington, Philadelphia, 9 April 1783, Edmund C. Burnett, ed., *Letters of Members of the Continental Congress* [LMCC], 8 vols. (Washington, D.C., 1921–36), VII:129.

[2]All monetary figures are given in 1787 dollars. In 1787, $2.50 was equivalent to £1 New York currency. A 1787 dollar was approximately twenty times the value of a 1984 dollar.

a hidden tax on consumers collected by merchants—a group not well represented in the ranks of the Clintonians. By forcing merchants to pay the impost, albeit through increasing the prices of imported goods, the Clintonians reduced the levies on real and personal property. In this way, the Clintonians championed yeoman farmers who supported the governor in his efforts to keep land taxes low.

Besides the impost, the Clintonians hoped to raise significant revenue from land sales. Almost $4,000,000 was raised from the sale of the confiscated Loyalist estates. Whig manor lords did not like to see these once glorious estates broken up and sold in small parcels. Nationalists also opposed the Clintonians' confiscation of Loyalist property in those territories recently evacuated by British troops in 1783. It was believed that Congress would suffer if the state violated the treaty of peace by confiscating Loyalist property.

The state's unsettled land was even more important than Loyalist property to the Clintonian program. This vast territory would guarantee huge revenues to the state for years to come, but the Clintonians saw a danger to this resource. New York's claim to the area known as Vermont was disputed by New Hampshire and Massachusetts. New York pursued its claims in Congress with little success. The state's congressional delegation reported to Governor Clinton on 9 April 1784 that Congress is determined "not to do any thing about that matter, expecting that in Time we shall be obliged to consent that [Vermont should] . . . become a seperate State." In the same letter, the delegates warned Governor Clinton about possible attempts to seize New York's northwestern territory. "Upon the whole Sir it is our opinion that the utmost Vigilence ought to be exercised to prevent any encroachment on our Territory as we are to expect no protection otherwise than from our own arms." Three weeks later, congressional delegate Ephraim Paine wrote that "it appears to be the general Sense" of Congress "that the western Country ought to be Considered as belonging to the united States in Common." Therefore, Paine concluded, "it is high time for our State to tak[e] the Same measures as though it was Sorounded with open and avowed Enemies." On 4 June 1784 Paine's fellow delegate Charles DeWitt repeated the warning: "I hope the Legislature have taken every precaution respecting the W. Territory. I believe Sir a Plan is formed and perhaps wrought into System to take that Country from us."[3]

[3]LMCC, VII:487–88, 504–5, 545.

The Clintonians thus clearly saw that any attempt to strengthen Congress probably would result in the loss of the state impost and future sales of lands from confiscated Loyalist estates, from Vermont, and from northwestern New York. If these sources of revenue were lost, real estate and personal property taxes would have to be raised significantly to pay the state debt and to meet the regular expenses of government. New York had already paid more than its rightful portion for the Union's independence from Great Britain. The Clintonians would not now allow Congress to wrest away the state's most productive sources of revenue.

The Depression of 1785–86

The end of the Revolution in New York was accompanied by a short period of prosperity followed by a serious depression, the "bad times" of 1785–86. These depression years were marked by public and private indebtedness, disorganization of trade, contraction of the circulating currency, and drastically reduced farm prices. In an effort to relieve the hardships of the depression, and to stimulate the economy, a demand arose for the state to create a land bank that would loan paper money on real estate collateral.

By spring of 1786 Governor Clinton supported the emission of paper money. He and his supporters saw the demand for paper money as an opportunity to aid distressed debtors and to improve their own political position. A provision was added to the paper money bill that appropriated $125,000 of paper money for a fund to pay the interest and principal on the entire state debt and on two kinds of federal securities owned by New Yorkers. The federal securities funded by the bill amounted to $1,400,000 and were owned by over 25 percent of all New York freemen. The remaining $3,600,000 in federal securities, owned by several hundred wealthy, anti-Clinton New Yorkers, was untouched by the bill. Clinton was, therefore, able to get the paper money bill enacted, cement his strength among state public creditors, and gain new support from the majority of federal public creditors, while not unduly benefiting his opponents. It was now in the interest of New York public creditors to support the state's financial interests over those of the Union.

The paper money act, passed on 18 April 1786, authorized $500,000 of paper currency—three-fourths earmarked for mortgages on real estate at 5 percent annual interest for fourteen years and the remainder to be paid to New York's public creditors. The paper money could be used to pay taxes and was legal tender in payment of private debts in case of suits. The paper money did not depreciate and it helped many hard-pressed yeoman debtors avoid bankruptcy and foreclosure proceedings. The paper money, along with revenue from land sales and the state impost, allowed New York to purchase large quantities of federal securities with interest-bearing and interest-paying state securities. By 1790 the state of New York owned federal securities worth over $2,880,000 in specie. The interest due New York on these securities more than equalled the annual requisitions on the state by Congress. New York had been transformed from a debtor state into one of the wealthiest creditor states in the Union. The interest of most New Yorkers had become connected with the state and its governor rather than with the general government.

Commerce

Although Governor Clinton made a concerted effort to attach yeomen to his policies, he also wholeheartedly encouraged merchants involved in foreign commerce. The more trade that came through the port of New York, the greater the revenue for the state treasury from the impost. Therefore, when commerce deteriorated in 1785–86, the Clintonians joined their political adversaries in seeking ways to stimulate trade. This Clintonian position explains why New York on 4 April 1785 adopted the authorization giving Congress commercial power to restrain trade with countries without commercial treaties with the United States. It also explains why the New York legislature responded so quickly and positively to Virginia's call for a commercial convention.

On 21 January 1786 the Virginia legislature appointed five commissioners to meet with commissioners from other states to consider trade problems. Governor Clinton submitted Virginia's proposal to the legislature on 14 March. The next day the Assembly resolved, and the Senate concurred on 17 March, that five commissioners be appointed to attend this commercial convention. Over a month later, on 20 April, the Assembly appointed Alexander Hamilton, Robert C. Livingston (of the upper manor family), and Leonard Gansevoort to the convention. On 5 May, the last day of the legislative session, the Senate accepted the Assembly's resolution with the addition of three more commissioners—Robert

R. Livingston, James Duane, and Egbert Benson. All six men had consistently supported greater power for Congress.

At least three commissioners were required to attend the convention and a report had to be made to the legislature. These commissioners were authorized "to take into consideration the trade and commerce of the United States—to consider how far an uniform system in their commercial intercourse and regulations, may be necessary to their common interest and permanent harmony." Before it could take effect, however, the report of the convention had to be approved by all of the states. Thus, the New York legislature was willing to consider a national commercial plan, but it reserved the right to reject any plan that might be detrimental to the state.

Only Alexander Hamilton and Egbert Benson attended the Annapolis Convention in September 1786, where they met with commissioners from New Jersey, Pennsylvania, Delaware, and Virginia. The commissioners agreed to a report drafted by Hamilton which acknowledged the sparseness of attendance, and therefore called for a general convention of all the states to meet in Philadelphia the following May to revise the Articles of Confederation.

The Impost of 1783

By the beginning of 1783 Congress' financial condition was desperate. During the first four months of the year, Congress debated measures to alleviate the economic morass. In April a unified program was adopted that included another request for a federal impost. The two New York delegates to Congress—Alexander Hamilton and William Floyd—divided the state's vote over the financial package. Ironically, nationalist Hamilton voted against the plan, while future Antifederalist Floyd supported it. Although Hamilton believed that the congressional proposal was too weak and that a stronger alternative should be presented to the states, he urged Governor Clinton to support the impost of 1783.

The Clintonians had hoped some other state would reject Congress' new attempt to seize New York's most lucrative revenue producer. But by spring 1786 all of the states except New York had adopted the impost in one form or another. New York could not remain aloof—it had to face the issue.

In order to sway public opinion in their favor, the Clintonians mounted a masterful newspaper campaign. With Abraham Yates,

Jr., in the lead, writing as "Sydney," "Rough Hewer," and "Rough Hewer, Jr.," the Clintonians emphasized the dangers inherent in giving Congress an independent source of revenue. With its own income guaranteed, Congress would soon "swallow up" the state legislatures; and with the disappearance of the states as viable political entities, freemen would lose many of their hard won rights. Thus, at least in the public debate, the issue was not primarily economic. New York, by rejecting the impost, could save the entire country from becoming a centralized despotism.

All attention was focused on the New York legislature as it debated the impost in May 1786. Clintonians were keenly aware that their motives would be questioned if the impost were rejected unequivocally. Consequently, the Clintonian legislature chose a middle ground. New York adopted the impost but refused to give up the right to supervise and remove the collectors of the impost. The state also reserved the right to pay the impost revenue to Congress in the recently issued state paper money.

On 4 May New York's conditional approval of the impost was submitted to Congress, which appointed a committee to examine the various state actions on the impost. The committee reported that New York's and Pennsylvania's ratifications were unacceptable, and on 11 August Congress requested Governor Clinton to call a special session of the legislature to reconsider the matter. Five days later the governor rejected this request, citing the state's constitutional provision that allowed the governor to call special sessions only on "extraordinary occasions." Congressional delegates condemned New York for endangering the entire country and sent a second appeal to Governor Clinton for a special legislative session. The governor again refused.

When the legislature convened in January 1787, the Hamiltonian forces tried to censure the governor for not calling an early session of the legislature. The Assembly, however, approved the governor's inaction by a vote of 39 to 9. Stephen Mix Mitchell, a Connecticut delegate to Congress, wrote that the Assembly's approbation of Clinton's action was tantamount to giving "Congress a Slap in the face."[4]

The Assembly submitted the impost to a three-man committee made up of two Hamiltonians and one Clintonian. On 9 February this committee reported a bill granting Congress the

[4]To Jeremiah Wadsworth, New York, 24 January 1787, LMCC, VIII:531.

impost with the power to supervise and remove collectors. Within a week the Assembly voted 38 to 19 to remove the clause giving Congress authority over the collectors. Despite the efforts of Hamilton and his allies, New York had not changed its position—revenue from duties collected on imported goods coming through the port of New York would still flow into the state treasury. The Assembly's action had, according to James Madison, "put a definitive veto on the Impost." Madison described the politics of New York as "directed by individual interests and plans, which might be incommoded by the controul of an efficient federal Government."[5]

Congress Calls the Constitutional Convention

By 20 September 1786 Congress had received the report of the Annapolis Convention calling for a general convention. In order to remove any doubt about the constitutionality of the general convention, Congress had to sanction such a meeting. Consequently, the Annapolis Convention report was turned over to a committee of Congress on 11 October. Because of the end of the federal year, however, no further action was taken in 1786.

The new federal year began when Congress attained a quorum on 12 February 1787. By this time several states had already appointed delegates to the general convention. On 19 February the congressional committee appointed four months earlier endorsed the Annapolis Convention report by a one-vote majority. When Congress took up the committee report on 21 February, New York delegates Melancton Smith and Egbert Benson made a motion to postpone consideration of the report in order to consider another resolution. On 20 February they had been instructed by their legislature to move in Congress for the appointment of a general convention empowered to consider "alterations and amendments" to the Articles of Confederation that would "render them adequate to the preservation and support of the Union."

Some delegates to Congress viewed New York's proposal with skepticism, especially in light of the Assembly's recent defeat of the impost. Since New York's proposal ignored the Annapolis Convention report and the actions of those states that had already appointed delegates to a general convention, it was believed by some that New York was attempting to sabotage the entire convention movement by dividing Congress between two different proposals. Other delegates saw the value in the convention proposal originating from a state rather than from an extra-legal body such as the Annapolis Convention.

New York's motion was rejected by Congress four states to three with two states divided. Nathan Dane of Massachusetts then moved to postpone the committee report in order to consider another motion calling a convention. Dane's motion implicitly acknowledged the Annapolis Convention report and sanctioned the elections of the delegates that had already taken place. But the resolution limited the power of the proposed convention which was called "for the sole and express purpose of revising the Articles of Confederation." Any proposals from the convention would have to be approved by Congress and by the states before taking effect. This motion was adopted by Congress on 21 February 1787 by a vote of eight states to one.

New York Elects Delegates
to the Constitutional Convention

On 13 January 1787 Governor Clinton addressed the legislature and delivered a copy of the Annapolis Convention report. Ten days later the report and a copy of Virginia's act appointing delegates to a constitutional convention were submitted to a five-man Assembly committee. No record of a committee report exists. On 23 February 1787 Governor Clinton sent the legislature the congressional resolution calling a general convention. Three days later the Assembly resolved that five delegates be appointed to the convention by joint ballot of both houses. The Senate, objecting to its inferior status in a joint ballot, disagreed; and on 28 February proposed that three delegates be appointed by the two houses voting separately—the manner specified in the state constitution for the election of delegates to Congress. On 28 February Senator Abraham Yates, Jr., attempted to limit the power of the convention by proposing that the alterations and amendments suggested by the convention be "not repugnant to or inconsistent with the constitution of this state." Yates's resolution was strenuously debated and was finally rejected by the casting vote of Pierre Van

Cortlandt, the president of the Senate, after the senators had divided evenly nine to nine.

The Assembly agreed to the Senate's resolution and on 6 March the open balloting for convention delegates was held. Each assemblyman voted for three candidates. State Supreme Court Justice Robert Yates and Alexander Hamilton appear to have been previously agreed upon as two of the three delegates, because Yates received the unanimous support of all fifty-two assemblymen, and Hamilton received all but three votes. The real fight came over the third delegate. Albany Mayor John Lansing, Jr., was nominated with twenty-six votes, only three votes more than New York Mayor James Duane. Chancellor Robert R. Livingston received four votes, John Taylor two, and Melancton Smith one. The Senate also nominated Yates, Hamilton, and Lansing. The two houses met together in the Assembly chambers, compared lists, and adjourned to their separate chambers where they passed resolutions officially appointing the three men. On 16 April Alexander Hamilton moved in the Assembly and it was agreed that two more delegates be appointed to the convention. Two days later, however, the Senate rejected this attempt to enlarge the delegation.

New York in the
Constitutional Convention

New York's three delegates to the Constitutional Convention were respectable, but, unlike some other states, New York's most prestigious men either did not choose to be candidates or were overlooked by the legislature. Unlike his counterparts in New Jersey, Pennsylvania, and Virginia, Governor Clinton did not opt to become a delegate. Robert R. Livingston, Philip Schuyler, Lewis Morris, James Duane, and the other great manor lords were not delegates to the Convention. Egbert Benson, Richard Harison, John Jay, and Samuel Jones, the state's most prominent attorneys, also avoided the Convention as did the merchant captains of New York City.

Albany lawyer Robert Yates was the senior New York delegate. He was forty-nine years old and had served on the state Supreme Court since its establishment in 1777. Thirty-three-year-old John Lansing, Jr., was mayor of Albany and was perhaps the wealthiest member of the Clintonian party. He had studied law with Robert Yates, and had been a delegate to Congress in 1785 and a state assemblyman from 1780 to 1784 and again in 1786 when he served as speaker. Alexander Hamilton, a thirty-year-old New York City lawyer and Philip Schuyler's son-in-law, had distinguished himself in the army during the Revolution, and afterwards as a member of Congress in 1782–83, a commissioner to the Annapolis Convention in 1786, and as a state assemblyman in 1787. Hamilton's reputation as a strong nationalist was well known. Yates and Lansing, on the other hand, were thought to be opponents of any serious attempt to strengthen the general government, especially if that entailed the loss of the state's impost. James Madison, in New York City as a Virginia delegate to Congress, described New York's two Clintonian delegates as leaning "too much towards State considerations to be good members of an Assembly which will only be useful in proportion to its superiority to partial views & interests." In a letter to George Washington, Madison wrote that Yates and Lansing were thought "to be pretty much linked to the antifederal party here, and are likely of course to be a clog on their Colleague."[6]

Yates and Hamilton first attended the Convention on 25 May. Lansing first attended a week later on 2 June. The early days of the Convention were ominous for Yates. On 30 May he voted with the minority against his fellow New Yorker in opposing a motion that called for the Convention to create a "*national* Government." On 1 June the New York justice wrote to his uncle Abraham Yates, Jr., that he had grave doubts about the Convention.

During the Convention, both Yates and Lansing aligned with a minority of delegates who favored a revision of the Articles of Confederation that would strengthen Congress without relinquishing the sovereignty of the individual states. The two Albanyites usually voted in tandem against Hamilton, and it was said that Lansing usually followed the lead and was deferential to his former legal mentor.

On 16 June Lansing expressed his own position.[7] He believed that the mere consideration of a national government violated the resolution of Congress and the delegates' commissions from their states. New York, he said, "would never have concurred in sending

[6]To Edmund Randolph, New York, 11 March 1787, and to George Washington, New York, 18 March 1787, Rutland, *Madison*, IX:307, 315.

[7]Max Farrand, ed., *The Records of the Federal Convention*, 3 vols. (New Haven, Conn., 1911), I:249–50, 257–58, 263–64, 267.

deputies to the convention, if she had supposed the deliberations were to turn on a consolidation of the States, and a National Government." Furthermore, the states would never "adopt & ratify a scheme which they had never authorized us to propose and which so far exceeded what they regarded as sufficient." The people looked for, hoped for, and would "readily approve" only "an augmentation of the powers of [the Confederation] Congress."

Hamilton's stance was diametrically opposed to his fellow New Yorkers. On 18 June he delivered an impassioned, five-hour oration in which he "sketched" his outline of a plan of government.[8] His presentation was not submitted to the Convention as a formal proposal but "was meant only to give a more correct view of his ideas and to suggest the amendments which he would probably propose" later. Hamilton's plan called for a bicameral Congress. The lower house would be elected by the people and have a three-year term. The upper house or Senate would be elected by electors chosen by the people and would serve for life. The single chief executive was also to be elected by electors and would have life tenure. This president of the United States would be commander in chief and would have an absolute veto over acts of Congress. The supreme judicial authority was to be lodged in a court of twelve justices with life tenure. Congress could also create inferior courts. All state laws contrary to the United States constitution or federal laws would be considered null and void. All state governors would be appointed by the president and would have veto power over their state legislatures. No state was to have an army or navy and the militias were to be under the sole and exclusive direction of the United States.

Hamilton knew that his plan was too extreme for the Convention or for the public. But he believed that there were "evils operating in the States which must soon cure the people of their fondness for democracies." Once the populace tired of democracy, they would endorse his beliefs. Because of his sincerity and his eloquence, Hamilton was "praised by every body" in the Convention, but he was "supported by none."[9] He left the Convention frustrated at the end of June after being continually outvoted by his two companions.

As the Convention inexorably moved toward a more national government, Yates and Lansing became increasingly more disen-

8*Ibid.*, 282–93.
9William Samuel Johnson Speech, 21 June, *ibid.*, 363.

chanted. They finally left the Convention on 10 July and did not return.

Various reasons have been given to explain Yates and Lansing's departure from the Convention and their refusal to return. Early in the Convention, Lansing told his brother Abraham that he and Yates "had no prospect of succeeding in the measures proposed, and that he was at a stand whether it would not be proper for him to Leave."[10] Spanish Minister Don Diego de Gardoqui and French Consul Antoine de la Forest both mentioned the absence of the New York delegates from the Convention "in order not to ratify" the Constitution.[11] A short item in the *Massachusetts Gazette*, 20 November, implied that eight Convention delegates, including Yates and Lansing, had left early because they had opposed the proceedings. A response in the *Massachusetts Centinel*, 21 November, said that Yates and Lansing probably were "obliged by domestick concerns to return home prior to its [the Constitution] being signed." Luther Martin, a Maryland delegate to the Convention, said that Yates and Lansing "had uniformly opposed the system, and I believe, despairing of getting a proper one brought forward, or of rendering any real service, they returned no more."[12] Martin's assertion that the New Yorkers had not intended to return was contradicted by Daniel of St. Thomas Jenifer, another Maryland delegate.[13] According to George Mason of Virginia, Justice Yates and lawyer Lansing withdrew early because "the season for courts came on."[14] Both men did indeed participate in judicial business after they left the Convention. (The Supreme Court met from 31 July to 8 August and the circuit courts through the end of September.) On 26 August 1787 Lansing's brother reported that he found "but Little Inclination in either of them to repair again to Philadelphia, and from the General Observations I believe they will not go."[15] Also, Yates and Lansing

---

[10]Abraham G. Lansing to Abraham Yates, Jr., Albany, 26 August 1787, Yates Papers, New York Public Library [NN].

[11]Gardoqui to Conde de Floridablanca, New York, 23 September, and Forest to Comte de Montmorin, New York, 28 September, John P. Kaminski and Gaspare J. Saladino, eds., *Commentaries on the Constitution: Public and Private [Commentaries]*, 5 vols. (Madison, Wis., 1981–), 1:223, 259.

[12]Luther Martin, "Genuine Information," Baltimore *Maryland Gazette*, 4 January 1788, *Commentaries*, 3:255.

[13]*Pennsylvania Packet*, 14 February 1788.

[14]Ex relatione G. Mason, Gunston Hall, 30 September 1792, Farrand, *Records*, III:367.

[15]To Abraham Yates, Jr., Albany, Yates Papers, NN.

may have had heard the rumor that the Convention was far from
agreement and that it would continue to meet for several more
months. This in all likelihood convinced them not to return while
the circuit courts were still in session.

After Yates and Lansing left the Convention on 10 July, New
York was unrepresented. Hamilton returned to the Convention
after the Committee of Detail reported on 6 August, but under
the rules of the Convention, New York's vote was not counted
because only one delegate was present. Hamilton was absent again
from 20 August to 2 September. He was appointed to the Committee of Style on 8 September and signed the Constitution nine
days later as the only delegate from New York.

For some reason, Yates and Lansing waited a while before
publicly declaring their objections to the proposed Constitution.
As the regular session of the New York legislature approached,
they decided to make an "official" report. It was said that Governor Clinton "had a hand" in convincing Yates and Lansing to
write their report.[16] Finally, on 21 December 1787, ten days before
the scheduled legislative session, Yates and Lansing wrote Governor Clinton, giving their reasons for opposing the proposed Constitution and for not returning to the Convention. When a quorum
assembled on 11 January, Clinton gave the legislature the letter,
the report of the Constitutional Convention, and other public
documents.

In their letter, Yates and Lansing said that they opposed the
proposed Constitution because it created "a system of consolidated
Government" which was not "in the remotest degree . . . in con-
templation of the Legislature of this State." "If it had been the
intention of the Legislature to abrogate the existing Confederation, they would, in such pointed terms, have directed the attention
of their delegates to the revision and amendment of it, in total
exclusion of every other idea." Furthermore, "a general Government," such as the one proposed by the Convention, "must un-
avoidably, in a short time, be productive of the destruction of the
civil liberty of such citizens who could be effectually coerced by
it." They were convinced that the new Constitution could not
"afford that security to equal and permanent liberty, which we
wished to make an invariable object of our pursuit." Although

[16]Walter Rutherfurd to John Rutherfurd, 15 January 1788, Rutherfurd Collection, New-York Historical Society [NHi].

they were not present when the Convention signed the Constitution, they were convinced before they left that the Constitution's "principles were so well established . . . that no alteration was to be expected, to conform it to our ideas of expediency and safety. A persuasion that our further attendance would be fruitless and unavailing, rendered us less solicitous to return."

The Yates-Lansing letter was printed in the New York *Daily Advertiser* and *New-York Journal* on 14 January. The *Journal* also printed the letter in its Thursday issue (17 January) which had a more general country circulation. By the end of the month it was reprinted in six other New York newspapers, and by 10 March it was reprinted in the Philadelphia *American Museum*, a nationally circulated magazine, and in eleven other newspapers from New Hampshire to Georgia.

Yates and Lansing's letter, though widely circulated, generated relatively little response either inside or outside of New York. Edward Carrington of Virginia wrote that the letter was "in perfect uniformity with the purpose of their Mission . . ." which was to represent the interests of only New York—"a state whose measures have for a Number of Years been uniformly against the federal interests."[17]

The Constitution before Congress

Three New York delegates—Melancton Smith, John Haring, and Abraham Yates, Jr.—were present when Congress debated the Constitution from 26 to 28 September. They supported efforts to attach a bill of rights to the Constitution, but these efforts failed. A compromise was reached and the demand for an accompanying bill of rights was dropped in exchange for a bare transmittal of the Constitution to the states without a statement of approbation by Congress.

The Public Debate over the Constitution

The public debate over the Constitution in New York was an extension of the debate over strengthening the Articles of Confederation that had been going on since the Revolution. From

[17]To James Madison, Manchester, 10 February 1788, Rutland, *Madison*, X:493–95.

1783 to 1787 the debate had in large measure centered on the question of the federal impost. Beginning in February 1787, however, the debate enlarged and focused on the type of government best suited for the fledgling country. In February, March, and April 1787, three New York City newspaper items advocated dividing the country into three or four separate confederacies united by a loose federal alliance.[18] They maintained that the United States was a mixture of different climates, customs, and interests that would never be able to accommodate each other. Furthermore, the writers accepted the principle of Montesquieu and other eighteenth-century political theorists that republics could not exist over vast territories without eventually degenerating into despotisms. A "West Chester Farmer" totally disagreed.[19] He believed that the states should be reduced to the status of "civil corporations" and their laws should be null and void if they were contrary to the laws of the central government, which should consist of a parliament and a president assisted by a council of twenty-six. The president should be appointed by the state governors for five years and two councillors should be chosen by each state legislature for four years each. The president and council would have an absolute veto over the parliament. Another centralist proposed that Congress should be sovereign and should make all laws for the states. If this was impossible, this "Well Wisher to the United States of America" recommended that no state law ought to go into effect "without the Assent of Congress first."[20]

During the four months while the Constitutional Convention met, Federalists used the state's newspapers to prepare the public to receive whatever the Convention proposed. No opposition to the Convention or warnings about what might be proposed appeared in the press during these months. Even the future Antifederalist *New-York Journal* announced on 12 July that it was "incumbent on every public printer" "to blow the trumpet, and sound the alarm" about "the necessity of an immediate *Efficient Foederal Government!*" The *Albany Gazette*, 21 June, hoped that something would be done to stem "the prevailing rage of excessive democracy—this fashionable contempt of government—of public and private faith," while a writer in the *New-York Journal*, 16 August, announced that America would experience "*a new birth to glory*

[18]*Commentaries*, 1:54–59.
[19]New York *Daily Advertiser*, 8 June 1787, *Commentaries*, 1:128–30.
[20]*Observations on the Articles of Confederation*, 27 July, *Commentaries*, 1:180–81.

and *empire*" if the "delegated wisdom" of "the chaste body" would be accepted.

The trigger that apparently set off the New York public debate over the Constitution was the departure of the state's delegates from the Convention. Yates and Lansing, while on their way back home to Albany, probably stopped in New York City and discussed the Convention with Governor Clinton. The news from Philadelphia seems to have evoked some unguarded comments from the governor. Alexander Hamilton, also on leave from the Convention, charged, in a widely circulated article in the *Daily Advertiser*, 21 July, that Clinton had "in public company, without reserve, reprobated the appointment of the Convention, and predicted a mischievous issue of that measure." Clinton's attitude was "That the present confederation is, in itself, equal to the purposes of the union." Hamilton, however, maintained "that the general government is fundamentally defective; that the very existence of the union is in imminent danger." He believed that "industrious and wicked pains have been taken by parties unfriendly to the measures of the union, to discredit and debase the authority and influence of Congress." The derogatory remarks by Clinton against the Convention before its results were known proved that the governor was more attached "to his *own power* than to the *public good*, and furnishes strong reason to suspect a dangerous predetermination to oppose whatever may tend to diminish the *former*, however it may promote the *latter*." "A Republican," *New-York Journal*, 6 September, without admitting that Clinton had been disrespectful of the Convention, defended the governor's right to speak out. Any attempt to limit free speech was said to be "high treason against the majesty of the people." This newspaper exchange set the tone for the debate that followed and indicated the intractability on both sides.

In the months of public debate that followed, Antifederalists condemned the delegates to the Constitutional Convention for violating the Articles of Confederation, the instructions from their state legislatures, and the 21 February 1787 resolution of Congress. They believed that the Constitution would create a national government that would end in either aristocracy or monarchy. In time, this new government would destroy the state governments. They reprobated the lack of a bill of rights, especially since the new Constitution and laws and treaties made in pursuance thereof were declared to be the supreme law of the land with state judges bound thereby, notwithstanding state laws or constitutions to the contrary. The president and Senate were too powerful, and the Senate held legislative, executive and judicial powers. The House of Representatives was too small and Congress had dangerous powers, some of which were undefined. Officeholders would surely multiply under the new government and taxes would consequently rise. Jury trials in civil cases were not guaranteed and the appellate jurisdiction as to law and fact favored the wealthy. Various provisions in the Constitution recognized, condoned, protected, and even encouraged slavery. Antifederalists believed that the state conventions should not ratify the Constitution but should recommend amendments to another general convention. In this way, the people would obtain the best form of government with the least danger to their liberties.

Federalists responded that the new Constitution would create a confederated republic with powers divided among legislative, executive, and judiciary branches. Since the new government would have only delegated powers, it was unnecessary to have a national bill of rights. Federalists stressed the unanimity of the Convention in creating a constitution that was an accommodation among thirteen jarring interests. No new convention could hope to produce a more acceptable compromise. The illustrious Washington, the sage Franklin, and other prominent Americans were continually cited as strong supporters of the new government. Opponents were labeled selfish state officeholders, demagogues, debtors, Shayites, and tories. If the Constitution were to be rejected, anarchy would ensue, and, following the commonly accepted circular theory of government, a tyrant would eventually seize power, restore order, and establish a despotism. On the other hand, if the Constitution were adopted, commerce would revive, the economy would flourish, public creditors would be paid, land values would rise, paper money would be abolished, government expenses would decline, taxes would be reduced, and the prestige of America would rise. Once the new government was functioning, defects in the Constitution could be corrected through the system's own process of amendment.

The proposed Constitution was first printed in New York in the *Daily Advertiser* on 21 September. Three days later the first New York commentary on the Constitution in the state also appeared in the *Daily Advertiser*. The Constitution, it said, would "render us safe and happy at home, and respected abroad." Adoption of the new form of government would "snatch us from impending ruin" and provide "the substantial basis of liberty, honor and virtue." It was "the duty of all honest, well-disposed men, friends to peace and good government . . . to cultivate and diffuse . . . a spirit of submission" to the Constitution; which, although not perfect, was "much more so than the most friendly and sanguine expected."

Three days later the Antifederalist barrage began. "Cato" I, the first of seven essays said to be written by Governor Clinton, appeared in the *New-York Journal*, 27 September. "Cato" called on freemen to be prudent and cautious in considering the Constitution—"if you are negligent or inattentive, the ambitious and despotic will entrap you in their toils, and bind you with the cord of power from which you, and your posterity, may never be freed." "Beware how you determine—do not, because you admit that something must be done, adopt anything—teach the members of that convention, that you are capable of a supervision of their conduct." If the Constitution were found defective, another convention could consider amendments. The Constitution should be adopted if it were found acceptable, but if it were judged to be dangerous, freemen were urged to "reject it with indignation—better to be where you are, for the present, than insecure forever afterwards."

On 1 October, "Caesar," allegedly Alexander Hamilton, attacked "Cato" as a demagogue. "Caesar" asked "shall we now wrangle and find fault with that *excellent whole*, because, perhaps, some of its parts *might have been* more perfect?" Then he warned "Cato" and other Antifederalists that it would be wiser to accept George Washington willingly as the first president under the Constitution than to have the former commander in chief lead another army to establish the Constitution by force.

On 3 October the Poughkeepsie *Country Journal* printed the first original upstate commentary on the Constitution. It praised the new Constitution that would provide the vigorous administration necessary to protect American commerce, guard against civil dissension, and re-establish respect abroad. The article was probably written by James Kent, a twenty-four-year-old Poughkeepsie lawyer who "was determined to speak my Mind & not to be silenced by mere authority or Party." He vowed that "if any person attacks the new Government here in print, I intend to attack *him*."[21]

[21]To Nathaniel Lawrence, Poughkeepsie, 6 October 1787, *Commentaries*, 1:309n.

By mid-October 1787 New York newspapers teemed "with vehement & virulent calumniations," most of which were reprinted from Philadelphia.[22] Serialized essays abounded such as the Federalist "An American Citizen" (Tench Coxe), "A Countryman" (Roger Sherman), and "Landholder" (Oliver Ellsworth); and the Antifederalist "Centinel" (Samuel Bryan) and "An Old Whig." Individual pieces were also common such as the Federalist "Social Compact," "Grand Constitution," and "Foederal Constitution," or the Antifederalist "Address of the Seceding Pennsylvania Assemblymen" and "A Democratic Federalist." Speeches by Federalists James Wilson and John Sullivan were widely reprinted in New York, as were the published objections to the Constitution by Elbridge Gerry, George Mason, Richard Henry Lee, and the minority of the Pennsylvania Convention.

By 18 October the New York press had come of age. No longer did it rely primarily on out-of-state items. Antifederalist and Federalist propagandists were tireless in producing material for the state's newspapers. For the most part, New York newspapers were Federalist oriented, especially the upstate newspapers in Albany, Lansingburgh, Hudson, and Poughkeepsie. The New York City newspapers included three staunchly Federalists sheets— the *Daily Advertiser*, *Independent Journal*, and *New-York Packet*. The *New-York Morning Post* was fairly neutral, while the *New-York Journal* was rabidly Antifederalist. Printer Thomas Greenleaf of the weekly *New-York Journal* was inundated with articles which he had no room to publish. Consequently, with the patronage of a number of friends, Greenleaf increased publication to a daily. To assist in disseminating this Antifederalist material, both domestic productions and importations primarily from Philadelphia, a committee of gentlemen was formed in New York City. Led by Collector of Customs John Lamb and his merchant son-in-law Charles Tillinghast, this committee vigorously solicited, edited, published, and disseminated Antifederalist literature throughout New York and Connecticut, and to a lesser extent, throughout the entire country.

Antifederalist essayists took the initiative in New York as the first of sixteen essays by "Brutus" appeared in the *New-York Journal* on 18 October. Other Antifederalist series followed—"Cincinnatus" (Arthur Lee of Virginia), "A Countryman" and "Expositor"

[22]James Madison to George Washington, New York, 18 October, *Commentaries*, 1:408–9.

(Hugh Hughes), "A Countryman" (DeWitt Clinton), and "Sidney" (Abraham Yates, Jr.). Federalists responded with "Philo-Publiūs" (William Duer), "Americanus" (John Stevens, Jr., of New Jersey), "A Country Federalist" (James Kent), "Examiner" (Charles McKnight), and "Fabius."

The single most important Antifederalist publication in New York, and probably in the entire country, was the pamphlet *Observations Leading to a Fair Examination of the System of Government Proposed by the Late Convention . . . In a Number of Letters from the Federal Farmer to the Republican.* Published during the first week in November 1787, this forty-page pamphlet was reprinted in pamphlet editions in "different states, and several thousands of them" were sold. The Poughkeepsie *Country Journal* was the only newspaper in the country to reprint the entire pamphlet. Federalist James Kent admitted that "Federal Farmer" illustrated the defects of the Constitution "in a candid & rational manner." Virginia Federalist Edward Carrington said that "These letters are reputed the best of any thing that has been written" against the Constitution.[23]

By far the most admired New York essays were *The Federalist* written by "Publius" (Alexander Hamilton, James Madison, and John Jay). A total of eighty-five numbers were published between 27 October 1787 and 28 May 1788. The first essays had a fairly extensive nationwide circulation, but as the numbers kept pouring from the New York City press, their circulation diminished. Newspaper republication was also reduced after it was announced that the entire series would be published in a two-volume edition. The first volume containing thirty-six essays was published on 22 March 1788. The second volume containing forty-nine numbers appeared on 28 May. Federalists throughout the United States generally considered "Publius" as the best analysis of the Constitution. Some Federalists, however, thought that the essays were too "elaborate" and not "well calculated for the common people"; while Antifederalists like "Federal Farmer" believed that *The Federalist* had "but little relation to the great question, whether the constitution is fitted to the condition and character of the people or not."[24] Despite the significant place *The Federalist* has assumed in

[23]Kent to Nathaniel Lawrence, Poughkeepsie, 9 November 1787, and Carrington to Thomas Jefferson, New York, 9 June 1788, *Commentaries*, 2:75, 18n.
[24]Archibald Maclaine to James Iredell, Wilmington, N.C., 4 March 1788, and "Federal Farmer," *Commentaries*, 1:493–94.

American political thought, its impact on New York's reception of the Constitution was negligible.

Far more important in the political battle to get the Constitution ratified in New York was John Jay's *An Address to the People of the State of New York* signed by "A Citizen of New-York." In this nineteen-page pamphlet published on 15 April 1788, Jay methodically demonstrated the weaknesses of the Articles of Confederation and the necessity of "a national government *competent to every national object.*" He asked New Yorkers to unite with the other states "as a *Band of Brothers*; to have confidence in themselves and in one another . . . [and] at least to give the proposed Constitution a fair trial, and to mend it as time, occasion and experience may dictate." Jay's pamphlet reportedly had a "most astonishing influence in converting Antifederalists, to a knowledge and belief that the New Constitution was their only political Salvation."[25] George Washington, greatly impressed with the pamphlet, wrote Jay that "The good sense, forceable observations, temper and moderation with which it is written cannot fail . . . of making a serious impression even upon the anti foederal Mind where it is not under the influence of such local views as will yield to no arguments—no proofs."[26]

"A Citizen of New-York" was ably answered by Melancton Smith in a twenty-six page pamphlet entitled *An Address to the People of the State of New-York . . .* signed by "A Plebeian." Smith's pamphlet, published on 17 April 1788, maintained that "the indefinite powers granted to the general government" endangered the state governments and the liberties of the people "not by express words, but by fair and legitimate construction and inference." Smith objected to the idea that the Constitution should be adopted first and then amended. He asked, "why not amend, and then adopt it? Most certainly" this was "more consistent with our ideas of prudence in the ordinary concerns of life."

From mid-October 1787 through July 1788 a never-ending stream of essays, extracts of letters, poems, news items, filler pieces, and convention debates filled the state's gazettes. Nowhere else were the people as well informed about the Constitution as in New York.

[25]Samuel B. Webb to Joseph Barrell, New York, 27 April 1788, Webb Family Collection, Yale University [CtY].
[26]Mount Vernon, 15 May 1788, John Jay Papers, Columbia University Libraries [NNC].

Warm Work in Poughkeepsie—
The Legislature Calls a Convention

The New York legislature convened in Poughkeepsie on 1 January 1788 but did not attain a quorum until 11 January. According to the *New-York Journal*, 3 January, this session was "conceived by every class of people to be the most important one" since the Revolution because "the momentous subject of the new federal constitution is to be discussed." No one, however, knew exactly what to expect from the legislature. Thomas Greenleaf, the printer, believed that the Constitution's "merits will be fully and impartially investigated." New York City Federalist Walter Rutherfurd expected "warm work" in Poughkeepsie. James Madison wrote that the legislature was "much divided" on submitting the Constitution to a Convention—the Assembly was reportedly in favor of calling a convention; the Senate opposed. Albany lawyer Richard Sill was less optimistic—"tis doubted by the best friends to the New Government whether we shall have a Convention called by a Legislative Act, the opposition are determined to make their first stand here."[27]

On 11 January Governor Clinton addressed the legislature and turned over the proposed Constitution, the resolutions of the Constitutional Convention and the Confederation Congress requesting the states to call conventions to consider the Constitution, and the 21 December letter from Robert Yates and John Lansing, Jr., to the governor explaining their opposition to the Constitution. Clinton told the legislature that it would be "improper" for him "to have any other agency in the business."

The Assembly thanked the governor for the communications that "are highly important and interesting" and said that they would "claim our most serious and deliberate consideration." The Senate similarly told the governor that the documents would "claim the attention due to their importance." On 29 January Antifederalist Senator John Williams of Washington County expressed the hope that the Constitution would be submitted "to the people without either recommending or disapprobation; let the people

[27]*New-York Journal*, 3 January; Walter Rutherfurd to John Rutherfurd, 8, 15 January, Rutherfurd Collection, NHi; James Madison to Edmund Randolph and to George Washington, New York, 20 January, Rutland, *Madison*, X:398–99; Richard Sill to Jeremiah Wadsworth, Albany, 12 January, Wadsworth Correspondence, Connecticut Historical Society.

judge for themselves."[28] On the same day the Assembly examined
the several documents and ordered that the calling of a convention
be the order of the day for Thursday, 31 January.

On 31 January Assemblyman Egbert Benson of Dutchess
County, who was also state attorney general, proposed a resolution
calling a state convention.[29] Assemblyman Cornelius C. Schoonmaker of Ulster County proposed that the preamble to the resolution be changed to indicate that the Constitutional Convention
had exceeded its powers by reporting "a new Constitution" which,
if adopted, would "materially alter" New York's constitution and
government "and greatly affect the rights and privileges" of all
New Yorkers. Benson attacked Schoonmaker's change as "a fla-
grant violation of common sense." Schoonmaker replied that his
proposal was merely "a state of facts" that the people should be
made aware of. Assemblyman Samuel Jones of Queens County
seconded Schoonmaker's amendment. Benson, however, said that
there "was no good could arise from" the amendment that would
throw "an odium on the members of the Convention." Assemblyman Richard Harison, a New York City lawyer, agreed with
Benson that the Constitution should go to the people without "the
inference . . . that the Legislature disapproved of the measures of
the Convention." The legislature ought not to consider the merits
of the Constitution itself—"the only question" was whether the
Constitution should "be submitted to the people." The debate
continued when Benson interrupted Schoonmaker and, holding
up the written amendment, charged that the crossed-out section
at the bottom betrayed Schoonmaker's real purpose. The stricken
portion of the amendment had called for the New York legislature
to express its disapprobation of the proposed Constitution. Jones,
one of the state's most astute lawyers, rose and said that it was
"very unfair to infer any thing from what had been scratched out."
Benson "contended that it was perfectly fair. . . . People . . . did
not suddenly change their minds on a subject of such magnitude."
After more debate, some of which got personal, the vote on
Schoonmaker's amendment was called for and the proposal was
defeated 27 to 25. Jones then proposed that the Constitution be

[28]"An Extract of a Letter from John Williams, Esq. at Poughkeepsie, to his
Friends in Washington County, dated 29th January 1788," Albany *Federal Herald*,
25 February 1788.
    [29]For the Assembly's debates over the calling of the state ratifying conven-
tion, see the New York *Daily Advertiser*, 12 February.

submitted to the convention "for their free investigation, discussion, and decision"—an obvious attempt "to introduce the Idea of *Amendment*." Jones's motion was defeated 29 to 23, and Benson's original resolution was approved 27 to 25.

The Assembly resolution of 31 January called for the state convention to meet at the courthouse in Poughkeepsie on 17 June 1788. The election of delegates was to begin on 29 April and continue until completed, but not to exceed five days. For the first time in state history, all free male citizens twenty-one years old or older were eligible to vote by secret ballot for convention delegates, even though the state constitution required a property qualification for voting in state elections. Polling places were to be located in every town and precinct—not just in county seats as was previously the case. Convention delegates, assemblymen, and one-third of the state senators were to be elected at the same time and place. Apportionment of convention delegates coincided with Assembly apportionment, and convention delegates were to be paid by the state at the same rate as assemblymen.

On 1 February the Assembly's resolution was delivered to the Senate.[30] Antifederalist Senator Abraham Yates, Jr., of Albany proposed that the resolution be considered by a committee of the whole, but Federalist Senator James Duane, mayor of New York City, saw no need for such a delay—the Senate should vote on the resolution without any alterations. If the resolution was rejected, the Senate could draft its own resolution. There was no need for further discussion. "He imagined that every man's mind was made up on this great question." Yates said that the people should be told that the Constitutional Convention delegates "went beyond their powers. . . . they have not amended, but made a new system." As far as he was concerned, he had opposed every step taken toward this new Constitution, "nor is there a sentence in it that I ever will agree to . . . I would be for rejecting it altogether." The Senate then, by a vote of 12 to 7, defeated Yates's motion to commit the resolution. Senators John Williams, John Haring of Orange County, and Yates then tried to delay consideration of the resolution to another day, but the Senate agreed to examine the resolution immediately by paragraphs. Williams objected to the resolution allowing all adult males to vote when the state con-

[30]For the Senate debates over the calling of the state ratifying convention, see the New York *Daily Advertiser*, 8 February.

stitution required property qualifications for voters. He also objected to the election of convention delegates being held on the same day as the election of state assemblymen and senators. Senator Lewis Morris of New York City moved that the Assembly's resolution be approved, but Senators Yates and Cornelius Humfrey of Dutchess County moved for a postponement so that they could propose an amendment similar to the one proposed by Schoonmaker in the Assembly. Humfrey "did not wish it to appear, as if the Legislature had sanctioned" the Constitution. Williams agreed that the matter should be postponed to consider whether the state convention should be empowered to propose amendments to the Constitution. The Senate then voted 10 to 9 against postponement and 11 to 8 to approve the Assembly's resolution. James Duane carried the Senate's concurrence to the Assembly, which on 2 February ordered 500 copies of the resolution printed and distributed throughout the state.

Both parties seem to have favored delaying the meeting of the convention until mid-June 1788. Federalists, thinking that a majority of the state opposed the Constitution, wanted time to convince the populace that the Constitution had to be adopted. They hoped that ratification by nine states would occur before the New York Convention would meet. This would have two benefits: (1) no state would be adversely influenced by an early New York rejection of the Constitution, and (2) New York might be more amenable to ratify the Constitution if nine states had already adopted it. On the other hand, Antifederalists had their own reasons for a late convention. Clintonians adopted the same strategy they had used on the impost of 1783—they hoped that another state, especially a large state such as Virginia, would reject the Constitution thus taking the onus off New York. Furthermore, although opposition to the Constitution looked substantial, Antifederalists still were uncertain about their statewide strength. Clintonians also hoped to coordinate interstate activities in an effort to seek amendments to the Constitution through a second constitutional convention. Proposals for such a convention would be made at the New York ratifying convention, but it would take time to communicate with Antifederalists in other states.

A perplexing provision of the resolution was the universal adult male suffrage. Federalists proposed and supported this provision in the hope that usually ineligible males in towns and small tenants on the manors could be convinced to vote in favor of the

Constitution. Antifederalists in the Assembly did not comment on the suffrage provision, while Senate Antifederalists expressed bafflement. Senator David Hopkins of Washington County said that the provision "was a point that required time for consideration," while John Williams, his fellow north country senator, "thought it was a matter that ought to be explained." Even if Antifederalists opposed this part of the resolution, they had to tread softly because, as Williams said, they "did not wish it to be understood" that they "would deprive any man of his right of voting." When the ballots were counted, the universal adult male suffrage had increased the number of voters by perhaps 25 to 30 percent, but it appears that neither Federalists nor Antifederalists were appreciably affected by the larger turnout.

The Elections

Throughout the last four months of 1787 a great deal of uncertainty prevailed over New York's attitude toward the Constitution. The general consensus was that New York City warmly supported the new government, Governor Clinton and his party opposed it, and the state as a whole was either hostile or evenly divided. Confederation Secretary at War Henry Knox, in New York City, wrote George Washington on 11 December 1787 that "The warm friends of the new constitution say that the majority of the people are in its favor while its adversaries assert roundly that the majority is with them." The ambiguity in New York stemmed from the lack of open political activity in all arenas except the newspapers. Elsewhere in the country, state legislatures, towns, counties, associations, and individuals took strong public stances on the Constitution. This, for the most part, was not the case in New York. On 24 October James Madison wrote Thomas Jefferson that "There seems to be less agitation in this State than any where. The discussion of the subject seems confined to the newspapers. The principal characters are known to be friendly. The Governour's party which has hitherto been the popular & most numerous one, is supposed to be on the opposite side; but considerable reserve is practised, of which he sets the example."

Once the New York legislature set the date for the election of convention delegates, electioneering began with a fury unmatched in any other state. County committees were established to supervise the nomination of candidates. Town and county meetings of local political leaders abounded. County committees of correspondence were created to communicate within a particular county and with political leaders in New York City, Albany, and in other states. Nomination lists were formulated and published in unprecedented numbers. And writers in newspapers, broadsides, and pamphlets continued their daily onslaught on the electorate. "The New Constitution," it was said, was "the Sole Object of all our attention."[31] But, because most of the politicking was done on a local and county basis, and much of it was conducted secretly, the general mood on the eve of the elections was not much different from what it had been during 1787. Two days before the elections, New York City merchant-factor Samuel B. Webb wrote that "there is not a doubt we [will] carry the Federal ticket in this City four to one, and I am happy to add that in the other Counties we have flattering prospects; some are unanimous against us, but we think we have a good chance of geting at least an equal number of Federalists for the Convention. . . . in short equal bets are now taken that this State [will] adopt the New Constitution."[32]

Federalist hopes had been buoyed by the recent ratification of the Constitution by Massachusetts. Before he had heard the news, Federalist Philip Schuyler had written that if Massachusetts ratified, "I believe we shall have little contest here."[33] Antifederalist Melancton Smith wrote that "The decision of that State will certainly have great influence on the final issue of the business."[34] Webb, himself, noted that Massachusetts' ratification would "give a most powerful impression. . . . no Antifederalists show their heads, many indeed have changed their sentiments."[35] Federalist Brockholst Livingston wrote his father, Governor William Livingston of New Jersey, telling him that since the news about Massachusetts, "Converts to the new Constitution are daily making among us."[36]

The uncertainty about the eventual composition of New York's convention persisted well after the elections. The state's

[31]William Constable to the Marquis de Lafayette, New York, 4 January, Constable-Pierrepont Collection, NN.
[32]To Joseph Barrell, New York, 27 April, Webb Family Collection, CtY.
[33]To Stephen Van Rensselaer, Poughkeepsie, 8 February, Schuyler Papers, Library of Congress [DLC].
[34]To Abraham Yates, Jr., New York, 23 January, Yates Papers, NN.
[35]To Joseph Barrell, New York, 7 February, Webb Family Collection, CtY.
[36]15 February, Livingston Papers, Massachusetts Historical Society [MHi].

election law of 1787 provided that ballots had to be sealed in county ballot boxes for four weeks after the election had begun. Therefore not until 27 May were county supervisors authorized to count the votes and report the results, after which they were supposed to destroy the ballots and election records. In most counties, poll watchers estimated the turn out of Federalist and Antifederalist voters, but only in a handful of counties was the margin of victory so one-sided that reliable predictions could be made of the results before 27 May. When the returns were counted, nine of the state's thirteen voting counties (Clinton County was not yet represented separately from Washington County) were solidly in the Antifederalist camp. Of the sixty-five delegates chosen, Federalists elected but nineteen to their opponent's forty-six. Antifederalists had swept to an amazingly one-sided victory much beyond anyone's expectations. This one-sided victory was the direct result of a concerted and coordinated effort by Antifederalists to mobilize the electorate coupled with fortuitous circumstances in several counties that created rifts within Federalists' ranks.

There was never any doubt that a large majority in New York City supported the Constitution. Antifederalists could only hope to chip away at this majority and perhaps elect the governor as one of the city's nine convention delegates.

By mid-April the election of convention delegates engrossed "all the Loose Chat" in New York City.[37] Both parties had nominated slates of candidates. Federalists boasted an impressive list headed by Confederation Secretary for Foreign Affairs John Jay, state Chief Justice Richard Morris, Chancellor Robert R. Livingston, Mayor James Duane, and recently elected congressman Alexander Hamilton. Other Federalist candidates were Judge John Sloss Hobart, lawyer Richard Harison, and merchants Nicholas Low and Isaac Roosevelt. Antifederalist candidates included Governor Clinton, Collector of Customs John Lamb, alderman and former Sheriff Marinus Willett, merchant-lawyer Melancton Smith, merchant and former Assemblyman William Denning, and lawyer Aaron Burr. Antifederalist expectations were so pessimistic, however, that the governor and Melancton Smith were also nominated in other counties, while Burr announced that he "declines serving . . . and that his Name has been given out without his Knowledge

[37]Peter Elting to Peter Van Gaasbeek, New York, 11 April, Peter Van Gaasbeek Papers, Senate House Museum, Kingston, N.Y. [NKS].

or Consent."[38] On the eve of the elections, Samuel B. Webb predicted that "The Governor & his party will probably meet with a great mortification, the great body of Cityzens are much displeased with his political sentiments and Conduct."[39]

On Tuesday, 29 April, the polls opened at 10:00 A.M. By 6:00 P.M. almost 1,500 votes had been cast for the Federalist ticket.[40] On this first day of ballotting, Antifederalists circulated a new ticket. It was folded in such a way as to appear to be the original Federalist ticket, but in reality it placed the governor's name at the head of the Federalist candidates. New Yorkers were warned to beware of this counterfeit.[41]

During the first three days of the elections, 29 April to 1 May, New Yorkers "laid aside their usual business, and paid their whole attention to the important business before them, all was conducted with perfect order and regularity, it was not a *contested Election*, the friends to an Energetic Foedral Government were so unanimous, that no danger was to be apprehended,—a small attempt was made by the Governors expireing party, in the first day, after which we heard no more of them, out of about 3,000 Votes, I much doubt if they have two Hundred."[42]

There was no question that Federalists had swept the city. The majority was said to be fifteen, twenty, or even thirty to one.[43] A total of 2,836 ballots were cast. John Jay received the highest number of votes (2,735), followed by Richard Morris (2,716). Hobart, Hamilton, and Livingston each received 2,713 votes. Nicholas Low, the least popular Federalist candidate received 2,651 ballots. Antifederalists were led by Governor Clinton, who obtained a mere 134 votes. Marinus Willett got 108 votes and William Denning 102. No other Antifederalist received more than 30 votes.

In the state's far western county of Montgomery, it was believed that Federalists would also be victorious. On 13 February

[38]*New-York Journal*, 30 April.
[39]To Catherine Hogeboom, New York, 27 April, Webb Family Collection, CtY.
[40]"Extract of a Letter from a Gentleman at New-York, to his Friend in this Town, dated April 30, 1788," *Maryland Journal*, 9 May.
[41]"One of Yourselves," New York *Daily Advertiser*, 1 May. This article was also published as a broadside.
[42]Samuel B. Webb to Catherine Hogeboom, New York, 4 May, Webb Family Collection, CtY.
[43]"Extract of a Letter . . .," *Maryland Journal*, 9 May; Morgan Lewis to Margaret Beekman Livingston, New York, 4 May, Robert R. Livingston Papers, NHi; "Extract of a letter from New York, dated, May 5," *Massachusetts Centinel*, 10 May.

1788 an extract from a letter published in the *Massachusetts Centinel* reported that "the federal cause gains strength daily" in Montgomery County. Federalist prospects were particularly optimistic in Montgomery because much of the property in the county was owned by wealthy Federalists from other counties. Chancellor Robert R. Livingston wrote to Philip Schuyler on 20 March and hoped "that Montgomery is not neglected." Nine days later Schuyler assured the chancellor that the Federal Committee of Albany County was diligently at work and "their Attention is Equally extended to Montgomery and I believe we shall obtain a majority of foedral constitutionalists there."[44] A gentleman in Montgomery County thanked his friend in Albany for sending copies of the Constitution which were "distributed among those who stood in need thereof." They made "numerous proselytes to federalism." Henry Livingston of the upper manor appealed to Albany patroon Stephen Van Rensselaer to use his "great Influence" in the county.[45]

Abraham Van Vechten, former law student and partner of John Lansing, Jr., was not so sanguine. "It is impossible to form a just Opinion at present of the general Sentiments of the Inhabitants of this County. . . . I have conversed with but few about it, and those few were either uninformed, or as usual much divided; and I am sorry to add, that in common those who bestow the greatest Attention on the new Constitution seem to regard it more with an Eye to party Interest, than as a System of future Goverment. . . . It is said by some Gentlemen here that a Majority of the best informed People of the County are (to use the most fashionable Language) on the federal Side, but for the Truth of these Assertions I can not undertake to vouch—In my opinion the Merits of the important Question before us are so little enquired into & understood by the Inhabitants in General, that very few indeed have yet deliberately & from Conviction made up their Minds respecting it."[46] One "Irish Landlord" was said to be "a violent Antifederalist, and denounces Vengeance against all who dare to differ from him, but unfortunately in the Transports of his Zeal he does not hesitate to declare that he scorns even to read the

[44]Livingston to Schuyler, New York, 20 March, Schuyler Papers, NN; Schuyler to Livingston, Albany, 29 March, Livingston Papers, NHi.

[45]"Extract of a letter from a gentleman in Montgomery County, to his friend [in] this city, dated April 2," Albany *Federal Herald*, 7 April; Livingston to Van Rensselaer, 1 March, New York State Library [N].

[46]To Henry Oothoudt and Jeremiah Van Rensselaer, 11 January 1788, James T. Mitchell Autograph Collection, Historical Society of Pennsylvania [PHi].

new Constitution."[47] County clerk Christopher P. Yates believed that "The adoption of the new Constitution will be attended with such bad Consequences that we conceive it our indispensable duty to oppose it."[48]

Federalists expected that Abraham Van Vechten would play a key role in winning the Montgomery County elections. They had nominated him for the convention and had "used Strenuous Exertions for his success" including the distribution of lists "with his Name inserted thro different Quarters of the County." On 7 April, however, after returning from Albany, Van Vechten informed fellow Federalist candidates Peter Schuyler and Josiah Crane that he wanted to be removed from the Montgomery County Federalist slate. Van Vechten said that "a variety of Circumstances have concurred to render it impossible for me to attend either the Convention or Assembly—You'll therefore oblige me much by striking my Name out of the List of Candidates held up in your District." Peter Schuyler was irate—"we deem it a late period for Mr V: Veghten to retract his intention and destroy the Effect of his assurances, knowing that his Friends are Solicitous for preserving him as a Member to Convention, We are apprehensive that the Consequence of his declining at this Crisis, will Create Confusion amongst the Election."[49]

Antifederalists made a clean sweep of Montgomery's six convention delegates. Christopher P. Yates, the most popular Antifederal candidate, received 1,209 votes; the lowest 1,199. The most popular Federalist candidate received 811 votes; the lowest 756. Van Vechten, despite his effort to withdraw from the race, received 806 votes, second highest among Federalist candidates.[50] Although tenant farmers supported Federalist candidates to a degree, Antifederalists clearly were favored by the more numerous yeoman farmers.

In Columbia County, Federalists also had high hopes because of the influence of the Livingstons. The campaign started propitiously in the intense winter cold when on 12 January the grand jurors of the county court of general sessions at Claverack en-

[47]Ibid.

[48]To George Herkimer, Fry's Bush, 9 April, Herkimer Papers, Oneida Historical Society, Utica, N.Y.

[49]Van Vechten to Peter Schuyler and Josiah Crane, 7 April, Abraham Van Vechten Papers, NHi; Peter Schuyler to Unknown, 8 April, Peter Schuyler Papers, NHi.

[50]New-York Journal, 5 June.

dorsed the Constitution which "has in our opinion every safe guard, which human foresight can suggest, for perpetuating to our posterity the blessings of Freedom."[51] On 11 March "some of the first characters in the county" met in Claverack to nominate Federalist candidates. A committee "of the most respectable characters from each district" nominated a slate of candidates for the convention, Assembly, and Senate which "the Gentlemen present approved of & pledged their honors to support."[52] A week later Antifederalists met in Claverack and nominated their candidates.[53] Federalist convention candidate Peter Van Schaack wrote that "We have some very great men among us, and a wonderful degree of information among the common people. Public speaking is much in vogue." It evoked images for Van Schaack "of the days of ancient Greece and Rome." The campaign, however, was intense—not merely "a war of tongues, but a few bloody noses have been the consequence."[54] Peter Ten Broeck wrote from the upper Livingston manor that "all we hear here is a Constitution talk: as for my part I troble my head but very little about: relying that like all other evils it will work its own Cure—tho I could wish it to be adopted as in my Juvenile opinion with a few alterations it to be a very good one & without any alteratn. better than none. sensible that something of the kind must [be] done without which this is a ruinous Country & nation & every Citizen must naturally see & feel it: if not remedied at this time at this very Junctive (we have no time to delay) it must be adopted or we will sink beneath the gripe of remedy."[55] Despite these favorable reports, Chancellor Livingston wrote Philip Schuyler about his "fears relative to the conduct of our friends in Columbia." Schuyler responded that Livingston's fears were "unhappily but too well founded;—all was in confusion there."[56]

When Schuyler left the legislature in Poughkeepsie to go home to Albany, he stopped along the way in Columbia. There he found that John Livingston had withdrawn as one of the Fed-

[51]*Albany Gazette*, 17 January (supplement).

[52]*Hudson Weekly Gazette*, 13 March.

[53]*Hudson Weekly Gazette*, 20 March.

[54]Peter Van Schaack to Henry Walton, Kinderhook, 3 June 1788, Henry C. Van Schaack, ed., *The Life of Peter Van Schaack...* (New York, 1842), 425.

[55]To Peter Van Gaasbeek, Manor Livingston, 7 April 1788, Peter Van Gaasbeek Papers, NKS.

[56]Livingston to Schuyler, New York, 20 March, Schuyler Papers, NN; Schuyler to Livingston, Albany, 29 March, Livingston Papers, NHi.

eralist candidates for the Assembly and had refused to support Thomas Jenkins of Hudson, another Assembly candidate. The thriving settlement of Hudson, recently founded as a commercial venture by New Englanders, had little good will toward the Livingstons, and John Livingston declared that he would be opposed to "every person unfriendly to his family." Schuyler "expostulated with him on the impropriety, if not danger of such a determination; attempted to shew the disgrace which must result to his family, to me, and to all our friends.—but in vain, he adhered to his opinions." Schuyler asked James Duane, John Livingston's brother-in-law, to intercede, but that too failed. Schuyler and Peter R. Livingston, John's brother, again pleaded for a change of heart, and "after a long conversation, he promised not to interfere one way or the other, but still refused to stand a candidate." When Schuyler went to Claverack, however, he "learnt that Mr. Jenkins had also declared, that he should injure the common cause, as Mr. John Livingston was so much opposed to him."[57]

Peter Van Schaack then threatened to withdraw as a convention candidate "if such discordant Ingredients still prevail."[58] Schuyler hurried a letter to Van Schaack in which he pleaded with him to stay on the ticket: "You stand so well at Hudson, Claverack, & Kinderhook that I must entreat you not to withdraw your name from the nomination. If you do, the opponents will gain a decided victory,—If you do not [withdraw] we will at least have one from Columbia to support the Cause."[59] Schuyler was also informed that Judge Isaac Goes "was offended" because he had not been invited to the nomination meeting and that Goes "would probably be in opposition." All of these "circumstances Induced" Schuyler to recommend another nomination meeting at which he hoped Henry Livingston would be replaced by the more popular Peter R. Livingston, the chancellor's brother-in-law. Schuyler's suggested change in candidates "was not relished." The Federalist peacemaker then tried to mend fences by visiting the "chagrined" Goes at Kinderhook. Schuyler apologized for General Robert Van Rensselaer's oversight in not inviting Goes to the first meeting. Goes was informed of the second meeting and was assured "that he would be called" to attend. Goes said that he would attend, and

[57]Ibid.
[58]To Philip Schuyler, 3 April, Schuyler Papers, NN.
[59]8 April, Schuyler Papers, NHi.

Schuyler believed that Goes would "sincerely Join in every measure which may promote the foedral Interest."[60]

In leaving Columbia, Schuyler lamented that Federalists' "hopes of Success in that County, are small indeed."[61] To make matters worse, within a week Schuyler was informed that the tenants in eastern Columbia were involved in "Controversies about their Lands" and that they were "wonderfully poison'd" against all the manor lords.[62] Assemblyman Dr. Thomas Tillotson of Redhook in Dutchess County asked Chancellor Livingston to "come up early enough to take a few pains in the Elections [in Columbia and Dutchess counties]. I think you might revive the Foederal cause."[63]

On 30 April Dr. Alexander Coventry of Hudson wrote in his diary that "Few people [attended] at the election." Coventry also reported that a Mr. Delemeter was "committed to jail for challenging Hezekiah Dayton, one of the board, for putting a different ticket into the box, from the one he received from one of the electors."[64] Robert Livingston, Jr., third lord of the Manor of Livingston, reported that Federalist poll watchers saw "a number of [Antifederalist] emissarys daily going about to poison the Tenants. . . . they do considerable mischief among the Ignorant but hope all they can do will not prevent our obtaining the Desired End."[65] Federalist lawyer John C. Wynkoop wrote that about 300 votes had been evenly cast at Hudson and 719 votes had been registered at Kinderhook. Wynkoop felt "sure of a federal delegation from" Columbia County. Peter Wynkoop, Jr., believed that Antifederalist candidates had received a slight majority of the votes cast at Kinderhook. He also stated that the "common report" was that the districts of King's, Hillsdale, Claverack, and Camp were Antifederalist; while Hudson, Clermont, and Manor Livingston were Federalist. It was expected that the county election hinged on the outcome in Livingston Manor. Peter Wynkoop believed that the results would "be in Favour of the Federal Party" because

[60]Schuyler to Robert R. Livingston, Albany, 29 March, Livingston Papers, NHi.

[61]*Ibid.*

[62]Peter Van Schaack to Schuyler, 3 April, Van Schaack, *Life of Peter Van Schaack,* 425.

[63]Poughkeepsie, 31 March, Robert R. Livingston Papers, NHi.

[64]NHi.

[65]To James Duane, Manor Livingston, 30 April, Duane Papers, NHi.

of the "Compulsive Measures . . . used to lead the Tenants."[66] Despite these predictions of a narrow Federalist victory, the three Antifederal convention candidates got almost 55 percent of the vote and defeated their Federalist opponents by an average of 1,852 to 1,488.

Federalist support was weakest in Ulster County, the Clinton family home. On 14 February the freeholders and inhabitants of Kingston met and unanimously voted to oppose the new Constitution. A committee was appointed that drafted a circular letter to Ulster County justices and supervisors encouraging them to adopt "a spirit of alacrity, firmness, and unanimity" in electing Antifederal candidates to the convention.[67] It was reported that Ulsterites burned a copy of the Constitution and an effigy of Alexander Hamilton.[68]

Six Antifederal convention candidates were nominated for Ulster County including the governor, his older brother James, and Assemblyman Cornelius C. Schoonmaker. When New York City Antifederalists realized their strength in Ulster, they decided to switch Governor Clinton's candidacy to Federalist Kings County. It was believed that Clinton could still be elected in Kings, thus defeating a Federalist candidate there. Clinton's Antifederal replacement in Ulster would also surely win. In this way, Antifederalists would gain an additional seat in the convention. The idea seemed sound, but as the election neared, Clinton's candidacy in Kings was viewed with skepticism. Furthermore it was believed that "If we dont Continue" Clinton in Ulster, "many People will be Cool and many will suspect A design or Trick is intended. this you know is very easy to imprint on the Minds of the more Ignorant People."[69] Schoonmaker was thus given the unpleasant task of telling Melancton Smith and the New York City Antifederalist committee that Ulster would not give up their favorite son. On 4 April Schoonmaker wrote Samuel Jones and informed him that Ulsterites would "not *hazard* the Election of the Governor in Kings

[66]John C. Wynkoop to Adrian Wynkoop, Kinderhook, 3 May, Peter Van Gaasbeek Papers, NKS; Peter Wynkoop, Jr., to Peter Van Gaasbeek, Kinderhook, 5 May, Franklin D. Roosevelt Collection, Roosevelt Library, Hyde Park, N.Y. [NHpR].

[67]*New-York Journal*, 29 February.

[68]Brockholst Livingston to William Livingston, 15 February, Livingston Papers, MHi.

[69]Peter Van Gaasbeek to Cornelius C. Schoonmaker, Kingston, 31 March, Peter Van Gaasbeek Papers, NKS.

County for fear that the federal Machinations in the City of New York may probably disconcert our plans and the Election of the Governor be lost, and that we were determined that he shall be voted in this County."[70] Coincidentally, New York City Antifederalists reached the same conclusions. They realized that Clinton's chances of being elected in Kings were remote, therefore they decided to run him in both New York City and Ulster County. In this way, perhaps Federalists would be denied a delegate from New York City without any danger to Clinton's candidacy. Melancton Smith rationalized: "For he had better be chosen in two Places, than not to be elected at all."[71]

George Clinton received 1,372 votes in Ulster, the highest total. His brother received 905 votes, the lowest total of any victorious candidate. The three unsuccessful Federalist candidates for the convention received 68, 35, and 29 votes each.

Except for the brief interest in running Governor Clinton from Kings, little is known about the election in this Long Island county. A correspondent in the New York *Daily Advertiser*, 20 February, advised citizens of Kings County to "Look about . . . for two honest, thinking, independent freeholders, to represent you in Convention; be governed as much as may be in your choice, by the policy on this subject, which predominates in the city of New York; be persuaded that *your interest* is inseparably connected with *that* of the city, and be assured at the same time, that a general energetic Government is best calculated for *both*, and that they are enemies to your prosperity, whether they know it or not, who maintain the contrary." This writer attacked the county's assemblymen, Charles Doughty and Cornelius Wyckoff, who had opposed a state ratifying convention. "Dismiss them therefore from your service, they are unworthy of your confidence. To say nothing of their abilities, they are both" under the influence of Queens Assemblyman Samuel Jones, who was himself a tool of the governor. Although the writer nominated no particular candidates, he warned the people of Kings "to beware of that insidious influence which will very probably creep under various disguises among you when you take this important business up. Caution and cun-

---

[70]Schoonmaker to Peter Van Gaasbeek, 7 April, Franklin D. Roosevelt Collection, NHpR.
[71]To Cornelius C. Schoonmaker, New York, 6 April, John Lamb Papers, NHi.

ning will be practised, which must be opposed by steadiness and circumspection."

By early April Federalist strength was so evident that two fairly inconspicuous candidates (Judge Peter Lefferts and Sheriff Peter Vandervoort) were selected to run against the state's most successful politician. Chancellor Livingston and Congressman Leonard Gansevoort foresaw no danger as they predicted an overwhelming Federalist victory. Even Melancton Smith soon realized that it would "not be prudent to hazard" Governor Clinton's election in Kings. Most men in Kings could agree with "A Flat-Bush Farmer" who wrote "that every time I read it [the Constitution], I think it more perfect than I before believed it to be. . . . the peace, happiness, and prosperity of our country depends" on the adoption of the Constitution. As the election closed, Morgan Lewis announced that Federalists "have succeeded in King's County beyond Doubt."[72]

Dutchess County was one of the strongest centers of support for Governor Clinton. Since 1782 only one man with federal principles—Attorney General Egbert Benson—represented the county in the Assembly. Because of this political tradition, it was expected that Dutchess would elect Antifederal delegates to the state convention. On 22 May Federalist Dr. Thomas Tillotson wrote that "Our affairs wear a very gloomy appearance at this time & *the Great Superintendant* of human affaires only can brighten the scene." Tillotson asked Chancellor Livingston to come to Dutchess County to "revive the Foederal cause."[73] For his part, Chancellor Livingston was disappointed with the efforts of Dutchess County Federalists. The chancellor confided in Philip Schuyler: "Benson & our friends in Dutchess County as far as I have yet learned are unpardonably negligent. Endeavour if possible to cause them to exertion."[74]

"A large number of respectable citizens from ten precincts of Dutchess County" met in Oswego on 26 February and unanimously agreed to a slate of convention delegates. The slate was

[72]Livingston to Philip Schuyler, New York, 20 March, Schuyler Papers, NN; Gansevoort to Peter Gansevoort, New York, 18 March, Gansevoort-Lansing Papers, NN; Smith to Cornelius C. Schoonmaker, New York, 6 April, Lamb Papers, NHi; "A Flat-Bush Farmer" (Broadside, New York, 21 April); Lewis to Margaret Beekman Livingston, New York, 4 May, Robert R. Livingston Papers, NHi.

[73]Tillotson to Robert R. Livingston, Poughkeepsie, 22, 31 March, Livingston Papers, NHi.

[74]New York, 20 March, Schuyler Papers, NN.

composed of Judge Zephaniah Platt, Melancton Smith, Surrogate Gilbert Livingston, Senator Jacobus Swartwout, Assemblyman John DeWitt, Ezra Thompson, and Quaker Jonathan Akins.[75] This slate was unusual in that it contained Melancton Smith but excluded some powerful county leaders, which gave "dissatisfaction" to some Antifederalists. Smith, a merchant-lawyer, had recently moved to New York City after having lived most of his adult life in Poughkeepsie. Recognized as one of the state's leading Antifederalists, Smith knew that he could not be elected to the convention from Federalist New York City. He thus sought election from his former home county where he still maintained personal and business connections and owned a sizeable estate.

Dutchess County Federalists had two goals in the elections. First and foremost, they hoped to defeat Melancton Smith and thus deprive Antifederalists of one of their generals in the convention. A second and probably unattainable goal was to so divide the Antifederalist voters that a unified Federalist slate of candidates might eke out a victory. Dr. Thomas Tillotson hinted at the Federalist strategy: "We prefered secret to open measures in order that the other party might divide before we come forward with our nominations."[76]

On 4 March the Poughkeepsie *Country Journal* published not only the Oswego Antifederalist slate, but also another slate recommended by "Many ANTIFEDERALISTS." This second Antifederalist slate was, in reality, a Federalist plant. In an opening address "To the Free Electors of Dutchess County," "Many ANTIFEDERALISTS" condemned the omission of prominent Dutchess County politicians from the Oswego slate as well as the inclusion of outsider Melancton Smith. Voters were told to beware of Smith because he had softened his opposition to the Constitution. The new Antifederalist list included only one candidate from the Oswego slate—Jacobus Swartwout. The newly recommended candidates were Judge Cornelius Humfrey, General Lewis Duboys, Sheriff Herman Hoffman, Colonel Morris Graham, Colonel John Drake, and Dr. Barnabas Payne.

The second Antifederalist slate immediately evoked public comment in the Poughkeepsie *Country Journal*. On 18 March "Cassius" denounced Federalists for this new slate which was "pur-

---

[75]Poughkeepsie *Country Journal*, 4 March.
[76]To Robert R. Livingston, 22 March, Livingston Papers, NHi.

posely designed, to divide" the Antifederalist vote. "Cassius" told
Dutchess County Antifederalists that their opponents "are sensible
that you greatly exceed them in number and respectability.—They
well know, that unanimity in you, will defeat and ruin their prospects in this country, and, that the only method for them to bring
about their purposes, is, to raise up jealousie among you, and to
set you at variance." "Cassius" defended the selection of Melancton Smith as a Dutchess County candidate, and affirmed what was
"universally known," i.e., "that there is no man in the State more
firm in his opposition to the new constitution than Mr. Smith; no
man that more fully harmonizes in sentiment with you concerning
it; and no man that would serve you with greater fidelity in the
convention." "A Landholder," however, satirized Smith's candidacy in the *Country Journal* on 8 April by proposing a slate of seven
New York City merchants who would be Dutchess County's candidates for the Assembly. Included in the list were Melancton
Smith and Federalists Comfort Sands and Nicholas Low. On 1
April General Duboys, Judge Humfrey, Colonel Graham, and
Sheriff Hoffman told the public not to vote for them for the convention. A week later, "One of the Many" reaffirmed his support
for these four "self-denying" statesmen. "As in the concernments
of the tender passions commend me to the coy withdrawing maiden,
shrinking even from herself; so in politics, give me the men who
must be *forced* from their retreats to mount the important theatre
of public life."

On 18 March the *Country Journal*; announced a meeting to
be held on 8 April in Nine-Partners district to select a new slate
of convention candidates. The meeting unanimously endorsed
seven Federalists including Egbert Benson. The meeting also approved an address "To the Independent ELECTORS in Dutchess
County" that was published in the *Country Journal* on 15 April.
The meeting believed that Americans were in the midst of "a
CRISIS in the progress of our national Existence." The new Constitution was said to be "founded on the true Principles of Republican Liberty—that its powers are no more than equal to the
proper objects of a national Government, our general Union, Protection and Prosperity; and that a due portion of power as a safe
guard against usurpation and oppression is still to remain in the
several State Governments." Finally, the meeting maintained that
"it would be advisable for the [New York] Convention after having
ratified the Constitution to propose such amendments as on dis-

cussion shall appear proper, and to be referred to the Congress. Such a mode of Revision is practicable and safe, every other pursuit is fallacious and may be ruinous."

On the same day that Federalists met at Nine-Partners, the annual meeting of the Constitutional Society of Dutchess County met in the town of Amenia. The society believed that the outcome over the Constitution was "an event of the greatest importance, whereon depends our liberties, privileges, and national safety." It was agreed that the ratification of the Constitution by New York would "involve ourselves in many difficulties incompatible with a free people," consequently the society endorsed the Oswego slate of Antifederalist candidates.[77]

Many of the persons at the Oswego meeting reiterated their support for their slate in an address to the electors in the *Country Journal* on 15 April. They denounced the Federalists' appeal for the proposal of amendments after New York ratification. "Certainly a system of government which contains such obvious defects as to require immediate correction is unworthy the adoption of a free and enlightened people." The writer reminded the electors "that the strength of a party in a great measure consists in their unanimity; adhere therefore to this maxim, and you may be assured of success."

Dutchess County voters adhered to this advice as almost 67 percent of them supported the Oswego slate. The average Oswego candidate received 1,750 votes compared to only 881 votes for the Federalist candidates. A Federalist correspondent in the *Country Journal*, 3 June, rationalized this one-sided result. To obtain one-third of the vote was a real victory because at the beginning of the year only one-twentieth of the population would have supported Federalist candidates. "So far from being chagrined at the result of the Election in this County," the correspondent viewed "it as a source of consolation and triumph." Antifederalists, however, elected all seven of their candidates.

The most heated election in the state occurred in Albany County. Federalists were confident of victory. The city of Albany, long voting in tandem with New York City, was believed to be strongly Federalist. The countryside was filled with vast manors and estates of Federalist aristocrats—the Schuylers, the Van Rensselaers, the Duanes, the Ten Broecks, the Gansevoorts, and the

---

[77]Poughkeepsie *Country Journal*, 15 April.

Cuylers. The only Antifederalist landed aristocrats of any size in Albany County were the Lansings, the Ten Eycks, the Douws, and the lesser Van Rensselaers.

On 12 February Albany Antifederalists met and formed a committee to direct the county's election campaign. Party politics raged as Antifederalists worked tirelessly to convince the people of the dangers inherent in the proposed Constitution. Major William North of Duanesburgh, Inspector of the Continental Army and James Duane's son-in-law, reported that "The Centinel, the farmers letters, & every other publication against the Constitution are scattered all over the County."[78] Despite these tireless efforts, Leonard Gansevoort believed that the Antifederalists could not succeed—"the Minds of the People are well impressed that the present Government is inefficient . . . and embrace the present plan as the only one held out."[79] North, however, was not so optimistic: "if the Federalists do not exert themselves . . . they will be beaten."[80] Antifederalists, in fact, surprised themselves. Abraham G. Lansing wrote that "Our Measures have hitherto a most favorable aspect and if we Continue our Exertions—we have the greatest prospect of success."[81]

Federalists followed their opponents' example and created an election committee led by Albany merchant Robert McClallen. On 12 March McClallen wrote James Duane asking him to use his "influence among the Inhabitants of Duanesburgh" and requesting him to write to the other landed aristocrats in Albany County to urge them to assist in the campaign.[82]

Both election committees campaigned hard. Judge Henry Oothoudt, an Antifederal convention candidate, wrote that not "since the settlement of America" had "such exertions . . . been made upon a question of any kind as the present upon the New Constitution. Those who advocate the measure are engaged from morning untill evening they travel both night and day to proselyte the unbelieving antifederals—They have printed in hand Bills their lists . . . by thousands."[83] On 12 March the small northern district of Scatakoke met "for the purpose of knowing the sentiments of

[78] To Henry Knox, Albany, 13 February, Knox Papers, MHi.
[79] To Peter Gansevoort, Albany, 13 February, Gansevoort-Lansing Papers, NN.
[80] To Henry Knox, Albany, 13 February, Knox Papers, MHi.
[81] To Abraham Yates, Jr., 12 March, Yates Papers, NN.
[82] Duane Papers, NHi.
[83] To John McKesson, Albany, 3 April, McKesson Papers, NHi.

the people on the *Important Subject* . . . when there appeared a majority" of 27 to 5 in favor of the Constitution.[84] The Lansingburgh *Federal Herald* could not predict who would win the county elections, but on 5 May it announced that four-fifths of Lansingburgh was "federal" and that the district had "a majority of near 300 federal voters." Despite this favorable projection, Federalist convention candidate Jeronemus Hoogland of Lansingburgh warned Philip Schuyler about the Antifederalists' attempt "to Divide the Federalist [vote by] publishing a Variety of Lists of persons held up for members of the Intended Convention." Hoogland suggested that Federalists print one or two thousand handbills for Albany County "Recommending proper persons for our members, Setting forth the Designs of the Antifederalists & those Sign'd by a few of the most Influential Characters who are for our measures in the County—it would be well I think to have some men of Activity who can be Depended on to attend each District Election, with a parcell of those hand Bills with them—Depend on it the Enemies of the New Constitution are making great Efforts to carry their favourite point & I have Reason to think they make too great a Progress in their business. They will be united while I fear we will without great care be Divided."[85] Chairman of the Antifederal committee Jeremiah Van Rensselaer was confident, but he warned some of his district lieutenants to "attend at the Polls constantly until it is closed to see that all Matters are properly conducted. We rely on your Exertions and from the fair Prospects in every Part of the County we have no doubt of Success—We expect a decided Majority in this City." Van Rensselaer also warned the district leaders about an attempt to pressure manor tenants. "We are told that the Patroon Tenants are to fold up their Ballots in a particular Manner—if they do, you will direct the anti Voters to do the same."[86]

The Albany County board of supervisors met from 27 to 29 May. Before counting the ballots, the supervisors invalidated the votes from Stephentown, a district twenty miles east of Albany, because a majority of that district's election inspectors had failed to sign the ballots.[87] When the results of the county election were announced, Federalists were "much Crest fallen and have very

[84]Lansingburgh *Federal Herald*, 17 March.
[85]Lansingburgh, 1 March, Schuyler Papers, NN.
[86]To Benjamin Egbertsen, Jonathan Niles, and others, Albany, 20 April, N.
[87]Proceedings of the Supervisors of the City and County of Albany, N.

Little to say."[88] Antifederalist candidates "had a Majority in every District except the City of Albany" where Federalists had won a "respectable majority." A total of 7,449 votes were cast for convention delegates.[89] All seven Antifederal candidates, including Robert Yates and John Lansing, Jr., were overwhelmingly elected. The seven Antifederalists got an average of 4,670 votes each; the seven Federalist candidates received an average of 2,618 votes apiece.

Little is known of the elections in Queens, Orange, and Washington counties. Federalist Leonard Gansevoort reported in mid-March that Queens was "somewhat divided but our Friends are very sanguine that they will carry their whole ticket of nomination."[90] Three weeks later, however, the New York City Antifederalist Committee wrote "that the people begin to pay attention to the subject of the proposed Constitution and the opposition is formidable and increasing."[91] On the day after the elections closed, Morgan Lewis, the chancellor's brother-in-law, felt confident that Federalists had won at least two of the county's four convention seats.[92] Despite this prediction, Antifederalists continued their dominance in Queens. The New York *Daily Advertiser*, 7 June, reported that Antifederalists had swept the elections in Oyster Bay, North Hempstead, and South Hempstead; while Federalists were successful in the less populous Jamaica, Flushing, and Newtown. Antifederalist candidates received 518, 517, 484, and 476 votes compared to 416, 415, 411, and 401 for the Federalists.

Agricultural Orange County strongly supported Governor Clinton's policies. Abraham Yates, Jr., predicted that the elections in Orange would "be Carried entirely By the opposers of the Constitution."[93] The New York *Daily Advertiser*, 14 June, printed an extract of a letter from Orange County in which only Antifed-

[88]Abraham G. Lansing to Abraham Yates, Jr., 27 May, Yates Papers, NN.

[89]Matthew Visscher to Abraham Yates, Jr., John McKesson, and Melancton Smith, Albany, 30 May, Yates Papers, NN. William North reported that "it rained almost continually" during the five election days and that "The roads are exceedingly bad." He said that the election at Schoharie went against the Federalists by "a Majority of 3 to 1." To [James Duane], Duanesburg, 4 May, William North Papers, N.

[90]To Peter Gansevoort, New York, 18 March, Gansevoort-Lansing Papers, NN.

[91]To Gentlemen, 6 April, Lamb Papers, NHi.

[92]To Margaret Beekman Livingston, New York, 4 May, Robert R. Livingston Papers, NHi.

[93]To Abraham G. Lansing, Poughkeepsie, 28 February, Yates Papers, NN.

eralists were said to have received votes for the convention. Jesse Woodhull, the most popular candidate, received 340 votes; the other three Antifederalists candidates received 332, 331, and 221 votes, respectively.

Antifederalists had strong support in agricultural Washington County. Federalist Leonard Gansevoort, upon hearing that the popular Senator John Williams had decided to run for the convention, lamented that "the federalists will be overpowered in that Quarter." Federalist success in Washington County could only be achieved if Albany County Federalists campaigned in Washington.[94] But Albany County Antifederalists were also aware of their own important role in the state's northern settlements. Throughout March and April they sent Antifederalist agents and literature to Washington County from which they reported that "our political Affairs wear a favorable Aspect."[95] No results of the convention elections were published in the state's newspapers, but the *New-York Journal*, 7 June, reported that "it is supposed that the antifederal ticket will be carried by a respectable majority."

Most New Yorkers expected Staten Island (Richmond County) to be solidly aligned with New York City in support of the Constitution. Leonard Gansevoort predicted that Richmond would "be unanimously federal."[96] In early April Assemblyman Abraham Bancker reported that the election was the only news in Richmond—"the Spirit of Electioneering has not risen to so high a Pitch for three Years past." Bancker told his cousin Evert that he intended to stand for election to both the Assembly and convention. Bancker believed his chances of being elected were as good as anyone else's, but because "Party seems much to prevail," it was difficult to predict the results. In any case, if Bancker was elected it would "be by the free and unbiassed Suffrages of the people," in which case he would "be free to serve" the people. Bancker would not "officiate" in any other "Capacity."[97] Throughout the next month, Abraham Bancker continually appeared "among the People" as a candidate. "Much Policy and Chicanery," he said, "has been used by certain Characters, I am

[94]To Peter Gansevoort, New York, 18 March, Gansevoort-Lansing Papers, NN.

[95]Albany Antifederalist Committee to John Lamb, 12 April, Lamb Papers, NHi.

[96]To Peter Gansevoort, New York, 18 March, Gansevoort-Lansing Papers, NN.

[97]3 April, Bancker Family Correspondence, NHi.

apprehensive that by low and subtile Craftiness, I shall fall short of the Convention, but even that is conjecture." He had the righteous feeling, however, that he had "acted an upright Part, neither made Interest for myself, nor denied it to be made by others."[98] Bancker's upright role succeeded as he was the top vote-getter "without Soliciting One Vote to the Great Disappointment of Some individuals."[99] Federalist Judge Gozen Ryerss was also elected to the convention from Richmond.

Federalists and Antifederalists in New York City were both optimistic about election prospects in Suffolk County. Geographically the Long Island county was allied with Federalist New York City, but demographically the county was almost totally agricultural with no cities or landed, aristocratic gentry. Politically Suffolk County had been divided between Clinton's friends and opponents. Leonard Gansevoort believed that Suffolk County would "be unanimously federal," while Melancton Smith wrote that "Appearances on Long Island are favourable to our cause, and I have strong hopes, if proper exertions are made that all will go well." The New York City Antifederal Committee echoed Smith by writing that the opposition to the Constitution on Long Island was "formidable and increasing."[100]

By the first week of April a Federalist slate of candidates was circulating in Suffolk calling for the election of George Smith, Judge Selah Strong, Benjamin Hunting, Nathaniel Gardiner, and Senator Ezra L'Hommedieu. On 5 April Assemblyman Jonathan N. Havens wrote John Smith that he was not eager to become a convention candidate. Two days later Havens wrote a supplement to John Smith. Havens was unsure whether Smith would even consider being a convention candidate. Havens, himself, said that he did not care "a fig about it," but he told Smith that what concerned him was "the ridicule that may be thrown upon us both at home and abroad, for it will be said we were dropt on account of our being antis."[101]

[98]To Evert Bancker, Staten Island, 4 May, Bancker Family Correspondence, NHi.

[99]Adrian Bancker to Evert Bancker, Staten Island, 29 May, Bancker Family Correspondence, NHi.

[100]Gansevoort to Peter Gansevoort, New York, 18 March, Gansevoort-Lansing Papers, NN; Smith to Cornelius C. Schoonmaker, New York, 6 April, Lamb Papers, NHi; Antifederalist Committee Circular Letter, New York, 6 April, Lamb Papers, NHi.

[101]Sagharbour, John Smith Misc. Mss, NHi.

When news of the Federalist slate reached New York City, Antifederalists there were irate. New York County Surrogate David Gelston, until recently a resident of Suffolk, wrote John Smith a scathing letter on 9 April. "*For Shame*—you must *Stir yourself* meet your Friends some where—agree upon a good list—hold them up—persevere—even to the end—Characters you know—go through the County—don't lie Idle."[102] Gelston's goading had its effect. By 21 April Judge Thomas Treadwell was travelling throughout the county with an Antifederalist list. Treadwell painted "the dredful consiquences that will follow this adoption of the Constitution in as high coulers as the Prophet Daniel did the distress of the Babilonians previous to their destruction."[103]

New York City politicians took nothing for granted. They inundated Suffolk County with pamphlets written by John Jay and Melancton Smith. John Smith believed that if copies of Melancton Smith's pamphlet "had been generally despersed through the County two or three Weeks sooner they would have convinced the greater part of the People of the impropriety of adopting the New Constitution previous to its being amended."[104]

No vote totals are available for Suffolk County. The election, however, must have been close because as late as 15 May Federalist Ezra L'Hommedieu believed that he had been elected to the convention.[105] Not until 2 and 5 June did the *New-York Journal* announce that Antifederalists had carried the county.

The outcome in Westchester County was also uncertain. Westchester had extensive manors—many, however, were in the process of being divided. The county's assemblymen had vacillated over the last several years, sometimes supporting and sometimes opposing paper money and an unconditional federal impost. But Westchester's assemblymen had voted to elect John Lansing, Jr., instead of James Duane to the Constitutional Convention in March 1787 and they had voted to censure the Constitutional Convention for violating its instructions.

On 28 February 1788 Abraham Yates, Jr., reported that "Antiferal Business is Carried on in . . . Westchester with Spirit."[106]

---

[102]*Ibid.*

[103]John Smith to David Gelston [23–27 April], John Smith Misc. Mss, NHi.

[104]*Ibid.*

[105]To Leonard Gansevoort, Suffolk County, 15 May, Gratz Collection, Old Congress, PHi.

[106]To Abraham G. Lansing, Yates Papers, NN.

Connecticut Federalist Jeremiah Wadsworth worried about West-chester's Antifederalism. As he passed through the township of East Chester, Wadsworth "found the Ante's had been busy and too Successfull."[107] Leonard Gansevoort, however, happily wrote his son about the events in Westchester. Philip Van Cortlandt, the lieutenant governor's son, had become active in the campaign. Van Cortlandt had been called forth "as out of a Gothic Cloister, and the Air so strongly impregnated with federalism has infused into his nostrils the aromatic, his whole frame infected with the contagion has called him forth to Action and has transported him from extreme inaction to increasing exertion. he is making In-terest to be returned a Delegate and from the Influence which his Office as Commissioner of forfeiture has acquired him and his established reputation for probity and Integrity will doubtless in-sure him success. how it will go with the Members he is supporting in general is very uncertain, the People have in general a tincture of antifederalism. tho' it is said that six States having already adopted the Constitution stifles in a great Measure the latent sparks."[108] Lewis Morris, the elderly lord of Morrisania and brother of the state's chief justice, had tried to get his son William nom-inated to the convention. Westchester Federalists, however, sensed the danger and insisted that the manor lord himself stand as a candidate. To run the younger Morris "was putting too much at stake."[109] As the election closed, Morgan Lewis reported that Fed-eralists "have the most flattering prospects" in Westchester, "un-less the votes of Bedford should be rejected, on Account of some Irregularity in the Appointment of their Inspectors."[110] The an-ticipated problem in Bedford apparently never materialized. An extract of a letter from a gentleman in Westchester, published in the New York *Daily Advertiser*, 2 June, reported "that the *Federal Ticket* . . . has prevailed by a majority of two to one. So decisive a victory, I frankly confess, has exceeded my most sanguine expec-tations." In fact, Federalists swept Westchester County with 64 percent of the vote. The six Federalist candidates averaged 655

[107]To Henry Knox, 17 April, Knox Papers, MHi.
[108]To Peter Gansevoort, New York, 18 March, Gansevoort-Lansing Papers, NN.
[109]Kenneth Rendell Catalog 78, Item 92 (1972):31.
[110]To Margaret Beekman Livingston, New York, 4 May, Robert R. Liv-ingston Papers, NHi.

votes to their opponents' 374. Abraham Yates, Jr., bemoaned the way that Westchester had "been most Shamefully taken in."[111]

No single factor can explain the county divisions over the Constitution. Various explanations have been suggested: north vs. south, merchant vs. farmer, tory vs. whig, debtor vs. creditor, aristocrat vs. democrat, and states rights vs. nationalism. All of these elements were indeed present in New York politics, although no one dichotomy totally explains the election of convention delegates. One overriding issue seemed to tie all of New York's conflicts together. To a remarkable degree the contest over the election of convention delegates was a conflict between Clintonianism and the proposed Constitution. It was suggested that Clinton, "The *Helmsman* leads a majority by the nose just as he pleases."[112] Another correspondent believed that Governor Clinton "is at the head of the opposition, and it is believed that if he would say *yea*, nineteen twentieths of the anti-federalists would say so too. If it be so, the opposition in this state, though apparently formidable, is in fact involved in one man."[113]

Whatever the reasons for the division over the voting, a correspondent in a widely circulated newspaper essay lamented the party spirit that had developed. "Wherever the spirit of party reigns, the public weal generally falls a sacrifice to it." Despite the one-sided Antifederalist victory, it was hoped that the convention would give the Constitution "a fair discussion." "But if blind prejudice, predetermined opposition, and '*silent negatives*' are to be characteristic of our Convention, our reputation as a Sovereign State will be deservedly lost forever!"[114]

The Convention

At 11:00 A.M. on Saturday the 14th of June 1788, Governor Clinton and a number of other Antifederalist delegates left New York City without fanfare aboard a Poughkeepsie sloop "determined

[111]To Abraham G. Lansing, 1 June, Yates Papers, NN.

[112]"Extract of a letter from New York, July 20, 1788," *New Hampshire Spy*, 29 July.

[113]"Extract of a letter from a gentleman in New York, to his friend in this City, dated May 24," Charleston *Columbian Herald*, 19 June. John Vaughan, a Philadelphia merchant, wrote John Dickinson that Governor Clinton's "opposition is the only formidable one." Whatever direction Clinton would take, "New York follows of course." N. d., Dickinson Papers, Free Library of Philadelphia.

[114]*New-York Packet*, 6 June.

not to adopt [the Constitution] without previous amendments tho all the others should."[115] Seven hours later James Duane, John Sloss Hobart, and other Federalist delegates started their trek up the Hudson, cheered on by the "loud acclamations" of "a great concourse of citizens" and saluted by thirteen discharges of cannon from the battery.[116] As the delegates converged on Poughkeepsie, they realized the critical situation of the state and country. Eight of the required nine states had already ratified the new Constitution and the New Hampshire and Virginia conventions were in session. It was expected that New Hampshire would ratify; Virginia's decision was uncertain.

Sixty-one of the sixty-five delegates attended the opening session of the New York Convention at noon on 17 June. Governor Clinton was unanimously elected president, other convention officers were appointed, and the doors of the convention were ordered open to the public. After the legislature's resolution calling the state convention was read and a rules committee was appointed, the convention adjourned to 11:00 the next morning. On the 18th, the convention agreed to the rules brought in by the committee, read the Constitution and the resolutions of the Constitutional Convention and Congress, and ordered these documents printed so that each member of the convention would have his own copy. Albany delegate John Lansing, Jr., moved that the convention meet the next day as a committee of the whole to discuss the Constitution.[117]

That evening "Federalists intimated their wish" that Chief Justice Richard Morris be made chairman of the committee of the whole. Antifederalists, however, had other plans. On Thursday morning, 19 June, Judge Henry Oothoudt was elected chairman and Federalists "acquiesced without opposition."[118] After the Constitution and other papers were read in the committee of the whole, Chancellor Robert R. Livingston rose and delivered an hour-long oration in a low voice that was hard to hear amid the noise of the

[115]Abraham Yates, Jr., to Abraham G. Lansing, New York, 15 June, Yates Papers, NN.

[116]New York *Daily Advertiser*, 16 June.

[117]The manuscript and printed journals of the convention are brief skeletal outlines of the proceedings. For greater details of the events including reports of debates taken by Francis Childs, see *The Debates and Proceedings of the Convention of the State of New-York...* (New York, 1788).

[118]John Lansing, Jr., to Abraham Yates, Jr., Poughkeepsie, 19 June, Gansevoort-Lansing Papers, NN.

crowded convention. The chancellor expounded on the deficiencies of the Articles of Confederation and condemned New York's inflexible policy on the federal impost. He warned the delegates of the dangers facing New York outside the Union. Staten Island might be seized by New Jersey and Long Island by Connecticut. Northern New York would be endangered by Canadians and land-grabbing Vermonters, while western New York would be increasingly threatened by the British and their Indian allies. Livingston thus urged that the delegates consider the new Constitution objectively, not from the point of view of interested state office-holders, which many of the delegates were, but with the open minds of citizens with the best interests of the state and country at heart. In closing, he moved that the Constitution be discussed by paragraphs and that no votes be taken on the Constitution or any parts of it until the whole had been discussed. Antifederalists agreed to Livingston's motion with the proviso that amendments to the Constitution could be proposed and debated at any time.

The vote on Chancellor Livingston's motion was critical. A number of Antifederalists both in and out of the convention were displeased with the decision. John Lansing feared "some Injury from a long delay," while David Gelston in New York City was disappointed that the convention did not adjourn "immediately after reading *the Constitution*."[119] Abraham G. Lansing, the Albany County surrogate and younger brother of John, was apprehensive that "we will eventually be injured by delays, notwithstanding the decided majority."[120] Federalist delegate Alexander Hamilton, on the other hand, reported to James Madison on 19 June that "there is every appearance that a full discussion will take place, which will keep us together at least a fortnight." Two days later Hamilton again wrote Madison that "the only good information I can give you is that we shall be sometime together and take the chance of events."[121] Federalists had won the first major battle of the convention—they had avoided an immediate adjournment or rejection—they had won a three to four week reprieve during which time they hoped to hear that New Hampshire and Virginia had ratified the Constitution. Abraham G. Lansing feared the influence of these other states on Antifederalist delegates, but he was more fearful that "our Country Friends with whom it is now the

Busy Season," might leave the convention to tend to their farms. He therefore appealed to Abraham Yates, Jr., then in New York City attending Congress, "to write Swart, Vrooman, Yates, etc. urging them to stay until the Business is compleated."[122]

Many Antifederalists saw little danger from considering the Constitution by paragraphs. Only a handful of delegates had come to the convention with the idea of an immediate rejection of the Constitution. A greater number of Antifederalists thought that the convention might adjourn quickly to reconvene perhaps in the spring or summer of 1789. In any event, with the advantage of a two-to-one majority, Antifederalists did not wish to give the impression that they were unfair. They would listen to the arguments of their opponents.

Antifederalists were also buoyed by recent news from Virginia. Patrick Henry, George Mason, and other Virginians had sent a copy of their proposed amendments to the Constitution and asked the New York Convention "to agree on the necessary Amendments" and communicate them to Virginia as soon as possible.[123] New York Antifederalists appointed a committee of correspondence, chaired by Robert Yates, an Albany delegate, that responded to their Virginia counterparts on 21 June. "We are happy to find that your Sentiments with respect to the Amendments correspond so nearly with ours, and that they stood on the Broad Basis of securing the Rights and equally promoting the Happiness of every Citizen in the Union. Our Convention . . . yielded to a Proposal made by our Opponents to discuss the Constitution in a Committee of the whole, without putting a Question on any Part, provided that in the course of this Discussion, we should suggest the Amendments or Explications, which we deemed necessary to the exceptionable Parts—Fully relying on the Steadiness of our Friends, we see no Danger in this Mode and we came into it to prevent the Opposition from charging us with Precipitation. . . . We have . . . the fullest Reliance that neither Sophistry Fear or Influence will effect any Change" in the Antifederalists.[124] Other Antifederalists agreed that the "Unanimity and Harmony" among the Clintonians "shut out the Shadow of Hope in the Federalists, of creating Divisions."[125]

[122]22 June, Yates Papers, NN.
[123]John Lamb to George Clinton, New York, 17 June, Lamb Papers, NHi.
[124]Robert Yates to George Mason, Poughkeepsie, 21 June, Emmet Collection, NN.
[125]James M. Hughes to John Lamb, Poughkeepsie, 18 June, Lamb Papers, NHi.

Federalists, however, spied a glimmer of hope. Almost immediately, Hamilton, Livingston, and John Jay began "singling out the Members in Opposition (when out of Convention) and conversing with them on the subject."[126] Jay wrote his wife that "the Event" was uncertain, but "I do not despair . . . altho I see much Room for apprehension."[127] Hamilton said that "the minor partisans have their scruples and an air of moderation is now assumed. So far the thing is not to be despaired of."[128]

On 20 June John Lansing responded to Chancellor Livingston's oration by saying that the problems of the Confederation could be solved if Congress were given the power to raise men and money. Fear of the dissolution of the Union, however, should not be the reason to adopt the new Constitution. Lansing looked upon the abandonment of the Union "with pain," but it was better to break up the Union than to "submit to any measures, which may involve in its consequences the loss of civil liberty." Lansing also attacked Livingston's insinuation that state officeholders opposed the Constitution for selfish reasons. Such "an illiberality of sentiment," he maintained, "would disgrace the worst cause."

Dutchess County delegate Melancton Smith hoped that the convention would now discuss the Constitution by paragraphs. He was tired of "general observations." Addressing the convention, Smith said that "he was disposed to make every reasonable concession, and indeed to sacrifice every thing for a Union, except the liberties of his country." There was no doubt that the Confederation was defective, but that was no proof "that the proposed Constitution was a good one." He then turned the tables on Livingston by suggesting that some men supported the Constitution because they thirsted for federal office. After this digression, Smith addressed the first part of the Constitution. He objected to slaves being included in the apportionment of congressional representatives, to the small number of federal representatives, and to the ratio of one representative for every 30,000 inhabitants.

Hamilton immediately responded, referring to "the imbecility of our Union" under the Confederation and predicting "that a rejection of the Constitution may involve most fatal consequences." He agreed that "we ought not to be actuated by un-

[126]Charles Tillinghast to John Lamb, Poughkeepsie, 21 June, Lamb Papers, NHi.

[127]Poughkeepsie, 21 June, N.

[128]To James Madison, Poughkeepsie, 19 June, Rutland, *Madison*, XI:156.

reasonable fear, yet we ought to be prudent." He reprobated the idea of giving the Confederation Congress the power over men and money—"Will any man who entertains a wish for the safety of his country, trust the sword and the purse with a single Assembly?" To give the Confederation Congress such powers "would be to establish a despotism." Hamilton had much more to say but, after an hour, he asked the convention's leave because "I feel myself not a little exhausted."

On Saturday, 21 June, John Williams of Washington County addressed the convention for the first time. He believed "that all our present difficulties are not to be attributed to the defects in the Confederation." The extravagant consumption of foreign luxuries also contributed to the hard times of postwar America. He called for a thorough examination of the Constitution to see if it would "preserve the invaluable blessings of liberty, and secure the inestimable rights of mankind. If it be so, let us adopt it.—But if it be found to contain principles, that will lead to the subversion of liberty—If it tends to establish a despotism, or what is worse, a tyrannical aristocracy, let us insist upon the necessary alterations and amendments." He too objected to Chancellor Livingston's "imaginary dangers: For to say that a bad government must be established for fear of anarchy, is in reality saying that we must kill ourselves for fear of dying." Smith, Lansing, and Hamilton followed with long orations, the latter concluding "that a firm union is as necessary to perpetuate our liberties, as it is to make us respectable; and experience will probably prove, that the national government will be as natural a guardian of our freedom, as the state legislatures themselves."

Governor Clinton then reiterated some of the objections to the small number of federal representatives. He concluded by stating that the United States was a vast territory and that the states were dissimilar—"Their habits, their productions, their resources, and their political and commercial regulations are as different as those of any nation on earth." Hamilton attacked the governor's inference "that no general free government can suit" the states. He maintained that "the people of America are as uniform in their interests and manners, as those of any established in Europe." The governor was aghast at the "unjust and unnatural colouring" given to his statements. He declared "that the dissolution of the Union is, of all events, the remotest from my wishes." Hamilton, the governor said, wished "for a consolidated—I wish for a federal republic. The object of both of us is a firm energetic government: and we may both have the good of our country in view; though we disagree as to the means of procuring it."

On 24 June word arrived in Poughkeepsie by express rider that New Hampshire had ratified the Constitution. Although the news had been expected, no one really knew what the actual event would do to Antifederalist solidarity. Antifederalist delegates were pleased with the reaction. Chairman Oothoudt reported that the news "Does not seem to make an Imprestion. I Expect it will not."[129] Christopher P. Yates of Montgomery County wrote that "we stand firm we have as yet lost no ground. . . . there is not the most distant fear of a division among ourselves. . . . I observe no change in the countenances, the opinion or the resolution of any."[130] Governor Clinton wrote that "The Antis are Firm & I hope and believe will remain so to the End."[131] Antifederalist observers in Poughkeepsie agreed. DeWitt Clinton, the governor's nephew, believed that "The Republican Members are (to use an expression of the Plebian) united as one man."[132] Abraham G. Lansing reported that Antifederalists congratulated their opponents on New Hampshire's ratification and expressed "our satisfaction that they can now give the New System an Experiment without Interfering in the politics of the State of New York."[133]

Although not discouraged by New Hampshire's ratification, Lansing and other Antifederalists still worried about "the Length of Time which must necessarily elapse before the Business can be concluded." Lansing also believed that a report of ratification by Virginia will have "a more serious effect I fear upon the Spirits and determination of our Friends."[134] In New York City, Abraham Yates, Jr., was asked by several members of Congress what the state of New York would do now that the new government was going to be established. His response was that New Hampshire's ratification was irrelevant; New York would ratify the Constitution but "not without previous Amendments."[135]

[129]To Abraham Yates, Jr., Poughkeepsie, 27 June, Yates Papers, NN.
[130]To Abraham Yates, Jr., Poughkeepsie, 27 June, Yates Papers, NN.
[131]To Abraham Yates, Jr., Poughkeepsie, 28 June, Yates Papers, NN.
[132]To Charles Tillinghast, Poughkeepsie, 27 June, DeWitt Clinton Papers, NNC.
[133]To Abraham Yates, Jr., Poughkeepsie, 29 June, Yates Papers, NN.
[134]*Ibid.*
[135]To Abraham G. Lansing, New York, 25 June, Yates Papers, NN.

New Hampshire's ratification did have an effect on Melancton Smith, the Antifederalists' convention manager. Smith hoped that the news would convince his fellow Antifederalists "to consider what is proper to be done in the present situation of things," but he could "scarcely perceive any" change in attitude. Smith feared "that there will not be a sufficient degree of moderation in some of our most influential men, calmly to consider the circumstances in which we are and to accommodate our decisions to those circumstances." Perhaps, Smith believed, it would be best not to ratify the Constitution with conditions. Rather, Smith formulated in his own mind a new plan that called for the convention to ratify the Constitution unconditionally but with the proviso that New York would withdraw from the Union if a second constitutional convention was not called within a year or two. Smith proposed this scheme to his friend Massachusetts Congressman Nathan Dane, but did not present this new idea to the convention at this time.[136]

Philip Schuyler, observing the convention in Poughkeepsie, sensed a slight change in Antifederalist tactics. He believed that "the Antis do not seem inclined to make much speed in the business. they probably wish to learn the result of Virginia's convention."[137] The latest news from Virginia was discouraging to Federalists. James Madison had written Hamilton on 13 June about the critical state of affairs in Richmond. On 25 June Hamilton responded that "Our chance of success here is infinitely slender, and none at all if you go wrong." Two days later Hamilton wrote again that "our chance of success depends on you."[138]

Events, however, turned in the Federalists' favor, and on 25 June the Virginia Convention ratified the Constitution with recommendatory amendments. News of the important event reached New York City on 2 July at 2:00 A.M. Within ten hours the news reached Poughkeepsie by express rider. Federalists were elated; Antifederalists concerned. Outwardly Antifederalists again said that Virginia's ratification had made "no impressions upon the republican members," but slight signs of disunity began to appear.[139]

---

[136]Smith to Dane, Poughkeepsie, 28 June, Dane Papers, Beverly Historical Society.

[137]To Henry Van Schaack, 24 June, Henry Van Schaack Scrapbook, The Newberry Library, Chicago, Ill.

[138]Rutland, *Madison*, XI:179–80, 183.

[139]DeWitt Clinton to Charles Tillinghast, Poughkeepsie, 2 July, DeWitt Clinton Papers, NNC.

As soon as news of Virginia reached Poughkeepsie, Federalists adopted a completely different tactic in the convention. Up until that time, Federalists had delayed the convention proceedings hoping for favorable news from New Hampshire and Virginia. Now Federalists stopped debating. Queens County delegate Nathaniel Lawrence reported on 3 July that previously Federalists had "disputed every inch of ground but today they have quietly suffered us to propose our amendments without a word in opposition to them."[140] During its first two weeks, the convention had debated only the first eight sections of Article I. During the next five days, the remainder of the Constitution was sped through as Antifederalist amendments were submitted without Federalist comment.

What were Federalists up to? It seems as if Federalists had gotten all the benefits possible out of their strategy of delay. They now wished to see what Antifederalists planned to do with their amendments. Federalists believed that an outright rejection of the Constitution was unlikely. While hoping for unconditional ratification accompanied by recommendatory amendments, Federalists thought that adjournment was preferable to conditional ratification. Abraham Yates, Jr., warned Governor Clinton and Abraham G. Lansing that Federalists hoped to adjourn the convention so that during the recess the members "will be Seperated and open to their Management" while "the State would be in Continual Convulsion."[141]

On 7 July the convention finished discussing the Constitution and John Lansing read a bill of rights that was "to be prefixed to the constitution." For the next two days, no business was transacted in the convention as Antifederalists caucused in order to arrange their proposed amendments. Hamilton and John Jay sensed that the "Party begins to divide in their opinions." Some Antifederalists favored previous conditional amendments, others favored ratification for a number of years "on Condition that certain Amendments take place within a given Time," and still others favored unconditional ratification with recommendatory amendments. Federalists saw "some ground of hope."[142]

[140]To John Lamb, Poughkeepsie, Lamb Papers, NHi.
[141]To Abraham G. Lansing, New York, 29 June, and to George Clinton, New York, 27 June, Yates Papers, NN.
[142]Jay to George Washington, Poughkeepsie, 4–8 July, Washington Papers, DLC; Hamilton to James Madison, Poughkeepsie, 8 July, Rutland, *Madison*, XI:187.

On 10 July John Lansing submitted a plan of amendments which represented a compromise among Antifederalists. There were three kinds of amendments: (1) explanatory, (2) conditional, and (3) recommendatory. The first included a bill of rights and some explanation of unclear portions of the Constitution. The conditional amendments provided that, until a general convention considered these matters, Congress should not (1) call the state militia to serve outside New York for longer than six weeks without the consent of the state legislature, (2) regulate federal elections within New York, or (3) collect direct taxes in New York without first requisitioning the tax from the state. The recommendatory amendments, which were "numerous and important," would be considered by the first federal Congress under the Constitution. John Jay, Chancellor Livingston, and Richard Morris attacked the plan as "a gilded Rejection" that Congress would never accept as a valid ratification. Melancton Smith, Governor Clinton, and Lansing defended the plan—"this, Say they is our *Ultimatum*. We go not a Step beyond it." In fact, many Antifederalists "thought they had conceded too much." DeWitt Clinton wrote that "if the feds. had been friendly instead of being inimical to the proposal I have my doubts whether [a] majority of antis would not have voted against it—but the opposition of their political adversaries has reconciled them."[143]

On 11 July John Jay moved that the convention ratify the Constitution without conditions but with certain explanations and with recommendatory amendments. Antifederalist Samuel Jones of Queens County, thinking the final vote would take place, did not attend the convention. It was said that he was "very much terrified." He believed that the Constitution should be ratified but did not wish to vote against his party.[144] Despite Antifederalists' attempts to get a vote on their plan, debate continued for almost a week. Philip Schuyler believed that "the opponents are so evidently deranged and embarrassed by this measure, that It affords a hope of a better Issue than we have hitherto had a prospect of."[145] On 15 July Melancton Smith moved to amend Jay's motion

[143]Abraham Bancker to Evert Bancker, Poughkeepsie, 12 July, Bancker Family Correspondence, NHi; DeWitt Clinton to Charles Tillinghast, Poughkeepsie, 12 July, DeWitt Clinton Papers, NNC.

[144]David S. Bogart to Samuel B. Webb, Poughkeepsie, 14 July, W.C. Ford, ed., *Correspondence and Journals of Samuel Blachley Webb*, 3 vols. (New York, 1893–1894), III:104.

[145]To Stephen Van Rensselaer, Poughkeepsie, 14 July, Schuyler Papers, DLC.

to make it conform to Lansing's original plan of 10 July. Debate over this amendment continued for several days. With the situation again looking bleak, Federalist John Sloss Hobart of New York City moved on 16 July for an adjournment until 2 September so "that the Members might have an opportunity of going home to Consult their Constituents." On 17 July Hobart's motion was defeated 40 to 22. James Duane of New York City then moved that Smith's amendment be postponed in order to consider another variant of a conditional ratification. Duane's proposal was defeated 41 to 20.

After some debate on his amendment, Smith, with Judge Zephaniah Platt of Dutchess County, brought in a new plan of ratification. The convention would first declare that the Constitution was defective; but since ten states had already ratified, New York would also ratify preserving the right, however, to withdraw from the Union if Congress did not call a convention to consider amendments within four years. In introducing this plan, Smith said that he was convinced that Congress would not accept any conditional ratification, "and as he valued the Union, he was resolved that this State should not be excluded." Therefore, Smith announced that he would not vote for any form of conditional ratification.

Antifederalists were displeased with Smith's new proposal. Cornelius C. Schoonmaker of Ulster County believed that "the federalists will agree to" the new plan "as the most favorable to them, and having no great hopes of a better—they say the lesser Evil of the two. I believe the Antis will divide on this plan which will I fear be against us. It appears to me very little short of an absolute adoption."[146] The convention adjourned to the next day.

On 18 July it was expected that Smith's amendment plan would be postponed in order to consider his new proposal; but, when the time came for the motion to postpone, "a long Silence ensued—the [Antifederalist] Party seemed embarrassed—fearful to divide among themselves."[147] The convention adjourned so that Antifederalists could caucus.

With the new proposal in mind, Hamilton wrote James Madison, back in Congress in New York City, asking him whether

[146]To Peter Van Gaasbeek, Poughkeepsie, 18 July, Peter Van Gaasbeek Papers, NKS.

[147]John Jay to George Washington, Poughkeepsie, 17–[18] July, Jay Papers, NNC.

Congress would accept New York's ratification with a *"reservation* of a right to recede in case our amendments have not been decided upon in one of the modes pointed out in the Constitution within a certain number of years."[148] Antifederalists, however, rejected Smith's new proposal in caucus. Therefore, when the convention met on 19 July, Smith withdrew the plan. John Lansing then moved, and the convention agreed 41 to 18, that all of the other plans under consideration be postponed so that a new conditional ratification could be considered. The convention considered Lansing's plan from 19 to 23 July.

The convention was now divided into four groups: "one of which was for an Adoption with Conditions, one for a given time in order to withdraw if a General convention is not obtained in that time; one for an adjournment and one for an absolute Ratification."[149] For a while it looked as if the convention would adjourn. Such a move was favored by Federalists and a handful of Antifederalists. It was thought that it might be too inconsistent for Antifederalists to vote in favor of ratification "in the same session they have so violently opposed it—and a short recess may at least put a better coloring to their assenting to it. a little time and cool conversation with their friends at home no doubt will have a good effect."[150]

On 20 July convention delegate Dirck Swart arrived in Albany, much to the surprise of Abraham G. Lansing. Swart told Lansing that he had left Poughkeepsie the day before at 10:00 A.M. and that a motion for adjournment was expected to pass the convention. Lansing was irate. "If this Measure should take place, all the Exertions we have made and the anxiety we have experienced for the Liberty of our Country will end in nothing." Rather than adjourn, Lansing would forego previous amendments and would support a ratification with only recommendatory amendments. An adjournment would leave Antifederalists "without any prospect of Success. The Baneful Manor Interest will be exerted to obtain Instructions to the Delegates, and the poor deluded well meaning Yeominery of our Country, not having it in their power to follow the dictates of their own Consciences, will be compelled to sign these Instructions to keep well with their Masters. Our

[148][19] July, Poughkeepsie, Rutland, *Madison*, XI:188.
[149]Isaac Roosevelt to Richard Varick, Poughkeepsie, 22–[23] July, NHpR.
[150]Pierse Long to Nicholas Gilman, Portsmouth, N.H., 22 July, J.S.H. Fogg Autograph Collection, Maine Historical Society.

Friends in the City, and Numbers in the County—will decline signing counter Instructions, by the Meaneauvers of the Federalists who will hold out every Circumstance they can to alarm and Intimidate." To combat any move for adjournment, Lansing and other Albany Antifederalists wrote a letter to their delegates recommending "by all Means to finish the Business to a Close before they rise." Lansing castigated Melancton Smith, who was "charged with some improper steps," which "if it is True[,] he has injured the Cause of our Country more than any Federalist."[151]

No motion was made for adjournment at this time. On 23 July the convention considered John Lansing's form of ratification which called for New York to ratify the Constitution "upon condition" that certain amendments be accepted. Samuel Jones then moved that the words "upon condition" be expunged and be replaced by the words "in full confidence." Melancton Smith supported the change. "He was as thoroughly convinced then as he ever had been, that the Constitution was radically defective, amendments to it had always been the object of his pursuit, and until Virginia came in, he had reason to believe they might have been obtained previous to the operation of the Government. He was now satisfied they could not, and it was equally the dictate of reason and of duty to quit his first ground, and advance so far as that they might be received into the Union. He should hereafter pursue his important and favourite object of amendments with equal zeal as before, but in a practicable way which was only in the mode prescribed by the Constitution." Conditional ratification "must now be abandoned as fallacious, for if persisted in, it would certainly prove in the event, only a dreadful deception to those who were serious for joining the Union."[152] Dutchess County delegates Gilbert Livingston and Zephaniah Platt echoed Smith's sentiments. Governor Clinton replied that he would "pursue what he believed to be the sense" of Ulster County, which was a conditional ratification.[153] The vote on Jones's motion was taken and it was adopted 31 to 29. Antifederalists were stunned. If nothing new occurred, New York would ratify the Constitution unconditionally. But Antifederalists were not ready to give up—they "mean to rally their forces and endeavour to regain that Ground."[154]

[151]Abraham G. Lansing to Abraham Yates, Jr., 20 July, Yates Papers, NN.
[152]"Copy of a Letter from Poughkeepsie, dated Friday, July 25, 1788," New York *Independent Journal*, 28 July (supplement extraordinary).
[153]*Ibid.*
[154]John Jay to George Washington, Poughkeepsie, 23 July, Washington Papers, DLC.

The New York City Federal Procession, 23 July 1788

Ever since the end of the Revolution, Americans celebrated their independence on the 4th of July. In 1788 this day of celebration took on added meaning—supporters of the Constitution proclaimed not only the twelfth anniversary of independence but also the birth of a new general government adopted by the people of America.

Despite the general joy at the adoption of the Constitution by ten states, New York City Federalists faced a perplexing dilemma. They wished to honor the new Constitution on the 4th of July, but New York had not yet ratified the new form of government. To avoid any disrespect to the convention, New York City Federalists postponed their celebration first to 10 July, then to the 22nd, and finally to the 23rd. Despite rumors to the contrary, the planned procession would be delayed no longer even though the state convention had not yet acted.

At 8:00 A.M. Wednesday, 23 July, ten cannon shots signaled the gathering of what was to be the "most brilliant" display "ever seen in America." After two hours of organizing, the grand procession began the mile and a half trek down Broadway to Great Dock Street through Hanover Square, Queen, Chatham, Division, and Arundel streets. Finally the parade made its way down Bullock Street to Nicholas Bayard's house and the city's parade grounds.

The procession, led by two horsemen with trumpets and a company of artillery with a field piece, was divided into ten divisions. The first eight divisions were composed, seemingly at random, of tradesmen and artisans of every description—millers, bakers, brewers, hatters, etc. Each occupation carried its emblems, and some rode on elaborate floats. The ninth division was composed of lawyers, the philological society, the president, faculty, and students of Columbia College, and merchants and traders; the tenth division was made up of physicians, foreigners, and militia officers.

The high point of the procession appeared in the seventh division. A twenty-seven-foot frigate named *The Hamilton*, upon a carriage

On 24 July John Lansing proposed that the form of ratification include the right of New York to secede from the Union if amendments to the Constitution were not adopted within a certain number of years. Hamilton then read a letter he had recently received in which James Madison said that "a reservation of a right to withdraw" was "a *conditional* ratification" and as such New York "could not be received [in the Union] on that plan." After similar opinions from James Duane and Chancellor Livingston, the con-

Federal Ship HAMILTON.

concealed by canvas waves, was pulled by ten horses. The ship was manned by over thirty sailors and marines and carried thirty-two guns that were discharged at different times.

When the procession reached the parade grounds the marchers went to one of ten tables, each 440 feet long, radiating like the spokes of a half wheel from a hub composed of three raised pavilions connected by a 150 foot colonnade. The elaborate structure, designed by Pierre L'Enfant, seated over 6,000. The members of Congress were seated in the center pavilion flanked by the foreign diplomatic corps on the right and the officers of the Confederation government and the city's clergy on the left. The whole concourse was treated to a banquet provided by the trade associations. At 5:00 P.M. the procession retraced its march and the participants were dismissed at 5:30. Almost 5,000 individuals marched in the procession—one-quarter of the city's population—while estimates of up to 20,000 onlookers lined the streets.

For more on the New York City procession, see Whitfield J. Bell, Jr., "The Federal Processions of 1788," New York Historical Society *Quarterly* XLVI (1962):5–40. For contemporary accounts of the procession, see the New York *Daily Advertiser* and the New York *Independent Journal*, both 2 August 1788. By the end of August, fifteen other newspapers from New Hampshire to Virginia reprinted these accounts of the procession. Accounts of celebrations of the ratification of the Constitution by New York were also widespread. See: Albany, 8 August (*Federal Herald*, 11 August; *New York Packet*, 5 September); Ballston, Albany County, 30 July (*Federal Herald*, 4 August); Flushing, Queens County, 8 August (*Daily Advertiser*, 13 August); Half Moon District, Albany County, 13 August (*Federal Herald*, 25 August); Hurley, Ulster County, 12 August (*Country Journal*, 26 August); Newburgh, Ulster County, 26 July (*New York Packet*, 1 August); Poughkeepsie, Dutchess County, 11 August (*Country Journal*, 19 August); Red Hook, Dutchess County, 6 August (*Country Journal*, 12 August); Saratoga, Albany County, 13 August (*Federal Herald*, 18 August); and Schenectady, Albany County, 15 August (*Pennsylvania Mercury*, 4 September).

vention adjourned.[155] On 25 July Lansing's motion was rejected 31 to 28. The committee of the whole approved the final form of ratification by a vote of 31 to 28 and unanimously resolved that a circular letter be prepared to be sent to the states "pressing in the most earnest manner, the necessity of a general convention to

[155]James Madison to Alexander Hamilton, New York, [20] July, Rutland, *Madison*, XI, 189; "Copy of a Letter from Poughkeepsie, dated Friday, July 25, 1788," New York *Independent Journal*, 28 July (supplement extraordinary).

take into their consideration the amendments to the Constitution, proposed by the several State Conventions." On 26 July the convention approved the committee of the whole's report to ratify the Constitution with recommendatory amendments by a vote of 30 to 27. John Jay then brought in the proposed circular letter which was unanimously approved. Cornelius C. Schoonmaker lamented "that the Federalists have fought and beat us from our own ground with our own weapons."[156] According to Philip Schuyler, "perseverance, patience and abilities have prevailed against numbers and prejudice."[157]

New York: The Reluctant Pillar

Why then did the New York Convention, with a two-to-one Antifederalist majority, ratify the Constitution? As the debate over the Constitution progressed and as one state after another adopted the new form of government, a rising tide of public opinion came to favor adoption. It was felt that all of the ratifying states could not be wrong, and therefore the Constitution should be given a chance.

Convention Antifederalists were far from being unanimous. From the very beginning of the convention, most Antifederalist delegates opposed an outright rejection. Only a few leaders, among them Governor Clinton, were willing to hazard such drastic steps as rejection or adjournment. Federalist delegate Abraham Bancker of Richmond County believed that if Clinton had not so strenuously opposed the Constitution, the convention would have adopted it a month earlier than it did. Hamilton believed that the governor's adamancy stemmed from his desire "to establish *Clintonism* on the basis of *Antifoederalism*."[158] The other divisions within moderate Antifederalist ranks also made united action difficult.

Federalist strategy also contributed to the adoption. The ability to keep the convention in session during the first critical weeks ultimately set the stage for ratification. For the most part, though, Federalist strategists played a waiting game. They let John Lansing

---

[156]To Peter Van Gaasbeek, Poughkeepsie, 25 July, Marius Schoonmaker, *The History of Kingston, New York . . .* (New York, 1888), 394–96.

[157]To Peter Van Schaack, Poughkeepsie, 25 July, N.

[158]Abraham Bancker to Evert Bancker, Poughkeepsie, 28 June, Bancker Family Correspondence, NHi; Alexander Hamilton to James Madison, [2 July], Rutland, *Madison*, XI:185.

and Melancton Smith orchestrate the entire convention. The divisiveness among Antifederalists created opportunities for Federalists. Throughout the convention, Federalists tried to remain as conciliatory as possible. Their perseverance and stamina were important weapons, much more effective than their touted eloquence. Repeatedly, Federalists and Antifederalists said that oratory convinced no one to change his mind.

The single most important factor in obtaining ratification, however, was simply the course of events taking place throughout America. Hamilton admitted that "Our arguments confound, but do not convince—Some of the leaders however appear to me to be convinced *by circumstances.*"[159] The ratification by New Hampshire and, most important, by Virginia were determining factors. New York could not kill the Constitution by itself. The new government was going into effect with or without New York. Since New Jersey, Pennsylvania, and Delaware had ratified the Constitution, New York was isolated without a chance of establishing a middle confederacy. By staying out of the Union, New York would lose the federal capital and most of the benefit of its lucrative state impost. Furthermore, the threat of civil war within New York or among the states or the secession of the southern district from the state were real and serious concerns to New Yorkers. Finally, the all-important task of amending the Constitution seemed most obtainable if New York, within the Union, cooperated with other like-minded Antifederalists.

All of these factors convinced enough Antifederalists delegates to join with their Federalist colleagues and form a slim majority capable of unconditionally ratifying the Constitution. These assenting Antifederalists had not been converted to Federalism. For the most part, they maintained objections to the Constitution. They viewed ratification, however, as a lesser evil than the consequences of not ratifying the Constitution.

The most important Antifederalist delegate to be converted was Melancton Smith, the self-proclaimed convention manager. While attending the convention, Smith regularly corresponded with Antifederalist friends in New York City. On 28 June he wrote Massachusetts Congressman Nathan Dane saying that he wanted "to support the party with whom I am connected as far as is consistent with propriety—But, I know, my great object is to procure

[159]*Ibid.*

such amendments in this government as to prevent its attaining the ends, for which it appears to me, and to you calculated—I am therefore very anxious to procure good amendments—I had rather recommend substantial amendments, than adopt it [the Constitution] conditionally with unimportant ones, leaving our critical situation out of the question—I do not find these endeavors sufficiently seconded." Smith did not immediately reveal these sentiments to the convention; he asked Dane, however, "to communicate any observations you may think useful."[160]

Dane responded to Smith on 3 July with a lengthy, insightful letter. If the Constitution was not ratified, violence would surely occur—either civil war within the non-ratifying states or between the ratifying and non-ratifying states. The result of such violence would be "at least a system more despotic than the old one we lay aside, or the one we are adopting." Dane told Smith that "our object is to improve the plan proposed: to strengthen and secure its democratic features; to add checks and guards to it; to secure equal liberty by proper Stipulations to prevent any undue exercise of power, and to establish beyond the power of faction to alter, a genuine federal republic. to effect this great and desirable object the peace of the Country must be preserved, candor cherished, information extended and the doors of accommodation constantly kept open."

To accomplish these ends, amendments to the Constitution had to be proposed in the first federal Congress. "For any state now to stand out and oppose" the ratification of the Constitution would be a mistake. If New York did not unconditionally ratify, Dane believed that "the federal republicans or men who wish to cement the union of the states on republican principles will be divided and have but a part of their strength in Congress where they ought to have the whole." Although Dane still retained his "opinion respecting the feeble features, the extensive powers, and defective parts of the System, yet circumstanced as we are," he felt "no impropriety in urging" New York to ratify the Constitution. "Men in all the states who wish to establish a free, equal, and efficient government to the exclusion of anarchy, corruption, faction, and oppression ought in my opinion to unite in their exertions in making the best of the Constitution now established."[161]

[160]Poughkeepsie, Dane Papers, Beverly Historical Society.
[161]John Wingate Thornton Collection, New England Historic Genealogical Society.

A week later, Confederation Treasury Board member Samuel Osgood wrote Melancton Smith and Samuel Jones from New York City offering similar advice. According to Osgood, Antifederalists had already accomplished their goal—the country seemed ready to accept necessary amendments to the Constitution. In fact, Osgood wrote that "the Danger of not obtaining Amendments such as we would wish for, will in my Opinion be greatly enhanced by the Absence of New York."[162]

Melancton Smith responded to Dane saying "I entirely accord with you in Opinion." Smith, however, knew that he faced a divided Antifederalist party. "Time and patience," he said, "is necessary to bring our party to accord, which I ardently wish." He explained "that time & great industry is requisite to bring us to act properly—my task is arduous and disagreeable"; but despite the fact that he would surely antagonize some of his political allies, Smith said that he would openly "avow" the sentiments that he, Dane, and Osgood shared.[163]

Zephaniah Platt agreed with Smith. Platt explained that he voted for unconditional ratification "not from a conviction that the Constitution was a good one or that the Liberties of men were well Secured. No—I voted for it as a Choice of evils in our own present Situation." The Constitution, he wrote, "Must and would now go into operation. the only Chance remaining was to get a Convention as Soon as possible to take up our Amendments & those of other States while the Spirit of Liberty is yet alive." In sum, Platt said "that we have Endeavoured to consider all Sides of the question & their probable consequences—on the whole [we] desided on what we Suposed was for the Intrest and peace of our State under present Circumstances."[164]

[162]New York, 11 July, National Park Service, Collections of Federal Hall National Memorial, New York City.

[163]Smith to Dane, Poughkeepsie, [c. 15 July], John Wingate Thornton Collection, New England Historic Genealogical Society.

[164]To William Smith, Poughkeepsie, 28 July, Museum, Manor of St. George, Mastic Beach, Long Island, N.Y.

MATERIALS

A Guide to Sources for Studying the Ratification of the Constitution by New York State

GASPARE J. SALADINO

University of Wisconsin–Madison

Clarence E. Miner, in his pioneer study on New York's ratification of the Constitution, wrote that the party divisions of the 1780s had their origins in the "conflict between local and central authority which had been characteristic of the Revolution."[1] To better understand the politics of ratification, then, one must investigate the politics of the late colonial period. The seminal study is Carl Becker, *The History of Political Parties in the Province of New York, 1760–1776* (Madison, Wis., 1909). Becker viewed New York politics as a struggle between aristocrats and democrats. The Revolution in New York was a fight for home rule and who should rule at home. Most historians have either attempted to support, refute, rehabilitate, or refine Becker.

A good overview of the history of the "revolutionary generation" in New York can be found in volumes III–V of the *History of the State of New York*, 10 vols. (New York, 1933–1937), edited by Alexander C. Flick. This work includes the writings of a number of eighteenth-century specialists. The best single volume for the

---

[1] *The Ratification of the Federal Constitution by the State of New York* (New York, 1921), 13. Unless otherwise noted, New York is the state of publication.

colonial period is Michael Kammen, *Colonial New York: A History* (New York, 1975). The war years are the subject of Flick's edition of *The American Revolution in New York: Its Political, Social and Economic Significance* (Albany, 1926); and Jackson Turner Main's *The Sovereign States, 1775–1783* (New York, 1973). The standard study of New York in the Confederation is E. Wilder Spaulding, *New York in the Critical Period, 1783–1789* (New York, 1932). On the economy and society, Spaulding is supplemented by Thomas C. Cochran, *New York in the Confederation: An Economic Study* (Philadelphia, 1932); Curtis P. Nettels, *The Emergence of a National Economy, 1775–1815* (New York, 1962); and Main, *The Social Structure of Revolutionary America* (Princeton, N.J., 1965). The classic study of the American states in the 1780s is Merrill Jensen, *The New Nation: A History of the United States During the Confederation, 1781–1789* (New York, 1950).

There are good bibliographic aids for this period. The best are Milton M. Klein, comp., *New York in the American Revolution: A Bibliography* (Albany, 1974); and Ronald M. Gephart, comp., *Revolutionary America, 1763–1789: A Bibliography*, 2 vols. (Washington, D.C., 1984). Both works, covering the same period of time, are arranged topically and have succinct descriptions and analyses of printed primary and secondary sources. They are supplemented by the bibliographic essays in Kammen, *Colonial New York*, and Alfred F. Young, *The Democratic Republicans of New York: The Origins, 1763–1797* (Chapel Hill, N.C., 1967). Valuable also are Douglas Greenberg, "The Middle Colonies in Recent American Historiography," *William and Mary Quarterly*, 3rd ser., XXXVI (1979): 396–427; and David Maldwyn Ellis, "Recent Historical Writings on New York Topics," *New York History* LXIII (1982): 74–96.

Research and Publications in New York State History—an exhaustive annual bibliography of recent works—is published under the auspices of the New York State Museum, Division of Historical and Anthropological Services. Between 1952 and 1968 the state historian's office prepared an annual bibliography that was printed in the July issue of *New York History*. In 1969 the state assumed direct responsibility for publication and printed *Research and Publications* until 1972. No volumes appeared from 1973 to 1975, but publication was revived in 1976.

Constitutional Convention

On 21 February 1787 the Confederation Congress called a constitutional convention to meet in Philadelphia on 14 May. On 6

March the New York legislature appointed Robert Yates, John Lansing, Jr., and Alexander Hamilton delegates to the Constitutional Convention. The state legislature's resolutions and proceedings on this appointment are in *Constitutional Documents and Records, 1776–1787*, volume I of Merrill Jensen et al., eds., *The Documentary History of the Ratification of the Constitution* (Madison, Wis., 1976–).

Yates and Lansing attended the convention until 10 July; Hamilton remained until the last day, 17 September, although he was absent on several occasions. Each man took notes of the debates. Yates's and Hamilton's are in Max Farrand, ed., *The Records of the Federal Convention*, 3 vols. (New Haven, Conn., 1911).[2] Hamilton's notes and other convention papers are also in volume IV of Harold C. Syrett, ed., *The Papers of Alexander Hamilton*, 26 vols. (New York, 1961–1979). Lansing's notes are in Joseph Reese Strayer, ed., *The Delegate from New York, or Proceedings of the Federal Convention from the Notes of John Lansing, Jr.* (Princeton, N.J., 1939).

Legislative and Executive Records

On 11 January 1788 Governor George Clinton addressed the state legislature at Poughkeepsie and turned over to it a copy of the proposed Constitution and a 21 December 1787 letter from Yates and Lansing explaining why they opposed the Constitution. On 31 January the New York State Assembly adopted a resolution calling for a state convention to meet in June in Poughkeepsie and for the election of convention delegates. The New York State Senate concurred the next day.

The contemporary printed Journals of the Assembly and Senate for this legislative session (9 January–22 March) are available on microfilm and microcard. On microfilm, the printed Journals are in the *Records of the States of the United States of America* (Washington, D.C., 1951–52)—a collection brought together by William S. Jenkins. On microcard, the Journals are in Clifford K. Shipton, ed., *Early American Imprints, 1639–1800* (Worcester, Mass., 1955–1964). The manuscript Journals of neither house exist.

The proceedings and debates of both houses on this resolution were published in the New York *Daily Advertiser* and the

---

[2] A fourth volume, published in 1937, has a general index and an index of the clauses of the Constitution.

New-York Journal from 14 January to 21 February. (See below for a description of these newspapers.) Francis Childs of the *Daily Advertiser* attended the legislature and took shorthand notes. Thomas Greenleaf of the *New-York Journal* arranged to have reports on the legislature sent to him by correspondents. On 14 January both newspapers printed Governor Clinton's speech and the Yates-Lansing letter. Clinton's speech is also in Charles Z. Lincoln, ed., *Messages from the Governors, Comprising Executive Communications to the Legislature and Other Papers Relating to Legislation* ... [1683–1906], 11 vols. (Albany, 1909), II:281–83. On 8 February the *Daily Advertiser* published the Senate debates of 1 February in two pages. The Assembly debates of 31 January were printed in the *Daily Advertiser* on 12 February. The *New-York Journal* printed its version of the Assembly debates on the 21st. Very few letters have survived that shed much light on the actions of either house.

The extant executive papers are sparse. In the disastrous 1911 fire at the New York State Library, forty-two of the fifty-two volumes of Governor George Clinton's Papers were lost. The volumes that survived were badly damaged. Copies of some relevant documents in these papers, however, had been made for historian George Bancroft in 1880 and are among the Bancroft Transcripts in the New York Public Library.

The extant manuscript records of the legislative and executive departments are now housed in the New York State Archives in Albany and are described in *Guide to Records in the New York State Archives* (Albany, 1981). The work also lists the archives' holdings of material relating to the state convention (see below). The reader should also examine the Klein and Gephart bibliographies (above) for the guides to New York's official records that were published before 1974. These early works help to determine the type and amount of material that was lost in the 1911 fire at the state library. A detailed (but unpublished) description of the present state of the Clinton Papers has been prepared by the state archives.

Personal Papers

There are many collections of personal papers for New York's ratification of the Constitution; both Federalists and Antifederalists are well represented. The most serious deficiency is the paucity of letters for the period September–December 1787. Political correspondence did not become heavy until February 1788, after the state legislature called the state ratifying convention. The New-York Historical Society, the New York Public Library, and the Columbia University Libraries have valuable collections. The historical society has the papers of such Federalists as Abraham, Adrian, and Evert Bancker (Bancker Family Papers), James Duane, Robert R. Livingston, Walter Rutherfurd, and Richard Varick; and such Antifederalists as John Lamb, John Smith of Mastic, Long Island, and Abraham B. Bancker. The Lamb Papers are rich in information for the interstate and intrastate cooperation among Antifederalists and for the work of Antifederalist committees in New York State. The New York Public Library owns the papers of such Antifederalists as Abraham Yates, Jr., Abraham G. Lansing, John Lansing, Jr., Gilbert Livingston, and George Clinton. The Yates Papers, which are especially rich, include letters from Antifederalist politicians, drafts of his own newspaper essays, and a draft of his history of the movement for the Constitution. Federalists are represented in the papers of Leonard Gansevoort and Philip Schuyler. There are also a few good items in such business papers as the Constable-Pierrepont Collection, the Collin MacGregor Letterbooks, and the Lewis Ogden Letterbook. Columbia University Libraries (Rare Book and Manuscript Library) owns the DeWitt Clinton Papers, including a brief journal that this young Antifederalist kept at the state convention. Columbia also has the largest collection of the papers of John Jay. The Van Schaack Family Correspondence contains the letters of Federalist Peter Van Schaack.

Several libraries outside New York City also have important collections. The papers of Antifederalist Melancton Smith at the New York State Library in Albany include Smith's notes of debates in the Confederation Congress that sent the Constitution to the states in September 1787,[3] a number of Smith's letters, and a wide variety of material on the state convention. The correspondence of Antifederalist Peter Van Gaasbeek is in the Senate House Mu-

[3]These notes are printed in John P. Kaminski and Gaspare J. Saladino, eds., *Commentaries on the Constitution: Public and Private*, volume 1 (Madison, Wis., 1981), volume XIII of Merrill Jensen et al., eds., *The Documentary History of the Ratification of the Constitution*, the first of five volumes presenting the day-to-day regional and national debate over the Constitution that took place in letters, newspapers, magazines, broadsides, and pamphlets.

seum in Kingston and at the Franklin Delano Roosevelt Library in Hyde Park.[4] The correspondence between Van Gaasbeek and Cornelius C. Schoonmaker is especially illuminating. The Museum, Manor of St. George, at Mastic Beach, Long Island, has a few Antifederalist letters to Judge William Smith.

The Library of Congress has the papers of Antifederalist Hugh Hughes, which include drafts of his newspaper essays, and the largest and most varied collection of the papers of Alexander Hamilton. Some of Hamilton's letters are in the James Madison and George Washington papers, while the Washington Papers also include letters from John Jay. The Webb Family Papers at Yale University include the letters of Federalist Samuel Blachley Webb, a commercial agent in New York City. The Henry Van Schaack Scrapbook at the Newberry Library in Chicago has a few letters of Peter Van Schaack and Philip Schuyler.

As the seat of the Confederation Congress, New York City was filled with congressmen, members of the executive departments, and foreign diplomats—many of whom wrote letters about the Constitution. The Massachusetts Historical Society has Secretary at War Henry Knox's papers, while Postmaster General. Ebenezer Hazard's letters are in its Belknap Papers. The letters and papers of all congressmen are being collected and published by Paul H. Smith and his staff at the Library of Congress as the *Letters of Delegates to Congress, 1774–1789* (Washington, D.C., 1976–). The Library of Congress also has the correspondence of French, English, Spanish, and Dutch diplomats based in New York City. This correspondence is available, with good finding aids, on photostats, microfilm, or transcripts.

Most of the libraries mentioned above have some fine autograph collections and collections of miscellaneous manuscripts that contain letters on New York ratification. For example, James Kent wrote several informative letters that are scattered in such collections at the New-York Historical Society, the Historical Society of Pennsylvania, and the Morristown National Historical Park, Morristown, N.J.

The basic guides to manuscript collections are Philip M. Hamer, ed., *A Guide to Archives and Manuscripts in the United States* (New Haven, Conn., 1961); and *The National Union Catalog of Man-*

---

[4]For an analysis of the papers at Kingston, see Michael D'Innocenzo and John Turner, "The Peter Van Gaasbeek Papers: A Resource for Early New York History, 1771–1797," *New York History* [NYH], XLVII (1966): 153–59.

uscript Collections, a continuing publication of the Library of Congress. The guides to New York manuscript repositories published before 1974 are listed in the Klein and Gephart bibliographies (above). These bibliographies also list the published correspondence and personal papers of some New York politicians and the biographies of others that include letters and other documents. A full listing of New York manuscript repositories, arranged by towns and counties, is in the *Directory of Archives and Manuscript Repositories in the United States* (Washington, D.C., 1978). This directory—compiled by the National Historical Publications and Records Commission—briefly describes the holdings of these repositories and includes the guides to these holdings. The national data base for this bibliography is regularly updated and a revised edition will soon be published. This commission is also a cosponsor of an important project begun in 1978 by the New York Historical Resources Center, Olin Library, Cornell University. The center has been surveying manuscripts and archives collections in New York State repositories and has begun to publish guides for each of the state's sixty-two counties. When completed, the guides will list the manuscripts and archival materials for almost three thousand historical agencies, public libraries, colleges, and universities. The center also submits all information to the National Historical Publications and Records Commission for its national data base. Lastly, the New York State Library has surveyed its manuscripts collections and has prepared a guide that is in press.

Newspapers

Newspapers are perhaps the most important source for studying the debate over the ratification of the Constitution in New York, especially for the first four or five months after the Constitutional Convention adjourned on 17 September 1787. Between 21 September and 4 October, nine New York newspapers published the Constitution.[5] Newspapers printed a wide variety of articles defending and attacking the Constitution, ranging from fillers or squibs to sophisticated political treatises. They reprinted propaganda material from out-of-state newspapers and reported on the progress of ratification outside New York. Newspapers carried the

[5] Leonard Rapport, "Printing the Constitution: The Convention and Newspaper Imprints, August-November 1787," *Prologue* II (1970): 69–89.

proceedings and debates of the New York legislature and ratifying convention, as well as the proceedings of public meetings. Lastly, newspapers included nomination lists of candidates seeking election to the legislature and the convention and the returns of these elections.

Between September 1787 and July 1788, thirteen newspapers and one magazine were published in the state at one time or another. Seven newspapers were printed in New York City, as dailies, semiweeklies, or weeklies. The dailies were *The Daily Advertiser*; *The New-York Morning Post, and Daily Advertiser*; and *The New-York Journal, and Daily Patriotic Register*. The Thursday issue of the *New-York Journal*, which circulated more generally in the country, was called *The New-York Journal, and Weekly Register*.

The *Daily Advertiser* printed numerous Federalist essays, including *The Federalist*. The printer Francis Childs took shorthand notes of the proceedings and debates of the state legislature and convention and printed them in his newspapers. William Morton's *New-York Morning Post* published both Federalist and Antifederalist material; its principal pieces were reprinted from out-of-state newspapers.

Thomas Greenleaf's *New-York Journal* was a prolific Antifederalist newspaper. Until 19 November 1787 the *New-York Journal* was a weekly, but it became a daily so that it could print the many Antifederalist articles that it received. The *New-York Journal* published such serialized essays as "Cato" (7 nos.), "Brutus" (16 nos.), "Cincinnatus" (Arthur Lee of Va., 6 nos.), "A Countryman" (Hugh Hughes, 6 nos.), and "A Countryman" (DeWitt Clinton, 5 nos.). It also reprinted prominent Antifederalist material from outside New York: seventeen of eighteen essays by "Centinel" (Samuel Bryan of Pa.), seven of eight numbers by "An Old Whig" ("a club" in Philadelphia), and all twelve installments of Marylander Luther Martin's *Genuine Information*. Often accused of being partial, Greenleaf tried to ease the criticism by printing Federalist articles, including some numbers of *The Federalist*.

Three of New York City's newspapers were semiweeklies— *The New-York Packet*; *The Independent Journal: or, the General Advertiser*; and *The New-York Museum*. The *New-York Packet*, owned by Samuel and John Loudon, and the *Independent Journal*, printed by J. M'Lean and Company, published all of *The Federalist*. With the issue of 2 July 1788, Archibald M'Lean was admitted to the firm of J. M'Lean and Company. There are few extant issues of John

Russell's *New-York Museum*, which was established on 23 May 1788. The city's only weekly, *The Impartial Gazetteer, and Saturday Evening's Post*, was established on 17 May 1788 by John Harrisson and Stephen Purdy, Jr.

The state's only magazine was Noah Webster's *The American Magazine* . . ., a monthly that was published in New York City beginning with the issue of December 1787. It was first advertised for sale in early January 1788. Webster, a Federalist propagandist, included many of his own writings in the *American Magazine.*

Albany had two weeklies—*The Albany Gazette* and *The Albany Journal: or, the Montgomery, Washington and Columbia Intelligencer.* The *Albany Gazette* was printed by Charles R. Webster and the *Albany Journal* by Webster and his brother George. The newspapers were Federalist, and they often shared articles. Despite Antifederalist hostility towards him, Charles R. Webster printed some Antifederalist material in the *Albany Gazette.* The *Albany Journal* was established as a semiweekly on 26 February 1788, but in about two months it became a weekly.

The *Northern Centinel, and Lansingburgh Advertiser*, a weekly published by Thomas Claxton and John Babcock, was Federalist. In January 1788 Claxton and Babcock moved the paper to Albany, and from 11 February to 14 April, they published it as *The Federal Herald.* The paper then returned to Lansingburgh and was published under the same name, but Ezra Hickok replaced Claxton.

Ashbel Stoddard's *The Hudson Weekly Gazette*, a Federalist weekly, printed Federalist and Antifederalist material. *The Country Journal, and the Poughkeepsie Advertiser*, another Federalist weekly, was owned by Nicholas Power. The *Country Journal* published Federalist and Antifederalist material, and it was the only newspaper in America to print, in its entirety, the *Letters from the Federal Farmer*, a major Antifederalist pamphlet. (See below for more on this pamphlet.)

The standard bibliography for newspapers is Clarence S. Brigham's *History and Bibliography of American Newspapers, 1690–1820*, 2 vols. (Worcester, Mass., 1947). A supplement to this work is in the *Proceedings* of the American Antiquarian Society, LXXI, Part I (1961): 15–62. The researcher should also examine Paul Mercer, *Bibliographies and Lists of New York State Newspapers: An Annotated Guide* (Albany, 1981); and *Newspapers on Microfilm, 1982*

(Washington, D.C., 1983).[6] For biographical data on New York newspapers and printers, consult Milton W. Hamilton, *The Country Printer, New York State, 1785–1830* (New York, 1936); Douglas C. McMurtrie, *A History of Printing in the United States . . . Volume II. Middle and South Atlantic States* (New York, 1936); Joel Munsell, *The Typographical Miscellany* (Albany, 1850); Munsell, *The Annals of Albany*, 10 vols. (Albany, 1850–1859); and A. J. Wall, "Samuel Loudon (1727–1813): (Merchant, Printer and Patriot), With Some of His Letters," *Quarterly Bulletin of the New-York Historical Society* VI (1922–23): 75–92.

Pamphlets and Broadsides

The pamphlet and broadside literature is another rich source for the study of ratification. The printers of New York published nine pamphlets and a two-volume edition of *The Federalist*. Five pamphlets were original treatises by New Yorkers; two were written by a South Carolina delegate to the Constitutional Convention and a resident of New Jersey; and two were Antifederalist material reprinted from other states. *The Federalist* was penned by two New Yorkers and a Virginian—Alexander Hamilton, John Jay, and James Madison.

Some bibliographers believe that Thomas Greenleaf of the *New-York Journal* published five Antifederalist pamphlets. These were: several editions of the *Letters from the Federal Farmer*;[7] a reprint of "A Columbian Patriot" (Mercy Otis Warren of Mass.), *Observations on the New Constitution . . .*; *An Additional Number of Letters from the Federal Farmer . . .*; "A Plebeian" (Melancton Smith), *An Address to the People of the State of New-York . . .*; and an anthology entitled *Observations on the Proposed Constitution . . .* that contains the writings of out-of-state Antifederalists.

Samuel and John Loudon of the *New-York Packet* published "A Citizen of New York" (John Jay), *An Address to the People of the*

---

[6]The Readex Microprint Corporation is in the process of putting all eighteenth-century American newspapers on microcard and a selected number of newspapers on microfilm.

[7]There is reason to believe that this pamphlet was written by a New Yorker, not Richard Henry Lee of Virginia. See Gordon S. Wood, "The Authorship of the *Letters from the Federal Farmer*," *William and Mary Quarterly* [WMQ], 3rd ser., XXXI (1974): 299–308; and Kaminski and Saladino, eds., *Commentaries on the Constitution*, 2: 15–16.

State of New-York. . . . Charles R. Webster printed *An Impartial Address* . . . *or, the Thirty-Five Anti-Federal Objections Refuted.* And John and Archibald M'Lean published *The Federalist* in two volumes. Francis Childs of the *Daily Advertiser* struck off South Carolinian Charles Pinckney's *Observations on the Plan of Government Submitted to the Federal Convention* . . .; and William Ross printed *Observations on Government* . . . by "A Farmer, of New-Jersey" (John Stevens, Jr., of Hoboken, N.J.).

New York printers published more than twenty-five broadsides on matters relating to the Constitution. For example, Thomas Greenleaf issued "Centinel" I–II and "Timoleon" (an original New York item) as a two-page broadside, and Ashbel Stoddard of the *Hudson Weekly Gazette* reprinted "The Dissent of the Minority of the Pennsylvania Convention" as a four-page broadside. During the months of March and April 1788, at least a dozen handbills appeared in New York City and Albany as Antifederalists and Federalists campaigned for the election of convention delegates. In early July two broadsides were run off announcing Virginia's ratification of the Constitution.

The bibliographic aids for this literature are Charles Evans, *American Bibliography* . . . [1639–1799], 12 vols. (Chicago, Ill., 1903–1934); and Roger P. Bristol, *Supplement to Charles Evans' American Bibliography* (Charlottesville, Va., 1970). Evans and Bristol are combined in Clifford K. Shipton and James E. Mooney, eds., *National Index of American Imprints Through 1800: The Short-Title Evans*, 2 vols. ([Worcester, Mass.], 1969). The imprints are on microcard in Shipton's *Early American Imprints, 1639–1800* (Worcester, Mass., 1955–1964), and *Supplement* (Worcester, Mass., 1966–). The reader should also consult G. Thomas Tanselle, ed., *Guide to the Study of United States Imprints*, 2 vols. (Cambridge, Mass., 1971). This work includes imprint bibliographies by town and city; studies of individual printers and publishers; and histories of the press by town and city.

Printed Primary Sources

Since the late nineteenth century, many of the essays and pamphlets mentioned in the two sections above have appeared in print. The pamphlets by the "Federal Farmer" (the first five letters only), "A Columbian Patriot," "A Citizen of New York," and "A Plebeian" are in Paul Leicester Ford, ed., *Pamphlets on the Constitu-*

tion . . . (Brooklyn, 1888); and the essays of "Cato," "Caesar," and "Sydney" (Abraham Yates, Jr.) are in Ford's *Essays on the Constitution . . .* (Brooklyn, 1892). The reader should be forewarned that Ford's identification of George Clinton as "Cato," Alexander Hamilton as "Caesar," Robert Yates as "Brutus" and "Sydney," Richard Henry Lee as the "Federal Farmer," and Elbridge Gerry as "A Columbian Patriot" have been challenged by a number of historians and political scientists. (See below for a brief discussion of this literature.) All of the letters from the "Federal Farmer," along with a lengthy analysis of them, appear in Walter Hartwell Bennett, ed., *Letters from the Federal Farmer to the Republican* (University, Ala., 1978). William Jeffrey, Jr., has analyzed, discussed the authorship of, and published the "Brutus" essays in "The Letters of 'Brutus'—A Neglected Element in the Ratification Campaign of 1787–88," *University of Cincinnati Law Review* XL (1971): 643–777. In volumes 2 and 6 of *The Complete Anti-Federalist*, 7 vols. (Chicago, Ill., and London, Eng., 1981), Herbert J. Storing has included all of the New York Antifederalist essays and pamphlets mentioned above, as well as several other essays. His first volume is a general analysis of Antifederalist political thought.

Some of the writings of New York Federalists and Antifederalists appear in John P. Kaminski and Gaspare J. Saladino, eds., *Commentaries on the Constitution: Public and Private*, 5 vols. (Madison, Wis., 1981–), volumes XIII–XVII of Merrill Jensen et al., eds., *The Documentary History of the Ratification of the Constitution*. The editors provide editorial notes that fully discuss the authorship of, circulation of, and commentaries upon a wide variety of newspaper essays, broadsides, and pamphlets. The sections on authorship include discussions of the writings of historians and political scientists who have identified the writers of anonymous or pseudonymous articles and pamphlets or who have disputed the authorship of various articles and pamphlets. The remaining documents on New York will appear in volumes IX–X and an accompanying microfiche publication. These two volumes, the microfiche, and *Commentaries on the Constitution* will represent the most comprehensive collection of documents ever published on New York ratification.

The Federalist

Eighty-four numbers of *The Federalist* were published in New York City between 27 October 1787 and 28 May 1788. Alexander Ham-

ilton wrote fifty essays, James Madison fourteen, and John Jay five.
The most recent scholarship generally suggests that Madison wrote
the remaining disputed essays.[8] The first seventy-six essays were
originally printed in four city newspapers—the *Independent Journal*,
the *New-York Packet*, the *Daily Advertiser*, and the *New-York Journal*.
All of these essays, including the first printings of the last eight
essays, were published by John and Archibald M'Lean in a two-
volume book edition. The first volume appeared on 22 March
1788; the second on 28 May. The M'Lean edition contains eighty-
five essays because newspaper number 31 was divided into two
parts. The *Independent Journal* and the *New-York Packet* printed all
the essays; the *Daily Advertiser*, nos. 1–50; and the *New-York Journal*,
nos. 23–39. The *Albany Gazette* reprinted nos. 1–6, 8–10, 12–13,
and 17; the *Hudson Weekly Gazette*, nos. 1–11; the Lansingburgh
Northern Centinel (later Albany *Federal Herald*), nos. 1–10 and 69;
and the Poughkeepsie *Country Journal*, nos. 14–21.

The best edition of the essays is Jacob E. Cooke, ed., *The
Federalist* (Middletown, Conn., 1961). The texts are from the newspapers, with emendations from three authorized book editions—
the M'Lean edition of 1788, the George F. Hopkins edition of
1802, and the Jacob Gideon edition of 1818. Cooke included an
introduction about the publication of *The Federalist* and the historical controversy surrounding its authorship. This introduction
and Hamilton's essays are reprinted in volume IV of Harold C.
Syrett, ed., *Hamilton Papers*, for which Cooke served as associate
editor. Madison's contributions, along with editorial notes discussing authorship, are in volume X of Robert A. Rutland, ed.,
The Papers of James Madison (Charlottesville, Va., 1977). Jay's five
essays, including drafts of four of them, will appear in volume III
of Richard B. Morris's edition of the papers of John Jay. All of
The Federalist will be published with editorial notes discussing the
authorship and circulation of the essays and commentaries upon
them in Kaminski and Saladino, eds., *Commentaries on the Constitution*. For the first time, *The Federalist* essays will appear in their
proper context—surrounded by other Federalist and Antifederalist essays. Recently, the study of the concepts in *The Federalist*
has been aided by Thomas S. Engeman, Edward J. Erler, and
Thomas B. Hofeller, eds., *The Federalist Concordance* ([Middletown,

---

[8]One exception is Linda Quinne Smyth, "*The Federalist*: The Authorship of
the Disputed Papers" (Ph.D. diss., University of Virginia, 1978).

Conn.], 1980). This concordance is keyed to Cooke's edition of
The Federalist.

The Sources for the
New York Convention

The elections for the delegates to the state convention took place
from 29 April through 3 May 1788. On 17 June the convention
met in Poughkeepsie and elected Governor George Clinton president, John McKesson and Abraham B. Bancker secretaries, and
Nicholas Power of the Poughkeepsie *Country Journal* printer. Except for Sundays, the convention met continuously until Saturday,
26 July, when it ratified the Constitution with an accompanying
declaration of rights and recommendatory amendments. It also
ordered the president of the convention to transmit to the executives of the other states a circular letter strongly recommending
a second general convention to consider the amendments proposed by the various state conventions.[9]

Election returns are in the *Daily Advertiser*, 29 May–14 June,
and the *New-York Journal*, 31 May–12 June. The *Journal* listed all
of the elected delegates and their party affiliations, concluding that
forty-six of the sixty-five delegates were Antifederalists. Together,
the two newspapers printed the vote totals for nine of the thirteen
counties. There are no vote totals for the counties of Kings, Richmond, Suffolk, and Washington (and Clinton). On 7 June the *Daily
Advertiser* carried the vote totals for Queens County by towns. The
John McKesson Papers at the New-York Historical Society have
all of the election certificates except those for Columbia County
and the City and County of New York. The certificate for the
latter is in the society's James Duane Papers.

The sources for the convention consist of the Journal (manuscript and printed); notes of debates taken by delegates and private reporters; drafts of manuscripts, such as resolutions and committee reports; newspaper summaries of proceedings and debates;
private letters written by members of the convention or by observers; and a brief journal by DeWitt Clinton.

[9]For a description of the meeting place of the convention, see Helen Wilk-
inson Reynolds, comp. and ed., "The Court House of Dutchess County . . .," Dutchess County Historical Society, *Year Book* XXIII (1938): 74–98; and Frederic A.
Smith, "Where New York Ratified the Federal Constitution," NYH, XVIII (1937):
218–19.

The manuscript Journal of the convention is in the records of the Department of State located in the New York State Archives. Lengthy fragments of smooth and rough Journals, from which this Journal was apparently constructed, are in the McKesson Papers at the New-York Historical Society. The McKesson Papers also include more than twenty roll calls for insertion in the Journal. The manuscript Journal in the New York State Archives contains a twenty-page pamphlet of the Constitution printed by Nicholas Power for the use of the delegates. The text is printed on one side of the leaves until page 17; after that the text is printed on both sides. At the end of the Journal is a copy of the circular letter signed by forty-seven delegates, including Clinton. These signatures do not appear in the official printed version of the Journal. The manuscript Journal, with the exception of this copy of the circular letter, formed the basis for the printed Journal.

The Journal was printed by Nicholas Power. By order of the convention, each delegate was to receive a copy and a copy was to be sent to each city, town, district, and precinct in the state. Both manuscript and printed Journals are on microfilm in William S. Jenkins, *Records of the States*; while the printed Journal is on microcard in Clifford K. Shipton, *Early American Imprints*.

The McKesson Papers include drafts of resolutions in the handwriting of such delegates as John Jay, Robert R. Livingston, Melancton Smith, and John Lansing, Jr. The papers also contain drafts of committee reports, recommended amendments, a declaration of rights, forms of ratification, and the circular letter. More drafts of recommended amendments, forms of ratification, and the circular letter are in the Melancton Smith Papers, New York State Library. These papers also include drafts of Smith's speeches. Drafts for speeches by other delegates are in the Robert R. Livingston Papers, New-York Historical Society; the George Clinton Papers, New York Public Library; and the Alexander Hamilton Papers, Library of Congress.

The debates of the convention must be reconstructed from several sources. For the most part, the fullest sets of notes cover the debates for the month of June; most of these accounts fall off badly in July. A full reconstruction of the debates has never been published, but the editors of the *Hamilton Papers*, in volume V, have printed several versions of Hamilton's speeches. The editors also describe their procedures and evaluate the quality of various notes of Hamilton's speeches.[10]

The most complete account of the convention debates was printed by Francis Childs of the *Daily Advertiser,* who published a pamphlet entitled *Debates and Proceedings of the Convention of the State of New-York. . . .* Childs's version is complete through 2 July, but then it becomes a summary of proceedings and must be supplemented by the convention Journal because Childs did not always supply a full account of proceedings.[11] Despite Childs's denials, Antifederalists considered him a "partyman" whose record of debates favored Federalist speakers.

Three newspapers—the *Daily Advertiser,* the *New-York Journal,* and the Poughkeepsie *Country Journal*—printed original accounts of debates and proceedings. The *Country Journal* carried the fullest reports of the first two days, and it was the first newspaper to carry the form of ratification and the circular letter. The *Daily Advertiser,* apparently with intentions of printing all of Childs's notes, published complete debates for 19 and 20 June but stopped such treatment in favor of summaries of debates and proceedings. The *New-York Journal* published the fullest summaries of debates and proceedings for July.

John McKesson and several delegates took notes of debates. The most extensive notes for June were kept by McKesson and Melancton Smith. Gilbert Livingston's notes, in the New York Public Library, surpass any set of notes for the period 14 to 26 July. Other note takers, whose notes are meager or difficult to use, are Alexander Hamilton, Richard Harison, Robert R. Livingston, and Robert Yates. The Hamilton and Harison notes are in the Hamilton Papers and the Yates notes are in the Edmund C. Genêt Papers—all at the Library of Congress. Robert R. Livingston's notes are in his papers in the New-York Historical Society. DeWitt Clinton's journal (15–19 July), in his papers at Columbia University, contains a brief account of speeches and

[10]For an example of the manner in which *The Documentary History of the Ratification of the Constitution* will reconstruct the debates for the state convention, see volume II, *Ratification of the Constitution by the States: Pennsylvania* (Madison, Wis., 1976).

[11]The Childs version is reprinted in volume II of Jonathan Elliot, ed., *The Debates in the Several State Conventions, on the Adoption of the Federal Constitution . . . ,* rev. ed., 5 vols. (Philadelphia, Pa., 1836–1845). A facsimile of the Childs version was printed by the Vassar Brothers Institute in Poughkeepsie in 1905.

convention gossip. The Morris-Popham Papers at the Library of Congress has a notebook that includes delegate Richard Morris's general comments on the Constitution and twenty-three numbered objections to the Constitution and Morris's replies to most of them. It is not clear if these notes were taken during the convention.

There are two copies of the form of ratification—one is in the records of the Department of State, New York State Archives, and the other is in RG 11, General Records of the United States Government, Certificates of Ratification of the Constitution . . ., National Archives, Washington, D.C. The latter is available in a microfilm publication of the National Archives (M-338).

A last source for the study of the convention is the large number of letters written by convention delegates and spectators. More than a dozen delegates wrote letters during the convention. Four of John Jay's ten letters were written to George Washington, and eight of Alexander Hamilton's ten letters went to James Madison. Among the Federalist spectators, Philip Schuyler wrote ten letters and Samuel Blachley Webb and David S. Bogart two each. Antifederalists are represented by delegates Cornelius C. Schoonmaker (6 letters) and George Clinton (3), and spectator DeWitt Clinton (5). A number of their letters (and those of other Antifederalists) went to John Lamb and his aides in New York City who coordinated activities with Antifederalists in other states with respect to amendments and a second general convention. Convention secretary Abraham B. Bancker penned eleven letters.

Secondary Accounts of Ratification

Studies on New York ratification have concentrated on the division between the state's two political parties over the issue of strengthening the general government; on the relationship of this issue to state issues, such as the state impost and paper money; on the formation, composition, principles, and strength of the two parties; on the methods that each party used to achieve its ends and goals; and on an explanation of why the overwhelmingly Antifederalist New York Convention ratified the Constitution. The early modern historiography of ratification by New York and other states was dominated by the sectional and class interpretations of Orin Grant Libby and Charles A. Beard. Beginning in 1955, a group of consensus historians and political scientists reacted negatively to these interpretations and denied the existence of a class struggle over the Constitution. Both Federalists and Antifederalists were committed to the idea of popular government. This school did not become dominant among historians as a group of neo-Progressive historians rushed to Beard's defense and tried to rehabilitate him, although they, too, were critical of him. The battle was apparently too intense for some historians who decided neither to defend nor criticize Beard; they attempted to ignore him.[12]

In 1894 Orin Grant Libby, a student of Frederick Jackson Turner, wrote the first scientific study of the ratification of the Constitution. His research was thin but his impact was formidable. In New York, Libby argued, the Constitution was supported by classes on the seacoast and on the Hudson River; these classes consisted of New York City merchants and commercial farmers of the southern counties and parts of the Hudson Valley, but not the great manor lords. The farmers in the isolated frontier counties of the north opposed the Constitution because the new government would put an end to the state impost and paper money.[13]

Two decades later, Charles A. Beard accepted Libby's thesis, but introduced new elements into the study of New York ratification. His work was tentative and suggestive. Beard believed that the state convention vote on ratification reflected the fight between the holders of real property (small farmers and manor lords) and the holders of personal property (merchants and public creditors). Sixteen of the thirty delegates who voted for ratification in the state convention in 1788 were creditors of the general government; the new government under the Constitution would redeem the Continental securities held by these individuals. The fight over the Constitution was a class struggle; men of property sought protection against the democratic spirit of the times. Had

[12]On the formation and ratification of the Constitution, see Jack P. Greene, "Revolution, Confederation, and Constitution, 1763–1787," in William H. Cartwright and Richard L. Watson, Jr., eds., *The Reinterpretation of American History and Culture* (Washington, D.C., 1973), 259–95; and James H. Hutson, "Country, Court, and Constitution: Antifederalism and the Historians," WMQ, 3rd ser., XXXVIII (1981): 337–68, and "The Creation of the Constitution: Scholarship at a Standstill," *Reviews in American History*, XII (1984): 463–77.

[13]*The Geographical Distribution of the Vote of the Thirteen States on the Federal Constitution, 1787–8* (Madison, Wis., 1894). On Libby's impact, see Robert P. Wilkins, "Orin G. Libby: His Place in the Historiography of the Constitution," *North Dakota Quarterly* XXXVII (1969): 5–20.

the Antifederalist counties not been underrepresented in the convention, New York would have rejected the Constitution.[14]

In 1921 Clarence E. Miner wrote the first full-scale study of New York ratification. He cursorily examined the politics of the 1780s and discovered two political parties—Hamiltonians and Clintonians—who were divided on paper money and most important, on the federal impost of 1783. In May 1786 the Clintonian legislature ratified the federal impost with conditions that were unacceptable to the Confederation Congress. Clintonians were concerned about the state's sovereignty, and they wanted to retain the state impost. The state's position on the federal impost "decided the fate of the Confederation." In analyzing the final votes of the state convention in 1788, Miner concluded that New Hampshire ratification was "a severe blow" but Virginia's was the "decisive blow." Melancton Smith's defection was critical; he and other Antifederalists feared that New York might be left out of the Union.[15]

In 1932 Thomas C. Cochran, *New York in the Confederation*, declared that the political alignments on the federal impost of 1783 and the Constitution were identical. New York's action on the impost wrecked the Confederation. Clintonians were defiant states' righters who wanted to keep the state impost and maintain the state's sovereignty.

In the same year, E. Wilder Spaulding, *New York in the Critical Period*, thoroughly investigated the politics of the 1780s and demonstrated clearly that the two political parties were divided on many issues. Clintonians supported the general government before 1783 but became either indifferent or hostile to it after the peace. They were interested in building the Empire State; they did not want New York to be dependent on Congress. Hamiltonians des-

---

[14]*An Economic Interpretation of the Constitution of the United States* (New York, 1913). For Beard's impact, see John Patrick Diggins, "Power and Authority in American History: The Case of Charles A. Beard and His Critics," *American Historical Review* LXXXVI (1981): 701–30.

[15]See note 1 above. Miner's doctoral dissertation was not the first printed on New York ratification. In 1901 or shortly thereafter, G. A. McKillip Dyess published a thirty-six page dissertation—*The Conflict over the Ratification of the Federal Constitution in the State of New York*—that he had written at New York University. Dyess argued that ratification was a struggle between democrats and aristocrats and between commercial and agricultural interests. The state convention ratified because of (1) New Hampshire and Virginia ratification; (2) the threat of secession by the southern counties; and (3) the "stupidity" and "fears" and tactical blunders of Governor Clinton.

perately wanted a strong central government and New York's position on the federal impost of 1783 made them more determined than ever. On ratification, Spaulding accepted the sectional division of parties and the commercial versus non-commercial interests, but listed the great manor lords as Federalists. The bitter struggle in the state convention was between social classes. Antifederalists were outmaneuvered but circumstances hurt them more. Governor Clinton could not hold the Antifederalists together because of (1) New Hampshire and Virginia ratification; (2) the threat of secession by New York City and the southern counties; and (3) the promise of a federal capital. The moderate Antifederalists who switched their votes were from areas closest to New York City or in the Hudson Valley.[16]

In 1955 Cecilia M. Kenyon launched the assault upon Beard, chiding him for not considering the theoretical foundations of the Constitution. She viewed Antifederalists, including those in New York, as "men of little faith." They were not democrats and they did not believe in national democracy. Ironically, the Federalists provided the framework for national democracy.[17]

The next year Robert E. Brown, Beard's severest critic, dismissed the notion that public securities determined the vote on ratification and scored Beard for uncritically using 1791 records to determine who held public securities in 1787 and 1788. There was no class struggle; society was basically democratic. Brown suggested that political and personal interests were most important. Most people sincerely believed that the Articles of Confederation were defective, and the prestige of the Constitutional Convention helped ratification.[18]

[16]For an appreciation of Spaulding's book, see Linda Grant De Pauw, "E. Wilder Spaulding and New York History," NYH, XLIX (1968): 142–55.

[17]"Men of Little Faith: The Anti-Federalists on the Nature of Representative Government," WMQ, 3rd ser., XII (1955): 3–43; and *The Antifederalists* (Indianapolis, Ind., and New York, 1966). For Kenyon's extended critique of Beard, see " 'An Economic Interpretation of the Constitution' After Fifty Years," *Centennial Review* VII (1963): 327–52. Richard W. Crosby agreed that the Antifederalists were "men of little faith" and that they were not true libertarians. Crosby declared that the Federalists "were the faithful libertarians." See "The New York State Ratifying Convention: On Federalism," *Polity* IX (1969): 97–116.

[18]*Charles Beard and the Constitution: A Critical Analysis of "An Economic Interpretation of the Constitution"* (Princeton, N.J., 1956). In line with Brown, Charles Edward La Cerra, Jr., rejected Beard's thesis that New York aristocrats supported the Constitution only out of self-interest. See "The Role of Aristocracy in New York State Politics During the Period of Confederation, 1783–1788" (Ph.D. diss., New York University, 1969).

Forrest McDonald presented his analysis of ratification in three studies published between 1958 and 1965. In 1786 Clintonians had a vision of the Empire State and refused to help Congress. These attitudes and Clinton's financial program (which benefitted his supporters) aroused the ire of Hamiltonians who fought back. McDonald put Beard to the test. He investigated the economic interests of state convention delegates and concluded that economic interests had no part in the showdown on ratification because neither group had a monopoly of these interests. (Much of his economic data has been questioned.) Although he presented little evidence, McDonald asserted unequivocally that the convention ratified because of the southern counties' threat to secede. The convention "degenerated comically" after New Hampshire and Virginia ratification. Antifederalists were not united in the convention.[19]

In 1960 Lee Benson concluded that Beard failed to realize that there is seldom total class solidarity. Beard was wrong about public securities, but right about the small number of New Yorkers who supported the Constitution. Benson recommended that historians also study ethnic and religious factors in determining classes, and he called for "a credible, systematic account of the sequence of events" in the state convention to explain why the Federalists won. The evidence on the threat of secession was too impressionistic.[20]

In 1960 and 1961 Jackson Turner Main defended Beard. Main wrote an exhaustive history of the Antifederalists in each state. He stated that during the 1780s New York's two parties were divided over many issues, especially paper money and the federal impost of 1783. The division over ratification was between commercial and non-commercial sections and classes and between aristocrats and democrats. The vote on ratification followed the votes on paper money and the federal impost. Public securities were an important factor. Antifederalist defectors were influenced

---

[19]*We the People: The Economic Origins of the Constitution* (Chicago, Ill., 1958); "The Anti-Federalists, 1781–1789," *The Wisconsin Magazine of History* XLVI (1963): 206–14; and *E Pluribus Unum: The Formation of the American Republic, 1776–1790* (Boston, Mass., 1965). For the paper money aspects of Clinton's financial program of 1786, see John Paul Kaminski, "Paper Politics: The Northern State Loan-Offices During the Confederation, 1783–1790" (Ph.D. diss., University of Wisconsin, Madison, 1972).

[20]*Turner and Beard: American Historical Writing Reconsidered* (Glencoe, Ill., 1960).

by New Hampshire and Virginia ratification; the threatened secession of the southern counties; and the belief that New York had to remain in the Union.[21]

Staughton Lynd's study on Dutchess County also reinforced the Beardian tradition. Lynd saw a sharp class conflict. The great landlords and their tenants were Federalists; the well-to-do freeholders and lesser landlords were Antifederalists. Dutchess elected seven Antifederalist delegates to the state convention. Four voted for ratification; two against; and one abstained. The four defectors were ambitious men of substance from the Poughkeepsie area; they were bound by economic and family ties. The two party stalwarts were from southeastern Dutchess which had a tradition of violent antilandlordism.[22]

In 1966 Linda Grant De Pauw announced that it was "time for Beard to leave the spotlight of the Constitution." In the most comprehensive study of New York ratification to date, De Pauw ignored Beard but challenged the conclusions of many other historians. She rejected the notion that political parties existed for the years 1781 to 1786. The Antifederalists of 1787–88, including Clinton, had always been friends to the general government; New York Antifederalism was compatible with a strong feeling toward this government. The emphasis that newspaper articles and convention speakers put on class divisions was mere rhetoric; both sides drew their strength from the middle class. New Yorkers were not overwhelmingly Antifederalist. The basic difference between the two groups in the state convention was how and when to ratify. Most Antifederalists wanted conditional ratification; none supported outright rejection. No Federalist opposed amendments on principle. Antifederalists were not disturbed by the news from

[21]"Charles A. Beard and the Constitution: A Critical Review of Forrest McDonald's *We the People*," WMQ, 3rd ser., XVII (1960): 86–102; and *The Antifederalists: Critics of the Constitution, 1781–1788* (Chapel Hill, N.C., 1961). Main's views about the importance of the public creditors in New York are shared by E. James Ferguson, *The Power of the Purse: A History of American Public Finance, 1776–1790* (Chapel Hill, N.C., 1961). For Main's fuller discussion of the state's two parties, see *The Upper House in Revolutionary America, 1763–1788* (Madison, Wis., 1967); and *Political Parties before the Constitution* (Chapel Hill, N.C., 1973).

[22]*Anti-Federalism in Dutchess County, New York: A Study of Democracy and Class Conflict in the Revolutionary Era* (Chicago, Ill., 1962). The reader should also consult Lynd's "The Mechanics in New York Politics, 1774–1788," *Labor History* V (1964): 225–46; and several essays in his *Class Conflict, Slavery, and the United States Constitution: Ten Essays* (Indianapolis, Ind., and New York, 1967). Melancton Smith, one of the four Antifederalist defectors, lived in New York City but he had been a Poughkeepsie merchant for many years.

New Hampshire and Virginia, and the threat of secession was inconsequential. Melancton Smith and other moderate Antifederalists voted for ratification because they realized that Congress would not accept a conditional ratification and they feared for the Union and Antifederalism. John Jay's conciliatory attitude helped win over some Antifederalists. Hamilton's brilliant oratory had no effect. Ratification was as much a victory for Antifederalists as Federalists. Amendments would be obtained through a second general convention.[23]

The same year Robert A. Rutland stated that his book was "neither a defense nor an attack on Beard." He wanted to discuss the personalities, problems, and apsirations of the Antifederalists. Rutland declared that in the state convention Antifederalists used the tactics of delay, not from design, but out of uncertainty. The threat of secession was a bluff, but they did not know how to call it. A confused Clinton gave up his leadership at the end; he could not stop the Antifederalist defections.[24]

In 1967 Alfred F. Young, *The Democratic Republicans of New York*, refused to allow Beard to expire, although he challenged him on certain points. Young demonstrated that there were two distinct political parties and that this division was in large part a class division. The Clintonians were led by men of the middle class and lesser aristocrats; some had attained wealth during the Revolution but they lacked social status or "tone." They were state particularists who feared the nationalist policies of the Hamiltonians. The Hamiltonians were the party of privilege, status, and wealth; this was the party of the merchants and manor lords who sought national solutions to the problems of the state and the Union. Mechanics lined up with the Hamiltonians because they believed that a strong central government would revive trade. The conflict in the state convention was a clear-cut class struggle; it reflected the old antagonism between the privileged aristocracy and the rep-

---

[23]*The Eleventh Pillar: New York State and the Federal Constitution* (Ithaca, 1966). On the second convention movement, in which New York played a major part, see De Pauw's general study, "The Anticlimax of Antifederalism: The Abortive Second Convention Movement, 1788–89," *Prologue* II (1970): 98–114; Edward P. Smith, "The Movement Towards a Second Constitutional Convention in 1788," in J. Franklin Jameson, ed., *Essays in the Constitutional History of the United States . . .* (Boston, Mass., 1889); and Robert Allen Rutland, *The Ordeal of the Constitution: The Antifederalists and the Ratification Struggle of 1787–1788* (Norman, Okla., 1966), chapter XV.

[24]See note 23 above.

resentatives of the people who had been oppressed by them. Beard was correct about public securities, and Main was right about the split along commercial and non-commercial lines. Several factors led to ratification: (1) the rising tide of public opinion in favor of the Constitution; (2) the serious division of opinion among Anti-federalists; (3) New Hampshire and Virginia ratification; and (4) the skill of the Federalists who used the threat of secession and offered conciliatory amendments. Melancton Smith was despised by Antifederalists for changing his vote.[25]

In 1969 Gordon S. Wood appeared to join the Beard forces. He believed that "The Constitution was intrinsically an aristocratic document designed to check the democratic tendencies of the period. . . ." It repudiated the Revolutionary ideals that New York Antifederalists wanted to preserve. Antifederalists strove to give people a greater role in government. As democrats, they feared a national government dominated by a natural aristocracy. To Federalists, the Constitution was the best means to protect republicanism which was being endangered by excessive egalitarianism in state politics. Federalists developed an elitist theory of democracy; they expected people to vote for the right leaders who would save republicanism.[26]

In 1976 and 1979 Steven R. Boyd asserted that New York Antifederalists were a well-organized, purposeful group throughout the ratification struggle. They failed, however, for several reasons: (1) the news of Virginia ratification; (2) Congress was moving toward the adoption of an ordinance calling for the first federal elections; and most important, (3) the Antifederalists in the state convention believed that they could get amendments from a sec-

[25]Also useful on the subject of New York's political parties and leaders are such unpublished doctoral dissertations as Edmund Philip Willis, "Social Origins of Political Leadership in New York City from the Revolution to 1815" (University of California, Berkeley, 1967); Leonard H. Bernstein, "Alexander Hamilton and Political Factions in New York to 1787" (New York University, 1970); and Dominick David De Lorenzo, "The New York Federalists: Forces of Order" (Columbia University, 1979).

[26]*The Creation of the American Republic, 1776–1787* (Chapel Hill, N.C., 1969). For detailed, unpublished doctoral dissertations on political thought in New York, see Theophilus Parsons, Jr., "The Old Conviction versus the New Realities: New York Antifederalist Leaders and the Radical Whig Tradition" (Columbia University, 1974); Jerome J. Gillen, "Political Thought in Revolutionary New York, 1763–1789" (Lehigh University, 1972); and Maria T. Eufemia, "The Influence of Republican Ideology on New Yorkers, 1775–1800: An Examination of the British Libertarian Tradition" (Fordham University, 1976).

ond general convention. Antifederalists decided to work within the system and change it.[27]

In 1981 Edward Countryman's study of New York society and politics demonstrated that the confrontation of 1787–88 was the culmination of a ten-year development. Between 1779 and 1788 two distinct, well-organized political parties developed; everyone knew the leaders and the issues. This partisanship was based upon class, sectionalism, economics, royalism, and the question of the extent of people's participation in government. The vote on ratification lay in regionalism and economic geography; the farther north a county, the more likely it was to be Antifederalist. Antifederalist delegates who lived closest to a city were most likely to switch their votes.[28]

Elsewhere in this volume, John P. Kaminski also sees two distinct political parties. Emphasizing their different attitudes to the central government, Kaminski concludes that the fight over the ratification of the Constitution was the most intense party battle between 1777 and 1788. In particular, the campaign to elect state convention delegates demonstrated how bitterly the parties were split. New York ratified for several reasons: (1) most important, after New Hampshire and Virginia adopted the Constitution New Yorkers feared that, if the state convention failed to ratify, New York would be isolated, civil war would break out, and the southern counties would secede; (2) an increasing number of people came to support the Constitution; (3) Antifederalists in the convention were badly divided, while Federalists were conciliatory and patient; and (4) the conversion of Melancton Smith was crucial.

Biographers of some state convention delegates also consider the process of ratification in New York. Many biographers of Alexander Hamilton, beginning in the middle of the nineteenth century, portrayed him as the key to understanding the struggle for ratification; without him, New York would not have ratified the Constitution.[29] This myth-making reached its apogee with the pub-

[27]"The Impact of the Constitution on State Politics: New York as a Test Case," in James Kirby Martin, ed., *The Human Dimensions of Nation Making: Essays on Colonial and Revolutionary America* (Madison, Wis., 1976), and *The Politics of Opposition: Antifederalists and the Acceptance of the Constitution* (Millwood, 1979).

[28]*A People in Revolution: The American Revolution and Political Society in New York, 1760–1790* (Baltimore, Md., and London, Eng., 1981).

[29]This literature is reviewed in Robin Brooks, "Alexander Hamilton, Melancton Smith, and the Ratification of the Constitution in New York," WMQ, 3rd ser., XXIV (1967): 339–58; and Philip R. Schmidt, "Virginia, Secession, and Alexander Hamilton: New York Ratifies the Constitution" (M.A. Thesis, University of Kansas, 1965).

lication of biographies by Broadus Mitchell in 1957 and Clinton Rossiter in 1964. Mitchell believed that New York ratification was Hamilton's foremost political exploit. He stressed Hamilton's great powers of reasoning and persuasion and his moral earnestness.[30] Rossiter stated that "The conversion of [Melancton Smith] was the most notable success of Hamilton's checkered career as a politician. . . . The Hamilton of Poughkeepsie was the best of all possible Hamiltons, not alone as politician and rhetorician but also as a political scientist." Rossiter, however, admitted that Hamilton was also "lucky"; several events helped Hamilton considerably.[31] In the 1960s Hamilton's role began to be deemphasized as several historians, among them Jackson Turner Main, Linda Grant De Pauw, and Robin Brooks, punctured the myth. Two of Hamilton's most recent biographers—Robert Hendrickson and Jacob E. Cooke—make no grandiloquent claims for their subject's role in bringing about the ratification of the Constitution in New York.[32]

Robin Brooks believed that Melancton Smith may well have been indispensable to New York ratification; Smith, not Alexander Hamilton, was the real hero of ratification. His decision to vote for the Constitution, in order to keep New York in the Union, was an example of high statesmanship. He gave up his political future to vote for ratification.[33] Richard B. Morris asserted that John Jay was more important than Hamilton. Jay realized that many Antifederalists in the convention did not want to reject the Constitution and he won some of them over by being moderate and conciliatory.[34] George Dangerfield gave no such credit to Robert R. Livingston, but he developed a sound interpretation of ratification. Dangerfield emphasized the character of the two groups and the class conflict endemic in the convention. Clintonians feared consolidation, aristocracy, and despotism, but they were divided, irresolute, stolid, and obstinate. Most important, they were unwilling to reject the Constitution outright. On the other hand, Federalists were united, energetic, resolute, purposeful, better educated, and willing to compromise.[35]

[30]*Alexander Hamilton: Youth to Maturity, 1755–1788* (New York, 1957).
[31]*Alexander Hamilton and the Constitution* (New York, 1964).
[32]Hendrickson, *Hamilton I (1757–1789)* (New York, 1976); Cooke, *Alexander Hamilton* (New York, 1982).
[33]See note 29 above.
[34]"John Jay and the Adoption of the Federal Constitution in New York: A New Reading of Persons and Events," NYH, LXIII (1982): 132–64.
[35]*Chancellor Robert R. Livingston of New York, 1746–1813* (New York, 1960).

New York, then, ratified the Constitution for a variety of reasons. The ratification of the Constitution by New Hampshire and Virginia, especially the latter, convinced a number of Antifederalists in the state convention that there would be no future for New York or Antifederalism outside the Union, and, therefore, New York had no choice but to ratify the Constitution. New York would be subjected to the hostility of neighboring states which had long chafed under New York's economic domination. The Union had to be preserved and a large, wealthy state like New York had to be part of it. The threat of secession by the southern counties would isolate the northern counties and would lead to civil strife and economic ruin. The promise of the retention of the federal capital in New York City and the growing support for the Constitution among the people in some parts of the state also influenced some Antifederalists.

These concerns could not have had such a significant impact had not the Antifederalists in the state convention been badly divided. As a group, Antifederalists lacked common goals and differed on tactics. Most important, they lacked strong effective leadership. At the end of the convention George Clinton, their principal leader, abdicated his leadership; he could not hold his group together. On the other hand, Federalists were united under a strong, energetic, and purposeful leadership. Federalist leaders, particularly John Jay, were realists who concluded that compromise was absolutely necessary in order to achieve ratification. They refused to allow the bitter class conflict revealed in the public and convention debates to destroy the chances for ratification. Alexander Hamilton was open to some concessions, but he was too widely distrusted by Antifederalists to have had any appreciable influence upon them. The defection of Melancton Smith, the principal Antifederalist speaker, was crucial. Smith led a group of Antifederalists who realized that New York had to remain in the Union. These Antifederalists represented commercial areas which would benefit from the ratification of the Constitution because the new government would have the power to regulate foreign and interstate commerce and pay the public debt. The vote on ratification of the Constitution resembled earlier votes in the New York legislature on the federal impost of 1783 and state paper money. The ratification struggle of 1787–88 was the culmination of ten years of party strife in New York. Lastly, the Antifederalist defectors sincerely believed that a second general convention would be called and that it would recommend amendments to the Constitution.

Local Histories and Genealogies

One last category of secondary material—local histories and genealogies—deserves some mention. Some of the historians mentioned above, especially Spaulding and De Pauw, have used these sources effectively. Town and county histories and genealogies often include primary sources that are no longer available or difficult to locate, biographical material on lesser known political figures, and descriptions of places and styles of living. Some local histories, in fact, attempt to cover every aspect of life. These sources, however, must be examined with a cool, critical eye. Many were written by amateur historians in the nineteenth century when standards of historical scholarship were not as rigorous as they have become. More recently, the study of local communities has become the province of some professional historians and the quality of these histories has improved considerably. An examination of the monthly *Dissertation Abstracts International, A: The Humanities and Social Sciences* (Ann Arbor, Mich.) reveals that, in recent years, the study of local communities has become popular among computer-oriented doctoral candidates.

The better local histories are listed in the Klein and Gephart bibliographies (above). More extensive guides are Charles A. Flagg and Judson T. Jennings, *A Bibliography of New York Colonial History*, New York State Library *Bulletin* No. 56 (1901), 291–558; and Harold Nestler, *A Bibliography of New York State Communities: Counties, Towns, Villages* (Port Washington, 1968). Many of the most recent local histories and genealogies are listed in *Research and Publications* and are reviewed in *New York History* and *The New York Genealogical and Biographical Record*. Before it stopped publication in early 1980, the *New-York Historical Society Quarterly* also reviewed this literature. Perhaps the finest collections of local history and genealogy in New York State are those in the New York State Library, Albany; the New York State Historical Association Library, Cooperstown; the Olin Library, Cornell University, Ithaca; and the New York Public Library, the New-York Historical Society, and the New York Genealogical and Biographical Society, all in New York City. Local historical societies, historic sites, and public libraries often have excellent holdings for their localities and contiguous areas. Guides to some of these places are listed in

Manuel D. Lopez, *New York: A Guide to Information and Reference Sources* (Metuchen, N.J., and London, Eng., 1980).

Suggestions for Further Study

Despite the flurry of historical activity, or perhaps because of it, a completely persuasive explanation of why New York ratified the Constitution has not emerged. Several subjects demand further investigation. The movement for a stronger central government among New Yorkers and the state's attitude toward the Confederation Congress must be studied systematically and exhaustively. In particular, close attention must be paid to the state's attitude toward the federal impost of 1783. Moreover, some of the more recent writers on New York ratification have been unwise in downplaying the Clintonians' desire to retain the state impost, their offices, and their hopes and aspirations for an Empire State. The further investigation of these topics will probably help to explain more fully why many Antifederalists, especially George Clinton and his more faithful followers, fiercely opposed the Constitution. The burgeoning conflict between this particularist philosophy and the nationalist philosophy of the Hamiltonians is one of the keys to understanding New York politics in the 1780s.

The public debate over ratification has not been sufficiently explored. Political writers on both sides were prolific and what they said and how they said it must be subjected to a critical analysis, not dismissed as mere rhetoric. How much impact did this avalanche of political writing have on the electorate? It probably had some effect because the Antifederalist majority in the state convention significantly exceeded the Antifederalist majorities in the most recent elections for the state legislature. *The Federalist* has long been considered the most significant American contribution to the history of political thought, but no adequate examination has ever been made to determine its impact on New York politics in 1787 and 1788. It must be remembered that the authors of *The Federalist* addressed their arguments directly to the people of the state of New York.

The factors that determined the vote in the state convention also need further study. The threat of secession, though admitted by most historians, has not been thoroughly examined. Lee Benson was certainly correct when he declared that the evidence for the threat of secession was too impressionistic. Moreover, did the threat of secession have any historical basis? Had the southern counties ever threatened to secede before? A number of historians have alluded to the importance of keeping the federal capital in New York City, but none has researched the question in depth.

Historians have closely examined the impact that economic and political factors have had on the composition of political parties and the vote on ratification, but they have not sufficiently considered the influence of ethnic and religious factors. The emphasis that historians of colonial New York are placing upon the state's extraordinary ethnic and religious diversity should be extended to include the period of the Confederation and the Constitution. New York society was perhaps the most complex of any American state. For decades, the state attracted large numbers of New Englanders who emigrated there in even greater numbers during the 1780s. This group undoubtedly changed the complexion of New York politics and its impact would be a worthwhile field of study. Certainly, a better understanding of the divisions among Antifederalists in the state convention is needed. These divisions were possibly of long standing and surfaced on such a critical issue as the ratification of the Constitution. If possible, we must try to discover how Federalists worked behind the scenes to convince some Antifederalists to change their votes.[36] It seems plausible that this happened, but the evidence presented to date has not been substantial.

More than twenty years ago, Lee Benson called for "a credible, systematic account of the sequence of events" in the state convention to explain why Federalists won. Unfortunately, no one has accepted his challenge. The scope of Linda De Pauw's monograph gave her the best opportunity, but her insistence that Antifederalists supported the Constitution prevented her from adequately investigating this sequence of events. These events must be tied together with the outside circumstances that have been emphasized by many historians. The material for such a study is perhaps too diffuse and it might not be possible to attempt the study until *The Documentary History of the Ratification of the Constitution* has brought together and published all of the primary material.

[36]Alice P. Kenney suggests that Federalist delegates exerted pressure on wavering Antifederalists through long-standing family, commercial, and religious ties. This kind of pressure, a tradition in New York politics, could not be duplicated by adamant Antifederalists (*The Gansevoorts of Albany: Dutch Patricians in the Upper Hudson Valley* [Syracuse, 1969]).

Fiction—Another Source

JACK VANDERHOOF
Russell Sage College

Remembering the past, recreating the past, honoring the past, and celebrating the past demand many different approaches and choices. The adoption of the federal Constitution is no exception to the rule. Scholarly works by Charles A. Beard, Edward S. Corwin, and others are important and necessary for certain levels of understanding and a more complete recreation of the past. Commentaries and correspondence of Federalists and Antifederalists serve as another avenue to understanding. Biographies and local histories are also useful. Many scholars of political and constitutional history would dismiss works of fiction as an appropriate means to understanding, honoring, or presenting a recreated past. This dismissal is unwarranted when one understands the role of fiction in studying the past and, more specifically, New York and the adoption of the federal Constitution.

When "history" and "fiction" are wed, the first image of the union is the sultry "historical romance." Dismiss this idea. Any novel is a historical novel either because it deals with some aspect of past reality, imagined reality, or past imagination or is itself of the past. Usually, "historical novels" is a term used to describe mediocre or poor efforts; if the work has merit it becomes literature or "belles-lettres." Consider *War and Peace* and classify it.

What should a novel accomplish if one is to use it as another useful way of approaching past reality? György Lukács in his splendid and thorough *The Historical Novel* supplies one answer.

> What matters therefore in the historical novel is not the retelling of great historical events, but the poetic awakening

of the people who figured in those events. What matters is that we should re-experience the social and human motives which led men to think, feel and act just as they did in historical reality.[1]

And Lukács continues:

> The historical novel therefore has to *demonstrate* by *artistic* means that historical circumstances and characters existed in precisely such and such a way. What in [Sir Walter] Scott has been called very superficially "authenticity of local colour" is in actual fact this demonstration of historical reality.[2]

The novel should give the reader an insight into the ordinary lives of the people in the story and it must, to be of value, set this ordinariness in the proper milieu. Thus, the function is *insight* for the former and *perspective* for the latter. Serendipity permits discovery of unexpected facets of the life and times of the subject under investigation. Valuable also, especially in the classroom setting, is the flavoring that conceals the real or imagined bitterness of the medicine. This, of course, assumes history as nonfiction is unadulterated cod liver oil and the novel is spearmint flavored oil. The novel also enhances the imagination and understanding of what it was like living in the past; and, if the novel is good, it underscores our great chain of being and confirms our humanity.

A caveat before a specific illustration of the use of the novel: Michael Kammen in *A Season of Youth* suggests that novelists were really relativists in their interpretations. He cites Hervey Allen:

> It is in this capacity to produce an illusion of reliving the past that the chief justification for the historical novel exists. Since no one, neither historian nor novelist, can reproduce the real past, one may infer that, if supremely well done, the historical novel, by presenting the past dramatically, actually gives the reader a more vivid, adequate, and significant apprehension of past epochs than does the historian, who conveys facts about them.[3]

Shad Run

Howard Breslin's *Shad Run* published in 1955 is set in Poughkeepsie, New York, during the year 1788, more precisely from

[1]György Lukács, *The Historical Novel* (London, 1962), 42.
[2]*Ibid.*, 43.
[3]Michael Kammen, *A Season of Youth* (New York, 1978), 151.

mid-March through 24 June.[4] As the title suggests, the spring shad run in the Hudson River is the overarching factor under which is set a series of romantic events, class conflict, and, with a seeming naturalness and almost inevitableness, the ratification of the new Constitution by New York.

How does Breslin in *Shad Run* meet the criterion of *perspective*? His depiction of the Hudson River milieu, late eighteenth century, is acceptable, believable, and accurate. The description of the ice breaking up on the mighty Hudson conveys to those who have not experienced this phenomenon a sense of presence. But for Breslin's heroine, Lancey, sixteen-year-old daughter of a river fisherman, it meant a real inconvenience for she had walked four miles from home and was planning to skate back. The breaking was worse for the traveler, Dirck, whom Lancey had to help get out of the river when his mare broke through the ice. Dirck was the son of the gentry family van Zandt of Rhinebeck. Here is a common and understandable liaison complicated by gentry and fishmonger antecedents.

The subject of the impending state ratifying convention is introduced in a natural fashion. It is a subject of conversation not because the fishermen were consumed with interest in and feelings about the Constitution but because the ratifying convention would attract more people to Poughkeepsie while the shad were running and it would mean increased demand and higher prices. The conversation about the Constitutional Convention that had met in Philadelphia was what one might expect of these folk.

> "It stands to reason," Pardon said, "that they didn't hold that meeting in Philadelphia for nothing. Every blessed time those high-cockalorums get together in Philadelphia something new comes out of it. For years now." He raised a big fist, snapped a finger upright as he made his points. "First off come a petition to King George, rot him. Then, come the war. Then, General Washington's appointment. Then, the Declaration. Lastly, the Confederation." (Breslin, 45)

The shad swam up the river and fishermen caught and sold them in what seemed a natural relationship. So the intrusion of the ratifying convention and the whole range of the political world was natural but with a priority a cut below the shad season. This

---

[4]Howard Breslin, *Shad Run* (New York, 1955). Hereafter, Breslin citations appear in the text.

is the perspective Breslin offers. For Breslin the novelist, the attitudes toward the Constitution were molded by simple and complex forces, informed study of the arguments, class antagonisms, acceptance of the positions of powerful political leaders and personalities, and gut feelings.

What *insight* does Breslin offer about the views of those caught up in the struggle over the ratification of the Constitution in New York? One of the leading characters is Justin, a Massachusetts man who escaped to New York after the collapse of Shays's Rebellion. He was unhappy with Governor George Clinton of New York because the governor marched an army to the border to prevent the routed insurgents from coming into New York. Justin introduced the standard connection between the Massachusetts action and the ratification of the Constitution.

> "Yes, he's [Daniel Shays's] safe in the Vermont Republic now." Justin shrugged, stared moodily at the ground. "But that isn't the worst of it, Lancey. In Massachusetts they used what we'd done as an argument in favor of this Constitution. So such an outrage could never happen again, they said. And folks listened, and voted to ratify." (Breslin, 230)

Justin was opposed to the Constitution and rehearsed a standard argument.

> "We won a war, Lancey, and every day it becomes less a victory. First we fought for our rights as English citizens. Then, because we couldn't get them otherwise, we fought to be free and independent states. And now we seem determined, state by state, to trade both freedom and independence for a government that grants only the rights it wishes!" (Breslin, 230)

Justin felt if New York stood firm and refused to ratify, the proposed new form of government could be defeated; but his dire prediction would never be realized.

As the adversaries gathered in the afternoon and evening of 16 June for the ratifying convention on the following day, one gets some idea of the leadership and the leanings of the local citizenry. Clinton, the first non-royal governor of New York, was a local hero. He was described as "valley born, river bred," a powerful figure in state affairs. Though he was not very effective as a military tactician during the American Revolution, he was regarded locally as a power in the state. As one character notes:

His had been one of the early voices raised against the Tory landlords, among the first to cry for independence. If, in the long struggle to keep the British from control of the Hudson, George Clinton had been a more willing than able general, he had proved his courage and his energy. The redcoats had driven him, and beaten him, but they had never crushed him. With Washington's help, he had managed, except for the raid that razed Kingston, to hold on to the upper river. (Breslin, 236–37)

He was there that evening with his Antifederalist supporters, including Melancton Smith, Zephaniah Platt, Gilbert Livingston, and DeWitt Clinton. The last described as "the elegant young fellow with the quiet smile . . . the governor's nephew." Though the governor was in his own element and was cheered as he rode to the Clear Everett house, the dominant figure was yet to appear.

Alexander Hamilton is presented as the protagonist. He had been, as all knew, Washington's aide and as one of the river folk commented, "Didn't hurt none either that he married a Schuyler!" There is some uncertainty reflected about the authorship of *The Federalist* papers, but one viewer indicates that if Hamilton did write all or some of them he was "a mighty sharp young man." He rode into Poughkeepsie as a conqueror, and though Breslin emphasizes the favorable impression he made upon the residents of the town, Hamilton was not held in warm regard by many of his fellow delegates. The thoughts of the heroine reveal Breslin's assumptions of Hamilton's performance at the convention.

> Listening, Lancey Quist realized she was witnessing something extraordinary, perhaps momentous. The girl lacked the words and the experience to recognize a great artistic performance, but she instinctively knew that this was a rare occasion, when a man and an historic moment blended in perfect harmony.

> He might have been born . . . for this cause and this convention. . . .

> Whoever won or lost, however the country was formed or governed, surely no man, not even Alexander Hamilton, could hope to reach brilliant perfection more than once in a lifetime. Here was a dominant will that held its audience enthralled. It was a triumph of personality over prejudice, of an eloquent conviction that convinced. (Breslin, 246)

New York's role in the ratification process is more fully presented by Breslin earlier in the novel. Before the convention met, news had arrived from New York City that Maryland's vote for adoption on 28 April brought the number of ratifications to seven; previously Massachusetts had also voted aye. New York had not yet decided nor had Virginia.

> "We are still the keystone," Lancey said. She was not travelled, but she knew her beliefs for truth. "By position, and wealth. Because of the river. Even the British realized that."
> "You forget one thing, Mistress," Master Venick said, "When nine states vote this Constitution into being, it has been adopted. Done. Set up. In force."
> "For those nine only!" (Breslin, 177–78)

Numbers come into play later, at the end of the novel.

> "Lancey, Hendrick, Hester! The word's just arrived. New Hampshire ratified!"
> Lancey recalled their stupefied questions, her own utter disbelief.
> "Are you sure, Dirck?"
> "When?"
> "I–I don't believe it."
> "It's true!" Dirck had sounded positive, as well as angry. "New Hampshire voted to adopt the Constitution on the twenty-first of June! New Hampshire, for God's sake!"
> "But–but doesn't that mean—"
> "Yes, Lancey! That makes New Hampshire number nine. The ninth state! It's the law of the land now, no matter what we decide here in Poughkeepsie!" (Breslin, 274)

It was true there would be arguments for a while. New York would be the reluctant eleventh pillar and the shad would run.

Breslin closes the novel on the day that the news reached Poughkeepsie that the ninth state had ratified the Constitution. One will not learn from the novel that the Federalists eked out a victory. Whether the Antifederalists snatched defeat from the jaws of victory or whether the Federalists snatched victory from the jaws of defeat will depend upon one's assumptions and one's predilections. No claim is made for the novel as the sole or the entire approach to understanding the past, merely for the novel as another approach to past reality.

Insight and perspective have been demonstrated by the nature of the experience. Serendipity by definition precludes example. Howard Breslin in *Shad Run* has created another view of the ratification process in New York, but more than that he has given us an opportunity to approach the ratification process in a proper and natural fashion. Not only does this modest novel have an immediacy about it in terms of the ratifying convention and the shad season, but there is also an element of timelessness about the work:

> "Granted," Justin Pattison said. "But some of us at Valley Forge, quick and dead, thought we were fighting for liberty. Not for any lousy piece of paper that says the rich get richer, and the poor man keeps his place!" (Breslin, 81)

Suggestions For Further Study

If the discussion to this point has been a spotlight on *Shad Run* and the New York ratification process as it centered in Poughkeepsie, perhaps a floodlight upon some paths that might be followed would help respond to the wider questions of ratification posed elsewhere in this collection. The same kind of approach might be applied to other novels with a potential for revealing something about the ratification process in other states. The readings to follow are to be seen as suggestive and not as knowingly fruitful or valuable for all concerned. They range from the center of ratification activity, as in Inglis Fletcher's *Queen's Gift* set in North Carolina, to Elizabeth Page's *The Tree of Liberty*, a sweeping novel with some helpful observations about the Constitution and its ratification. The net is cast wide to include antecedents of political and constitutional activity, such as Shays's Rebellion, and subsequent events as Aaron Burr's western intrigue.

If flights of imagination are to be generated by this essay consider the "what if" of the past as Robert Sobol has done in a splendid tour de force, *For Want of a Nail . . . If Burgoyne Had Won at Saratoga* (New York, 1973). For the purposes of this essay, what if New York had failed to ratify and remained determined to stay out of the newly organized federal system? The "what ifs" are innumerable and certainly a way of stating the implications and effects of ratification.

A Reading List[5]

Atherton, Gertrude F. *The Conqueror*. . . . New York, 1902. 546p. Life of Alexander Hamilton.

Barnhill, J. *Hatching the American Eagle*. New York, 1937. 399p. Philadelphia during the years 1766–89.

Belknap, Jeremy. *The Foresters, an American Tale: Being a Sequel to the History of John Bull the Clothier, in a Series of Letters to a Friend*. Boston, 1792. 216p. Allegory containing reference in Letter 15 to a debate between fiddlers and antifiddlers over a proposed plan of partnership.

Bellamy, Edward. *Duke of Stockbridge: A Romance of Shays's Rebellion*. New York, 1900. 371p.

Beyea, Basil. *The Golden Mistress*. New York, 1975. 380p. Life of Mme. Betsy Jumel (later married to Aaron Burr) to the 1790s.

Clemens, Jeremiah. *The Rivals: A Tale of the Times of Aaron Burr and Alexander Hamilton*. Philadelphia, 1860. 286p. Lives of Burr and Hamilton from the Revolution to their duel.

Degenhard, William. *The Regulators*. . . . New York, 1943. 598p. One of the best dealing with Daniel Shays in 1786–87.

Fletcher, Inglis. *Queen's Gift*. Indianapolis, 1952. 448p. The seventh in the author's Carolina series deals with North Carolina during 1788–89 with the ratification as pivot.

Gerson, Noel. *Yankee Doodle Dandy: A Biographical Novel of John Hancock*. New York, 1965. 352p. Life of Hancock from 1754 to 1789.

—————. *Give Me Liberty: A Novel of Patrick Henry*. New York, 1966. 347p.

Kelley, Welbourn. *Alabama Empire*. New York, 1957. 503p. Panorama of the early national period, 1789–93, with the first part set in New York City in 1789.

Markoe, Peter. *The Algerine Spy*. . . . Philadelphia, 1787. 129p. Covers years from 1783 to the Constitutional Convention.

Mudgett, Helen. *The Seas Stand Watch*. New York, 1944. 391p. Salem and New Bedford during the years 1780–1812 by a professional historian.

Muir, Robert. *The Sprig of Hemlock: A Novel about Shays' Rebellion*. New York, 1957. 314p.

[5]Citations taken from Jack VanDerhoof, *A Bibliography of Novels Related to American Frontier and Colonial History* (Troy, 1971) and from work currently underway by the author.

Page, Elizabeth. *The Tree of Liberty.* New York, 1939. 985p. Virginia family from 1754 to 1806.

Turnbull, Agnes. *The King's Orchard.* Boston, 1963. 467p. Pittsburgh during the years 1772–95, based on the life of James O'Hara, Revolutionary soldier, later appointed quartermaster general in 1792. Contains infrequent references to national events after the Revolution.

Van De Water, Frederic Franklyn. *Wings of the Morning.* New York, 1955. 335p. The third in the author's Vermont series involving New Yorkers *versus* Vermonters during 1777–91. Contains infrequent references to national events after the Revolution.

Vidal, Gore. *Burr: A Novel.* New York, 1973. 430p. Set in the 1830s with frequent references back to Burr's activities in the 1780s.

Wheelwright, Jere Hungerford. *Kentucky Stand.* New York, 1951. 279p. Life on the Kentucky frontier during 1777–92, with infrequent references to national events after the Revolution.

Works on History and Fiction

Blake, Nelson Manfred. *Novelists' America: Fiction as History 1910–1940.* Syracuse, 1969.

Feuchtwanger, Lion. *The House of Desdemona or the Laurels and Limitations of Historical Fiction.* Detroit, 1963.

Henderson, Harry B. III. *Versions of the Past: The Historical Imagination in American Fiction.* New York, 1974.

Inge, M. Thomas. *Handbook of American Popular Culture.* Vol. 1. Westport, Conn., 1978.

Klein, Milton M. *New York in the American Revolution: A Bibliography.* Albany, 1974.

Leisy, Ernest E. *The American Historical Novel.* Norman, Okla., 1950.

Levin, David. *In Defense of Historical Literature: Essays on American History, Autobiography, Drama, and Fiction.* New York, 1967.

Matthews, Brander. *The Historical Novel, and Other Essays.* New York, 1901.

Wilson, Rufus Rockwell. *New York in Literature: The Story Told in the Landmarks of Town and Country.* Elmira, N.Y., 1947.

A Biographical Gazetteer of New York Federalists and Antifederalists

compiled by
STEPHEN L. SCHECHTER
Russell Sage College

The debate over the adoption of the new Constitution was not an abstraction. It was a long and complicated process of many stages. At each stage there were real people debating specific issues and taking concrete actions in real places. This section offers two reference aids that can be used to locate the people and places of that debate in New York. The first aid is a biographical gazetteer consisting of 255 New York participants in the ratification debate. The second is an inventory of surviving homes of New York Federalists and Antifederalists, followed by an interpretive guide to historic sites open to the public. The final section includes chronologies of the key events of the debate in New York and the nation. Men, places, and events are only part of the story of ratification. Another reference aid, which would be of inestimable value, is a concordance of the key terms, political ideas, and historical allusions gleaned from the writings and speeches of Antifederalist and Federalist writers and politicians. This massive undertaking would enable the kind of intellectual comparisons now possible in the recently published concordance of *The Federalist*.[1]

---

[1]Thomas S. Engeman, Edward J. Erler, and Thomas B. Hofeller, eds., *The Federalist Concordance* (Middletown, Conn., 1980).

The biographical gazetteer is the most complete listing available of New Yorkers involved in the debate over the Constitution. Its search criteria are chronologically based and include: (1) New York delegates to the Confederation Congress in 1787 and 1788; (2) New York delegates to the Constitutional Convention of 1787; (3) members of the eleventh (January–March 1788) session of the New York State Assembly and Senate, responsible for calling the state ratifying convention; (4) Federalist and Antifederalist candidates campaigning in the spring of 1788 for the state ratifying convention; (5) Federalist and Antifederalist candidates campaigning in the spring of 1788 for the twelfth session of the New York State Assembly and Senate; (6) members of Federalist and Antifederalist county committees who helped organize the election campaigns of 1788; (7) Federalist and Antifederalist writers who played a role in articulating party platforms; and (8) printers who published the writings of these men.

Utilizing these search criteria, most of the active participants in the debate are identified. Most of the remaining gaps are due more to the unavailability of resources than to the limits of the criteria. It was not possible to locate consistently reliable lists of Federalist county committeemen. Also missing are records of defeated candidates (mainly Federalists) from approximately one-fourth of the state legislative and convention races of 1788, not a high figure considering the intervening vagaries of history. On the other hand, few known participants were missed because of the limits of the search criteria, and those that were missed are included as "partisans" without office or formal position.[2]

Sources

Various sources were used to identify the participants. The most reliable source for members of the Confederation Congress meeting in 1787 and 1788 is volume VIII of *Letters of Members of the Continental Congress*, 8 vols. (Washington, D.C., 1921–1936), edited by Edmund C. Burnett. State legislators, state convention del-

[2]Partisans missed in the formal search, but included in the final list, are of three basic types: (a) recent arrivals (such as Judge William Cooper from New Jersey, Rufus King from Massachusetts, and Gouverneur Morris, on a brief return from his Pennyslvania sojourn); (b) political mavericks and renegades (such as Peter Van Gaasbeek); and (c) fence-sitters on this issue (notably Lieutenant Governor Pierre Van Cortlandt).

egates, and statewide officers can be found easily in any one of the many state civil lists compiled in the nineteenth century. Primary reliance was placed on the edition of Edgar A. Werner, *Civil List and Constitutional History of the Colony and State of New York* (Albany, 1891). However, errors and discrepancies were discovered based on checks of the civil lists against the Minutes of the Council of Appointment; the Journals of the New York State Assembly, Senate, and Convention; and the election lists noted below. (Errors in and discrepancies between sources are noted in the biographical gazetteer.)

For the candidates, county tickets published in newspapers are especially important. They are supplemented by data found in the files of The Documentary History of the Ratification of the Constitution, located at the University of Wisconsin, Madison (hereinafter cited as the Ratification Project). The most complete list of candidates was published in the *New-York Journal* on 5 June 1788. This list is supplemented by a list in Steven R. Boyd's *The Politics of Opposition: Antifederalists and the Acceptance of the Constitution* (Millwood, N.Y., 1979), 80–81, that includes Antifederalist candidates for the state ratifying convention and the twelfth session of the Assembly.[3] Missing are some of the defeated candidates (most of them Federalists) for the state convention and the twelfth session of the Assembly. They are as follows: Federalist Assembly candidates for Montgomery, Suffolk, and Ulster counties; Federalist convention candidates for Orange County; Federalist Assembly and convention candidates for Washington County; and Antifederalist Assembly and convention candidates for Richmond County.[4]

---

[3]Additional sources are as follows: for Dutchess County, Federalist Assembly and convention candidates appeared in the Poughkeepsie *Country Journal*, 15 April 1788, and the New York *Daily Advertiser*, 6 June 1788, respectively. For Orange County, Federalist Assembly candidates were found in the New York *Daily Advertiser*, 14 June 1788. For Queens County, the Federalist convention candidates appeared by last name only in the *Albany Journal*, 16 June 1788. The full names of these candidates, along with the full names of defeated Federalist Assembly candidates, were given in Henry Onderdonk, *Queens in Olden Times* (Jamaica, N.Y., 1865), 71. For Suffolk County, Federalist convention candidates were listed in a letter from "St. Patrick" (Jonathan N. Havens) to John Smith, 5 April 1788, John Smith Misc. Mss, New-York Historical Society.

[4]In all likelihood, the maximum number of missing candidates closely approximates the total number of missing offices at stake (thirty-five, or 25 percent of the offices at stake). The minimum number of missing candidates would be six if every known Federalist candidate had run for both Assembly and convention seats.

For Antifederalist committeemen, the list compiled by Steven Boyd for his book, *The Politics of Opposition*, 80–81, was most useful. Consulted but not included is a longer list of "active Antifederalists" appearing in Theophilus Parsons, Jr., "The Old Conviction versus the New Realities: New York Antifederalist Leaders and the Radical Whig Tradition" (Ph.D. diss., Columbia University, 1974), Appendix. No comparable studies or credibly consistent lists could be found for Federalist county committeemen.[5] For some counties, the names of Federalist organizers (and the candidates for whom they campaigned) are probably lost forever; for others, a more careful sifting of manuscript collections may yield positive results.

The identification of Federalist and Antifederalist writers posed the special problem of attribution, since most used pseudonyms. At the risk of incompleteness, only those authors whose attribution is certain are included. Some of these were found in John P. Kaminski and Gaspare J. Saladino, eds., *Commentaries on the Constitution: Public and Private* (Madison, Wis., 1981–), of Merrill Jensen et al., eds., *The Documentary History of the Ratification of the Constitution*. For printers, primary reliance was placed on volume I of Clarence S. Brigham, *History and Bibliography of American Newspapers, 1690–1820*, 2 vols. (Worcester, Mass., 1947), supplemented by volume II of Douglas C. McMurtrie, *A History of Printing in the United States* (New York, 1936).

Organization

In 1788 the county was the basis of representation (and, hence, campaign politics) for the state Assembly and state ratifying convention; state senators were apportioned among four multi-county districts. (See Table 1.) For historical and practical reasons, the gazetteer is organized by the thirteen counties represented in 1788. The state's fourteenth county—Clinton—was created on 4 March 1788; however, Washington and Clinton counties were represented together in the twelfth legislative session and in the convention; and, in any case, no representative from Clinton County was elected in 1788. Hence, they are treated together here. The

---

[5]On the Antifederalist side, twenty-one persons (two to three per county), who were active only by virtue of their membership in a county committee, are identified. This provides one basis for estimating the number of similarly involved Federalists missing from this search.

TABLE 1
County Representation in 1788

Counties, by Senate District	State Senators		State Assembly & Convention Seats[a]		County Population, as a percent of state population, 1790
	No.	Percent	No.	Percent	
Southern District	9	37.6%	28	43.1%	28.6%
Kings	1	4.2	2	3.1	1.3
New York	3	12.5	9	13.8	9.7
Queens	1	4.2	4	6.2	4.7
Richmond	1	4.2	2	3.1	1.1
Suffolk	2	8.3	5	7.7	4.8
Westchester	1	4.2	6	9.2	7.0
Middle District	6	25.0	17	26.2	27.3
Dutchess	3	12.5	7	10.8	13.3
Orange	2	8.3	4[b]	6.2	5.4
Ulster	1	4.2	6	9.2	8.6
Western District	6	25.0	16	24.7	39.3
Albany	3	12.5	7	10.8	22.3
Columbia	1	4.2	3	4.7	8.2
Montgomery	2	8.3	6	9.2	8.8
Eastern District	3	12.5	4	6.2	4.6
Washington & Clinton	3[c]	12.5	4	6.2	4.6
TOTAL[d]	24	100.1	65	100.2	99.8

NOTES: The number of senators by district and assemblymen by county was fixed in the New York State Constitution of 1777, with provisions for reapportionment every seven years. The first reapportionment took effect in the fifteenth legislative session (1792) and was based on the census of 1790. Most of the imbalances reflected in the 1788 figures of the twelfth session were corrected by the 1792 reapportionment.

[a]The county allotment of delegates to the state ratifying convention was equal to the number of assembly seats assigned to the county.

[b]One of these Assembly seats was vacant in the twelfth session.

[c]One of these Senate seats was vacant in the twelfth session.

[d]Totals do not equal 100.0 due to rounding.

present-day counties included in the counties of 1788 are listed in Table 2 and, for convenience, in footnotes appropriately placed at the beginning of each county listing.

TABLE 2
New York State Counties of 1788 and Today

Counties of 1788	Present-day Counties	Substate Regions
Albany	Albany	Upper Hudson Valley
	Delaware, part of[1]	Delaware Valley
	Greene	Upper Hudson Valley
	Rensselaer	Upper Hudson Valley
	Saratoga	Upper Hudson Valley
	Schenectady	Mohawk Valley
	Schoharie, part of	Schoharie Valley
	Ulster, part of	Mid-Hudson Valley
	Washington, part of	Upper Hudson Valley
Columbia	Columbia	Upper Hudson Valley
Dutchess	Dutchess	Mid-Hudson Valley
	Putnam	Lower Hudson Valley
Kings[2]	Kings (Brooklyn)	New York City
Montgomery[3]	Fulton	Mohawk Valley
	Herkimer	Mohawk Valley
	Montgomery	Mohawk Valley
	Otsego	Susquehanna Valley
	Schoharie, part of[1]	Schoharie Valley
New York[2]	New York (Manhattan)	New York City
Orange	Orange, most of	Lower Hudson Valley
	Rockland	Lower Hudson Valley

Entries within counties are to individual participants arranged in alphabetical order. In the 1780s there were no general residency requirements for public office and few restrictions on the number of offices one could hold. Moreover, none of the latter restrictions (e.g., those barring the chancellor, supreme court justices, and sheriffs from holding other state offices) seems to have applied to the office of state convention delegate. Hence, it was not uncommon for convention candidates to run for office in a "safe" county instead of their home county, or to run for the same office in both safe and home counties, or to run for two offices (e.g., convention delegate and assemblyman) in their home county. Participants, then, are placed in each county where they sought and held office. For example, Melancton Smith is listed under New

TABLE 2
Continued

Counties of 1788	Present-day Counties	Substate Regions
Queens	Nassau	Long Island
	Queens (Queens)[2]	New York City
Richmond[2]	Richmond (Staten Island)	New York City
Suffolk	Suffolk	Long Island
Ulster	Delaware, part of[1]	Delaware Valley
	Orange, part of	Lower Hudson Valley
	Sullivan[1]	Delaware Valley
	Ulster, most of	Mid-Hudson Valley
Washington & Clinton	Clinton[1]	North Country
	Essex[1]	Upper Hudson Valley
	Franklin, part of[1]	North Country
	Warren[1]	Upper Hudson Valley
	Washington, most of	Upper Hudson Valley
Westchester	Bronx (The Bronx)[2]	New York City
	Westchester	Lower Hudson Valley

[1]No participant in the ratification debate of 1787–88 lived in the area now part of this county.

[2]Now a state-designated county (and city-designated borough) of the City of New York. Present-day Kings and Queens counties are included in the New York City region, even though they are situated on Long Island.

[3]The 1788 boundaries of Montgomery County included all the western lands claimed by New York. Included in this table are only those present-day counties formed from the areas of Montgomery County that were most heavily settled in 1788.

York County as a defeated convention candidate and under Dutchess County as a victorious convention candidate. Smith's other offices and positions are placed under his New York County entry because that was the county he represented or the county considered to be his place of residence during the terms of those offices.

Each entry contains five elements: the individual's full name, party affiliation, offices sought and held, town or ward represented, and its present-day place name. Footnotes accompanying entries are intended to explain or resolve peculiarities associated with the entry. Excluded from the footnotes are otherwise interesting points unrelated to the entry elements on the individual at the time of the ratification debate. These elements are briefly explained below.

Name of Participant. The first line of each entry, the full name of the participant, would seem to be the most straightforward of elements, but it is not. The eighteenth-century mind (predating the federal census and all it represented) was unaccustomed to standardization; New Yorkers were still wrestling with the differences between English and Dutch names; and successive generations of recorders have attempted to impose their own brand of standardization on eighteenth-century names.

For purposes of political identification, most of the participants listed herein are identifiable by a standard appellation that has become accepted over the generations. (Such a claim cannot be made for the subsequent task of searching personal and family records.) Where problems of political identification persist, they are of three basic categories: alternative spellings of one person's name, two or more persons with the same name, and erroneous attributions by subsequent recorders. Wherever possible, these sources of confusion are resolved in footnotes.

Two special features are included in this element. First, in the interest of readability, all footnote numbers are placed on the first line of the entry, regardless of which element they modify. Second, the names of state convention delegates are in CAPITALS AND SMALL CAPITALS. (Also in capitals and small capitals are cross-references appearing in footnotes.)

Party Affiliation. The second element of each entry indicates the party affiliation of the participant in 1787–88 on the issue of the ratification of the Constitution. In the 1788 elections, candidates for the state legislature and state ratifying convention were listed on tickets as Federalist or Antifederalist. And though there were often several nominating lists, there was typically one election list in each county that mirrored the final choice of Federalist and Antifederalist county committees of one kind or another. For convenience, the terms "party" and "partisanship" refer to these organizations and their ties of affiliation, mindful always of the eighteenth-century disinclination to use these terms.

Regardless of how one chooses to describe them, "Federalist" and "Antifederalist" were accepted terms of campaign politics in 1788. Problems in attributing affiliation are less over this general point than over three special cases: printers' preferences, candidates listed by both parties, and members of the eleventh session.

The newspapers of 1788 were owned, published, and often edited by printers. None of the newspapers covering the ratification debate were "party organs," in the sense that they were sponsored and subsidized by a party organization. (A close approximation is Thomas Greenleaf's *The New-York Journal, and Daily Patriotic Register,* begun on 19 November 1787 as a daily with the aid of generous Antifederalist subscribers and patrons.) None of the printers were, as far as could be determined, members of a county party committee. However, most printers had clear personal preferences; and, with the exception of Greenleaf, their preferences were generally Federalist. These preferences affected what came in through the transom and what was printed. And it is in this sense that printers' preferences, if not affiliations, are ascribed. (The first "party organ" in the state was *The Albany Register,* established by John and Robert Barber three months after New York's ratification vote, with the support of Antifederalists who had been displeased with the coverage by the Federalist-dominated press of Albany.)[6]

A different kind of problem respecting party attribution is concerned with candidates listed on both Federalist and Antifederalist tickets in 1788. These instances might have been part of a committee's effort to confuse the opposition or to develop a compromise slate with the opposition. Also involved may have been a candidate's own calculation that a listing on two tickets was better than one. Unfortunately, some of the lesser known candidates involved in these machinations left no indication of their true affiliation, if they had one. Where affiliations are attributable by other measures, they are so indicated; otherwise, the candidate is listed as "affiliation uncertain."

Yet another problem concerns the political affiliation of members of the eleventh session of the state legislature. Elected in the spring of 1787 before the Constitutional Convention met, they were expected to vote in 1788 on the Federalist *versus* Antifederalist issue of calling a state ratifying convention. For those members who did not run as Federalists or Antifederalists in the subsequent spring elections of 1788, policy stances are based solely on their recorded votes on key motions in the eleventh session.

In the Assembly, policy stances are based on votes cast for three Antifederalist motions (all defeated): (1) a motion by Cornelius C. Schoonmaker on 31 January that the Constitutional Con-

[6]On the *Albany Register,* see Douglas C. McMurtrie, *A History of Printing in the United States,* II:176.

vention had exceeded its authority; (2) a motion by Samuel Jones on 31 January to assure that the state convention had the right to propose amendments to the new federal Constitution; and (3) a motion by Samuel Jones on 22 January to insert the name of William Floyd (a neutral), instead of the partisan Alexander Hamilton, as a delegate to the Confederation Congress. (The motion to call the state convention was passed in the affirmative without a recorded vote, and the Assembly resolution was transmitted to the Senate.)

In the Senate, stances are based on votes cast for three motions: (1) a motion by Antifederalist Abraham Yates, Jr., on 1 February to commit the Assembly resolution to a committee of the whole (defeated); (2) a second motion by Yates on February 1 to postpone consideration of the Assembly resolution (defeated); and (3) a motion by Federalist James Duane on 1 February to concur with the Assembly resolution (passed). Inconsistent voting patterns are footnoted for both senators and assemblymen.

All affiliations, then, are for stances taken in 1788, whether those stances be on legislative or campaign issues. No serious effort is made to record all of the many changes in affiliation that occurred between 1783 and 1790. However, attempts are made to note those instances when someone temporarily switched affiliations on the issue of adopting the new federal Constitution.

Key Offices and Positions. The third element in each entry is concerned with the offices and positions held or sought by the participant in 1787–88. Items included are of two types: first are the key offices and positions directly related to the politics of the ratification debate. These are based on the selection criteria set out earlier, and they include seats held in the Confederation Congress and the Constitutional Convention, state legislative and state ratifying convention seats won and lost, county committee positions served, pseudonyms used, and newspapers published. (See "Key to Abbreviations" following this introduction.) Second are other state and county offices concurrently held by the participant. These include: state executive offices; supreme court judgeships; the state commission of forfeiture; the state councils of appointment and revision; and the county offices of clerk, sheriff, surrogate, and first judge of the county court.[7] These offices appear

[7]In 1788 the state supreme court was the highest court in the state; it was later renamed the court of appeals. The state commissioners of forfeiture were appointed and responsible for dispensing forfeited Loyalist property within districts

in brackets to set them off from key offices. (See "Key to Abbreviations.") Confederation offices are identified in footnotes, as are key city offices for Albany, Hudson, and New York. However, the items in this element, as in the other elements, are restricted to the participants' activities in 1787–88.

Also included in this element are the special electoral, voting, and attendance features for certain key offices. For the state convention, the votes of delegates on the final motion to ratify the Constitution are given. For the state Senate, those members who were newly elected to the eleventh and twelfth sessions are indicated.[8] For the state convention and the twelfth session of the state legislature, defeated candidates are identified. (Codes for the abovementioned features can be found in the "Key to Abbreviations.") In addition, footnotes are utilized to identify unusual elections, inconsistent voting records, and cases of nonattendance and early departures.

Towns of 1788. The remaining elements identify the participant's place of residence; first, by the town and city ward designations of 1788; then, by a present-day place name designation; and finally, by present-day county, if different from that of 1788. As explained below, this task is possible because the present town system was established just before the spring elections of 1788.

Today, every New York schoolchild learns that the state was subdivided into counties which were, in turn, subdivided into towns. Often missing from this lesson is its practical effect: everyone in

---

roughly conforming to Senate districts. Members of the state councils of appointment (empowered to fill certain state, county, and local offices) and of revision (empowered to revise or veto state laws) were appointed from the existing ranks of state government. The council of appointment was appointed by the Assembly and included one senator from each of the four Senate districts; the council of revision was composed of the three supreme court justices, the chancellor, and the governor.

The surrogate in each county was authorized to probate wills and determine other testamentary matters. A 1787 law empowered the governor to appoint county surrogates with the advice and consent of the council of appointment. The other county offices included here were appointed by the council. In New York City, the county court (a general trial court), was the mayor's court (civil) and court of sessions (criminal), with Mayor James Duane serving as presiding judge.

[8]In the state Senate, the terms of one-fourth (or six) of its members expired each year. Only five new senators were seated in the twelfth session: James Clinton (Ulster County); Ezra L'Hommedieu (Suffolk County); Paul Micheau (Richmond County); Isaac Roosevelt (New York County); and Peter Van Ness (Columbia County). The vacant seat was Ebenezer Russell's (Washington County). See the footnotes to Russell and Edward Savage, also of Washington County.

New York who lives outside a city or an Indian reservation lives in both a county and a town; and some may also live in a village (i.e., an incorporated city in miniature) or a hamlet (i.e., an unincorporated community). Invariably missing from this lesson in government is the origin of town government.

The present system of town government was brought into effect by the state legislature on various dates in March 1788, shortly before the state convention elections held between 29 April and 3 May. Over a period of several weeks, nearly ninety towns were created to replace the eclectic system of provincial and early state-created towns, precincts, and divisions. Curiously, scant attention has been devoted by historians to this statewide act of local reorganization; however, E. Wilder Spaulding suggests that the establishment of the town system was the latest in a series of challenges to the authority of the manors[9]; and it seems likely that the legislators acted with the impending legislative and convention elections in mind.

Whatever the historical reasons, the creation of the present town system in 1788 provides a standard and consistent basis for locating the participants in the ratification debate. Since 1788, new towns and cities have been split off from the original towns, and villages and hamlets have sprung up within towns. However, the towns of 1788 provided the basis for the first federal census of 1790, early state civil lists, and most local and county histories. Utilizing these sources, supplemented by the expertise of New York's municipal and other local historians, it has been possible to identify the location by town of most of the participants living outside the state's three cities (Albany, Hudson, and New York) and a few unincorporated commercial communities (such as Lansingburgh) that had been founded beyond the bounds of town and

---

[9]See *New York in the Critical Period, 1783–1789* (New York, 1932), 69–70. The state constitution of 1777 confirmed all previous land grants made by the British Crown. However, it also eliminated manor representation in the legislature (the manors of Cortlandt, Livingston, and Rensselaerwyck had district seats in the provincial legislature). Over the next decade, the state legislature chipped away at the manor system by eliminating the practices of entail and primogeniture (thereby enabling the division and alienation of manor lands), terminating feudal obligations and tenures (many of which had long since been forgotten), and enabling landowners to commute the quitrent (then used as a tax loophole owing to the difficulties of collection). The resulting nonfeudal manor system of landlord-tenant relations persisted until the 1840s when its essential features were declared unconstitutional by the state courts and banned by the state legislature.

manor control. (For ward designations, see "Albany and New York City Wards: An Historical Note," below.)

The identification procedure is as follows: beginning with two known facts (the participants' names and the counties they represented), participants are first located by town and city ward utilizing the 1790 federal census. This provided a starting point for follow-up research. Between 1788 and 1790, there were no significant changes in local designations (though the 1790 federal census incorporated the conversion from named to numbered wards that was finalized by New York City the next year). Hence, the principal objectives of follow-up research entailed checking for census errors, distinguishing the correct entry in the case of multiple entries, identifying the place of residence for participants not listed in the 1790 census, identifying those participants whose county of representation and residence differed, and identifying those participants who changed their town or ward of residence between 1788 and 1790.

Outside of New York City, these objectives were realized by relying on genealogies, local histories, and local records. These materials were initially perused in the biographical files of the Ratification Project. The support of municipal and other local historians was enlisted for more in-depth research. In the case of New York City, where mobility between wards was high in the late 1780s, the most reliable basis for determining residences in 1788 is the property tax lists (the only surviving city records organized by ward). However, these lists remain unindexed and could not be reviewed in their entirety. Instead, reliance was placed on the city directories for 1787 and 1789 (1788 was never issued), noting what appear to be major moves from one ward to another.

Present-Day Place Designations. The last element in each entry is the present-day local and county designation for the area in which the participant lived in 1788. A local designation is always indicated, even if it is the same as that used in 1788. A county designation is indicated only if the county is different from that of 1788. In researching this element, the expertise of municipal and other local historians has been especially useful. Wherever warranted, follow-up research, second opinions, and independent verification were sought. In the case of persistent uncertainties, present-day designations are indicated as "probable" (meaning likely), "perhaps" (indicating less certainty), or "unknown."

For one-third or more of the participants, surviving or recently standing homes provide evidence for determining present location. For roughly another third, local records or reliable histories sufficiently fix the location of the participant's home for the broad designations used here. Moreover, in many of these cases, and in others as well, boundaries and designations have remained relatively stable over time. Hence, this writer is reasonably confident about most of the entries; degrees of confidence in the remainder are noted.

Several regional patterns of changes emerge from this research. The greatest jurisdictional changes have occurred in the 1788 counties of Albany and Montgomery, where extensive boundaries have been steadily reduced by the formation of new counties, the erection of new towns from older towns, and the incorporation of cities (from towns) and villages (within towns). By contrast, the Upper Hudson Valley counties of Columbia and Washington have remained relatively stable. In the the Mid-Hudson and Lower Hudson valleys, the major changes have occurred in the southern portion of each county, where new counties were created (Bronx County and borough from Westchester, Putnam from Dutchess, and Rockland from Orange) or borders altered (notably resulting in the movement of southern Ulster County towns into the jurisdiction of Orange County). On Long Island, the most significant jurisdictional changes have involved the creation of Nassau County from Queens County and the conversion of the latter into a borough and county. The town boundaries in Suffolk and present-day Nassau counties have remained remarkably stable; however, within these towns, there has been a suburban proliferation of unincorporated communities with clear commercial centers and hazy boundaries. New York County (now Manhattan) is a special case. This introductory statement concludes with an historical note on the changes in the 1788 boundaries and place names of New York City and Albany.

Albany and New York City Wards:
An Historical Note

The City of Albany, according to the federal census of 1790, had a population of approximately 7,000, less than one-tenth the size of Albany County and roughly one-fifth the population of the coterminous city and county of New York. In the late 1780s the city of Albany was essentially confined to the area bounded by the Hudson River on the east, Patroon Street (now Clinton Avenue) on the north, Snipe Street (now New Scotland Avenue) on the west, and Gansevoort Street on the south. The most densely populated part of the city was further confined to two areas: one, between State and Patroon streets, up the hill from the Hudson River to Eagle Street; the other, an irregular area between State and Hudson streets, up the hill from the river to Washington Street.

The closest approximation of the city's ward boundaries in 1788 is from a "Plan of the City of Albany . . . 1794," surveyed by Simeon DeWitt, and reproduced by Historic Urban Plans (Ithaca, 1968). According to that plan, the city contained three numbered wards. (Unless otherwise noted, ward boundaries here and in New York City ran up the center of the streets named.)

First Ward, now known as the South End, included the area west of the Hudson River, between the city's southern boundary (near Gansevoort Street) and a northern ward line running up Mark Lane from the river, across Market Street, and up the hill parallel to, and just north of, State Street. The northern ward line then crossed Eagle Street on the south side of the public square, proceeding up Deer Street beyond Snipe Street where the plan of 1794 ends. In this ward, the plan depicts the Schuyler and Yates estates, separated by Beaver Creek; with the Pastures area located below the two estates.

Second Ward, now known as Capitol Hill, included the area west of Middle Lane (now James Street) between the State-Deer streets line and Patroon Street, up to Snipe Street and beyond. In this ward, the plan of 1794 shows the Arbor Hill block and the public square.

Third Ward, now known as Downtown Albany, was the most compact and densely populated section of the city. It included the area bounded by the Hudson River, Mark Lane, Middle Lane, and a line running through the blocks from Patroon Street to the river. The hub of this area was the market on Market Street.

The present-day area of North Albany was part of the town of Watervliet in 1788.

New York City's area of dense settlement in 1788 was confined to what is today Downtown (or Lower) Manhattan and the Lower East Side, south of Chambers Street on the west side and Broome Street on the east side. Contained in this area were all of five wards and the southern portions of two wards. Together, these seven wards were created by the Montgomerie Charter of 1731 which was confirmed by the state constitution of 1777. They remained essentially unchanged until 1791, when, among other things, the switch from named to numbered wards occurred. (The 1790 federal census used the numbered ward system.)

South Ward (later the First Ward), located between the Battery and Bowling Green, was bounded by a line up Broad Street from the East River, west on Wall Street at City Hall (then Federal Hall), then south on New Street, and west on Beaver Street to the Hudson River. The shorthand reference for this area is "above the Battery, inside Beaver & Broad sts."

Dock Ward (later the Fourth Ward), containing Fraunces Tavern, was bounded by Broad, Wall, and Smith (William) streets and the East River. The shorthand reference is "below Wall St., betw. Broad & William sts."

East Ward (later the Fifth Ward), containing the largest number of Federalist and Antifederalist leaders as well as most printers, was bounded by a line from Old Slip up Smith and William streets, and then down John Street to Burling Slip. The shorthand reference is "east of William St., betw. Old & Burling slips."

Montgomerie Ward (later the Sixth Ward), including the present-day South Street Seaport Restoration, was bounded by a line from Burling Slip up John Street, up William Street to Frankfort Street, then through the blocks to the Fresh Water Pond (where the Criminal Courts Building and "Tombs" now stand), east to the corner of Chatham and Roosevelt streets, and down the latter to the New Slip (just north of what is now the Brooklyn Bridge) via Cherry and James streets. The shorthand reference for the principal area of settlement in this ward is "east of William St., betw. Burling & New slips."

West Ward (later the Second Ward) included the area north of Beaver Street and west of a line running parallel to, and just east of, Broadway. In present-day terms, The World Trade Center area would dominate what were the most heavily settled parts of this ward. From south to north, the area then boasted the second Trinity Church (1788–1790), St. Paul's Chapel, and Columbia College (moved north in 1857). Richmond Hill (built in 1767) was then a "country mansion," located near today's intersection of Charlton and Varick streets. The shorthand reference is "Broadway area, below Chambers St."

North Ward (later the Third Ward) was located between West and Montgomerie wards, bounded by Wall Street on the south and the Fresh Water Pond area on the north. It included the Fields or Commons, a triangular plot fronting the almshouse, Bridewell, and the jail. The shorthand reference is "above Wall St., between Broadway and William St."

Out Ward (later the Seventh Ward), divided into Bowery and Harlem divisions, essentially included all of the island north of Montgomerie Ward and east of the West Ward. The "country estates" of Henry Rutgers and Nicholas Bayard were located in this ward at Rutgers Street and Bayard's Lane, respectively. In today's terms, the shorthand reference is "Lower East Side," for the principal area of settlement in which Federalist and Antifederalist leaders lived.

Ward boundaries are from Thomas E. V. Smith, *The City of New York in the Year of Washington's Inauguration, 1789* (New York, 1889), 54–55. For more information on New York City in 1787–88, see Sidney I. Pomerantz, *New York: An American City, 1783–1803, A Study of Urban Life* (New York, 1938).

Key to Abbreviations

Key Offices and Positions

A-11   Member, New York State Assembly, Eleventh Session
Poughkeepsie, 9 January–22 March 1788.

A-12   Member, New York State Assembly, Twelfth Session
Albany, 11 December 1788–3 March 1789.

Cong(87)   Delegate, Confederation Congress
New York, 6 November 1786–5 November 1787.[1]

Cong(88)   Delegate, Confederation Congress
New York, 5 November 1787–3 November 1788.[1]

Comm   Member, County Party Committee
Antifederalist unless otherwise indicated.

FedCon   Delegate, Constitutional Convention
Philadelphia, 14 May–17 September 1787.

RaCon   Delegate, New York State Ratifying Convention
Poughkeepsie, 17 June–26 July 1788.

S-11   Member, New York State Senate, Eleventh Session
Poughkeepsie, 11 January–22 March 1788.

S-12   Member, New York State Senate, Twelfth Session
Albany, 11 December 1788–3 March 1789.

Other State Offices and Positions

Appt(87)   Member, Council of Appointment, 1787

Appt(88)   Member, Council of Appointment, 1788

AttGen   Attorney General

Chanc   Chancellor, Court of Chancery

Forf   Commissioner of Forfeitures

Gov   Governor

LtGov   Lieutenant Governor

Rev   Member, Council of Revision

SCt   Justice, Supreme Court

[1]The official journals of Congress follow the federal year which then began on the first Monday of November. In 1787 and 1788 quorums were achieved on 17 January and 21 January, respectively.

Other County Offices and Positions

CoClk	County Clerk
CoJdg	First Judge of County Court
Sher	Sheriff
Surr	Surrogate

Electoral Characteristics

*	Elected in 1787 (S-11); elected in 1788 (S-12).
(d)	Defeated in election for office indicated.

Convention Votes

(no)	Voted against the final ratification motion.
(nv)	Not voting on the final ratification motion.
(yes)	Voted for the final ratification motion.

Local Jurisdictions

(boro.)	borough
(c.)	city[2]
(co.)	county
(t.)	town[2]
(v.)	village

[2]For cities and towns, an abbreviation is used only in those instances where confusion might otherwise arise.

Biographical Gazetteer

Albany[1]

Babcock, John[2]
Federalist
printer
town unknown
present place name unknown

Claxton, Thomas[3]
Federalist
printer
town unknown
present place name unknown

Cuyler, Jacob
Federalist
RaCon(d)
Albany, Second Ward
now Albany, Capitol Hill

Douw, Volkert P.[4]
affiliation unknown
S-11/ S-12
Albany, ward unknown
still Albany, area unknown

Duncan, John[5]
Antifederalist
A-12
Schenectady, South
now in Niskayuna
Schenectady Co.

Gansevoort, Leonard[6]
Federalist
A-11/ Cong(88)/ A-12(d)

[1]An original county, its bounds in 1788 include all of the present-day counties of Albany, Greene, Rensselaer, Saratoga, and Schenectady, and parts of the present-day counties of Delaware, Schoharie, Ulster, and Washington. In 1788 the county was in the western Senate district. (For Albany city wards, see the introduction to this gazetteer, section on "Albany and New York City Wards: An Historical Note.")

[2]Leading partner with THOMAS CLAXTON in publishing the short-lived *Northern Centinel, and Lansingburgh Advertiser* in 1787, the first newspaper of Lansingburgh. He removed to Albany for several months early in 1788 to establish *The Federal Herald* with Claxton, returning in April to Lansingburgh, where he continued *The Federal Herald* with EZRA HICKOK until 1790.

[3]Joining JOHN BABCOCK in publishing the short-lived Lansingburgh *Northern Centinel* and Albany *Federal Herald*, he became doorkeeper of the U.S. House of Representatives in 1789.

[4]Not to be confused with his cousin, Volkert A., who lived in the third ward and signed a statement of the Antifederalist Committee, 10 April 1788. Volkert P. may also have been an Antifederalist, but he is not recorded as voting on any of the key Senate motions. (For key motions in the Senate and Assembly, see the introduction to this gazetteer, section on "Party Affiliation.") Volkert P. Douw's residence in 1788 is not known, though he may have been living at the family home located at Douw's Point south of Crailo in what is now the city of Rensselaer, Rensselaer County.

[5]Schenectady, South, refers to one 1788 town, "Schenectady South of the Mohawk," from which the present-day city of Schenectady and the town of Niskayuna were formed. A second 1788 town, "Schenectady," was located across the Mohawk River.

[6]Not to be confused with his cousin Leonard, Jr. Though the 1790 census puts him in the first ward, his home and inherited family lot were probably on the northside of State Street in the third ward.

Albany, Third Ward
now Albany, Downtown

Gansevoort, Peter, Jr.[7]
Federalist
RaCon(d)
Albany, Third Ward
now Albany, Downtown

Gordon, James
Federalist
A-11/ RaCon(d)
Ballston
still in Ballston
now in Saratoga Co.

Hickok, Ezra[8]
Federalist
printer
Lansingburgh
now in Troy (c.)
Rensselaer Co.

Hoogland, Jeronemus
Federalist
RaCon(d)
Lansingburgh
now in Troy (c.)
Rensselaer Co.

Knickerbacker, John, Jr.[9]
Federalist
A-12(d)
Schaghticoke
still in Schaghticoke
now in Rensselaer Co.

Lansing, Abraham G.[10]
Antifederalist
Comm/[Surr]
prob. Watervliet
prob. now Colonie

LANSING, JOHN (TEN EYCK),
Jr.[11]
Antifederalist
RaCon(no)/ Cong(87)/
FedCon/ A-12(Speaker)/
Comm
Albany, Third Ward
now Albany, Downtown

[7]Elder brother of LEONARD. Between 1783 and 1790, he was probably attending his lumber business on the Snock Kill where he built a frame house in 1787. Snock Hill was then in the town of Saratoga, Albany County, but is now in the town of Northumberland, Saratoga County.

[8]Published *The Federal Herald* in Lansingburgh with JOHN BABCOCK (1788–90). Lansingburgh, then adjoining the Rensselaerwyck Manor, was not yet erected by the state legislature as a town or village.

[9]Probably Colonel Johannes II (1751–1827), son of Colonel Johannes I (1723–1802). Johannes II inherited his father's estate, including the Knickerbacker Mansion (begun in 1749, completed by 1772), and raised fourteen children. One of his sons was Harmon, "Prince of Schaghticoke," friend of Washington Irving, and believed to be the model for Irving's Diedrich Knickerbocker.

[10]Not to be confused with Abraham J., founder of Lansingburgh. Abraham G. was the son of Gerrit J., brother of JOHN, JR., and son-in-law of ABRAHAM YATES, JR.

[11]Brother of ABRAHAM G., he was mayor of Albany (1786–90). Delegate to both Congress and the Constitutional Convention in 1787, he did not attend the former and left before the conclusion of the latter.

McClallen, Robert[12]
Federalist
Comm(Chairman)
Albany, First Ward
now Albany, South End

Nicoll, Francis
Federalist
RaCon(d)
Watervliet
now in Bethlehem

OOTHOUDT, HENRY[13]
Antifederalist
RaCon(no)/ Comm/ [Forf]
Catskill
now Jefferson Heights, Catskill
Greene Co.

Schermerhorn, John W.[14]
Federalist
RaCon(d)
Philipstown
now in Nassau
Rensselaer Co.

Schuyler, Philip[15]
Federalist

S-11/ S-12/ [Appt(88)]
Albany, First Ward
now Albany, South End

Sickles, Thomas[16]
Federalist
A-11
Hoosick
still in Hoosick
now in Rensselaer Co.

Sill, Richard[17]
Federalist
A-12(d)
Albany, ward unknown
still Albany, area unknown

SWART, DIRCK[18]
Antifederalist
RaCon(nv)
Stillwater
still in Stillwater
now in Saratoga Co.

Ten Broeck, Abraham
Federalist
RaCon(d)/ [CoJdg]
Albany, Third Ward
now Albany, Downtown

TEN EYCK, ANTHONY[19]
Antifederalist

[12]McClallen was a long-time alderman and political leader for the First Ward.

[13]Leader with JEREMIAH VAN RENSSELAER of the Albany Antifederalist Committee, Henry Oothoudt was chairman, committee of the whole, state ratifying convention.

[14]Philipstown was located between Stephentown and Schodack (then a part of Rensselaerwyck Manor), but not yet erected by the legislature as a town. John was not the Schermerhorn living in the house now standing in Schodack Landing.

[15]Considered by many to be the leader, with his son-in-law ALEXANDER HAMILTON, of the Federalists in state politics. Schuyler was a spectator and correspondent at the state ratifying convention.

[16]Party designation based solely on votes cast in the eleventh session. In 1788 Sickles was probably living on a farm on the Walloomsack in Hoosick.

[17]Did not move into Bethlehem House (then in Watervliet and owned by his father-in-law FRANCIS NICOLL) until 1790. His wedding there in 1785 is said to have brought ALEXANDER HAMILTON, AARON BURR, and others.

[18]Left the convention on 19 July, arriving in Albany the following day.

[19]Though he did not vote on the final ratification motion, he voted the Antifederalist position on preceding motions at the convention.

RaCon(nv)
Rensselaerwick
now in Schodack
Rensselaer Co.

Ten Eyck, John de Peyster[20]
affiliation unknown
A-11
Albany, First Ward
now Albany, South End

THOMPSON, ISRAEL
Antifederalist
RaCon(no)
Pittstown
prob. still in Pittstown
now in Rensselaer Co.

Thompson, John
Antifederalist
A-12
Stillwater
still in Stillwater
now in Saratoga Co.

Van Dyck, Cornelius
Antifederalist
A-12
Schenectady, South
now in Schenectady (c.)
Schenectady Co.

Van Ingen, Dirck[21]
Federalist
A-11
Schenectady, South

now in Schenectady (c.)
Schenectady Co.

Van Orden, Hezekiah[22]
Federalist
A-11/ A-12(d)
Catskill
still in Catskill
now in Greene Co.

Van Rensselaer, Henry K.[23]
Antifederalist
A-12
Rensselaerwick
now in East Greenbush
Rensselaer Co.

Van Rensselaer, Jeremiah[24]
Antifederalist
A-12/ Comm(Chairman)/
    [Forf]
Albany, Second Ward
now Albany, Capitol Hill

[20]No votes recorded on key Assembly motions. Possibly Antifederalist, since three Ten Eycks (ANTHONY, Henry, and Jacob C.) appear on Antifederalist lists of one kind or another.

[21]Party designation based solely on votes cast in the eleventh session.

[22]Van Orden lived in that part of Catskill corresponding to the far southern section of the Great Inboght District of earlier years and near the present-day village of Catskill.

[23]Son of Kilian and brother of Philip who built Cherry Hill in 1787, Henry K. was of the "Fort Crailo" line (one of several Van Rensselaer lines). He lived in what later became known as the Van Rensselaer-Genêt House, no longer standing.

[24]Of many Jeremiahs, this is probably the son of Captain Hendrick of Claverack. As chairman of the Albany Antifederalist Committee, he helped supervise the county's defection from the Federalist ranks of STEPHEN VAN RENSSELAER (a distant cousin), PHILIP SCHUYLER, and others.

Van Rensselaer, Stephen[25]
Federalist
A-12(d)
Watervliet
now North Albany

Visscher, Matthew
Antifederalist
Comm(Secretary)/ [CoClk]
Albany, Second Ward
now Albany, Capitol Hill

Vrooman, Isaac
Federalist
A-12(d)
Schenectady, South
now in Schenectady (c.)
Schenectady Co.

VROOMAN, PETER[26]
Antifederalist
RaCon(nv)
Schoharie
now in Schoharie (v.)
Schoharie Co.

Webster, Charles R.[27]
Federalist

printer
Albany, First Ward
now Albany, South End

Webster, George[28]
Federalist
printer
prob. Albany, ward unknown
prob. still Albany, area
unknown

Yates, Abraham, Jr.[29]
Antifederalist
Cong(87,88)/ S-11/ S-12/
"Rough Hewer"/
"Sidney"/ "Sydney"
Albany, Third Ward
now Albany, Downtown

Yates, Peter W.
Antifederalist
Comm
Albany, First Ward
now Albany, South End

YATES, ROBERT[30]
Antifederalist

---

[25]Sixth and last lord of the Rensselaerwyck Manor, Stephen was of the so-called "patroon" line of Van Rensselaers. He was a son-in-law of PHILIP SCHUYLER and brother-in-law of ALEXANDER HAMILTON. His mansion was located off Tivoli Street, then in the town of Watervliet, now in the city of Albany.

[26]Linda Grant De Pauw speculates that he might have left the convention early. See *The Eleventh Pillar: New York State and the Federal Constitution* (Ithaca, 1966), 247.

[27]Foremost Albany printer, he published *The Albany Gazette*, the first long-lived newspaper of that city, from 1784 until shortly after 1820, with various partners, including his twin brother GEORGE who also joined in *The Albany*

Journal: or, the Montgomery, Washington and Columbia Intelligencer, briefly published as a semiweekly (26 January 1788–31 March 1788) and then as a weekly until 11 May 1789.

[28]Published the *Albany Journal* with his brother CHARLES R. In 1789 he joined his brother in publishing the *Albany Gazette* until shortly after 1820.

[29]Uncle of ROBERT, he attended Congress from 20 to 28 September 1787, but not from 13 to 21 February of that year.

[30]Delegate to the Constitutional Convention, he left before its conclusion. At the state ratifying convention, he was chairman of a committee of correspondence appointed by an Antifederalist caucus to work with Virginians in formulating "previous and absolute amendments" to the Constitution. In

RaCon(no)/ FedCon/ [SCt/
  Rev]
Albany, First Ward
now Albany, South End

Younglove, John[31]
affiliation uncertain
A-11/ A-12
Cambridge
prob. now in White Creek
Washington Co.

Columbia[32]

ADGATE, MATTHEW
Antifederalist
RaCon(no)/ A-12/ Comm
Canaan
now in New Lebanon

BAY, JOHN
Antifederalist
RaCon(no)/ A-12/ Comm
Claverack
still in Claverack

Ford, Jacob
Federalist

RaCon(d)
Hillsdale
now in Austerlitz

Jenkins, Thomas[33]
Federalist
A-12(d)
Hudson (c.)
still in Hudson (c.)

Kortz, John
Antifederalist
A-12
Germantown
still in Germantown

Livingston, Henry[34]
Federalist
RaCon(d)
Livingston
still in Livingston

Livingston, John[35]
Federalist
A-11/ A-12(d)
Livingston
still in Livingston

1789, a moderate Antifederalist, he was the Federalist nominee of anti-Clinton forces for governor. He was defeated in the election by GEORGE CLINTON.

[31]He voted the Federalist position in the eleventh session. For the twelfth session, he was listed on both Antifederalist and Federalist tickets, winning on the former. It is not known why he was listed on both tickets or where his stronger affiliations were placed.

[32]Columbia County was established in 1786 from Albany County with the support of the members of the Livingston Manor, the senior branch of the family, known as the "upper manor line." The county's boundaries have remained virtually unchanged since 1786. In 1788 the county was in the western Senate district.

[33]Hudson was incorporated as a city in 1785, the same year it was laid out as a planned community by Jenkins and other New Englanders. For twenty-eight of the next thirty years, members of the Jenkins family served as the city's mayor.

[34]Member, "upper manor line." Sixth and youngest son of Robert, Jr., third lord of the manor. Not to be confused with Henry (Poughkeepsie), clerk of Dutchess County (1777–89). In 1788 the upper Livingston manor and the town of Livingston were coterminous, as was the town and "lower manor" of Clermont associated with Chancellor ROBERT R. LIVINGSTON (see New York County entry).

[35]Member, "upper manor line." Fifth youngest son of Robert, Jr., and brother of Henry.

Ludlow, William H.
Federalist
A-12(d)
Claverack
still in Claverack

Powers, William
Federalist
A-11
Canaan
now in Chatham

Silvester, Peter
Federalist
A-11/ S-12(d)
Kinderhook
now in Kinderhook (v.)

Stoddard, Ashbel[36]
Federalist
printer
Hudson (c.)
still in Hudson (c.)

VAN NESS, PETER
Antifederalist
RaCon(no)/ S-11/ S-12*/
    Comm/ [CoJdg]
Kinderhook
still in Kinderhook

Van Schaack, Peter[37]
Federalist
RaCon(d)
Kinderhook
now in Kinderhook (v.)

Whiting, William B.
Antifederalist
Comm
Canaan
still in Canaan

Dutchess[38]

AKINS, JONATHAN
Antifederalist
RaCon(no)/ A-12
Pawling
still in Pawling

Bailey, Theodorus[39]
Antifederalist
Comm
Poughkeepsie
still Poughkeepsie

Barker, Samuel A.[40]
affiliation uncertain
A-12
Frederickstown
now in Kent
Putnam Co.

Benson, Egbert[41]
Federalist

---

[36]Sole printer in the city of Hudson at this time, he published *The Hudson Weekly Gazette* (a Federalist newspaper in the ratification debate), from 1785 through the end of 1803, initially with the support of CHARLES R. WEBSTER.

[37]Van Schaack/Van Schaick, the latter spelling appearing only on the Federalist ticket.

[38]An original county, its boundaries in 1788 include all of present-day Dutchess and Putnam counties. In 1788 it was in the middle Senate district.

[39]Not known is whether Bailey lived in that part of Poughkeepsie now in the city or town of the same name.

[40]Samuel A. (also Samuel Augustus) was listed on both Antifederalist and Federalist tickets for the twelfth session. Though he won on the former, his affiliation is not certain.

[41]Attorney General of New York (1777–89), he and ALEXANDER HAMILTON were the only New York delegates who attended the Annapolis Convention in 1786. In 1787 he attended Congress from 13 to 21 February, but not from 20 to 28 September. In 1788

A-11/ Cong(87,88)/
RaCon(d)/ A-12(d)/
[AttGen]
Rhinebeck
now in Red Hook

Bloom, Isaac[42]
affiliation uncertain
A-11/ A-12
Clinton
now in Pleasant Valley

Cantine, Peter, Jr.[43]
Federalist
A-11
Rhinebeck
now in Red Hook

Cary, Ebenezer
Federalist
RaCon(d)
Beekman
still in Beekman

Crane, Joseph
Federalist
RaCon(d)
prob. Southeast Town
now in Southeast
Putnam Co.

D'Cantillon, Richard
Federalist
RaCon(d)
Clinton
now in Hyde Park

DE WITT, JOHN, JR.
Antifederalist
RaCon(yes)/ A-11/ A-12
Clinton
still in Clinton

DuBois, Lewis[44]
Antifederalist
Comm
Poughkeepsie
still Poughkeepsie

Graham, Morris[45]
Antifederalist
A-11
Northeast
now in Pine Plains

Griffin, Jacob
Antifederalist
A-12
Fishkill
still in Fishkill

Hoffman, Anthony
Federalist
S-11*/ S-12/ [Appt(88)]
Rhinebeck
now in Red Hook

Benson's Assembly motion of 31 January became the basis for the legislative resolution to call the state ratifying convention.

[42]Listed on both Antifederalist and Federalist tickets for the twelfth session. Though he won on the former, his affiliation is not certain.

[43]Party designation based on votes cast in the eleventh session and on campaign activities in 1788.

[44]Dubois (also Duboys) was placed on a spurious Antifederalist ticket put forward by Federalists to divide the Antifederal vote. That ticket was reported in *The Country Journal, and the Poughkeepsie Advertiser*, 4 March 1788. Not known is whether Dubois lived in that part of Poughkeepsie which is now in the city.

[45]In the eleventh session, Graham voted the Antifederalist position on motions 1 and 3 and the Federalist position on motion 2. He was listed on the spurious Antifederalist ticket, reported in the *Country Journal*, 4 March 1788.

Hughes, Hugh[46]
Antifederalist
"A Countryman"/
    "Expositor"/
    "Interrogator"
town unknown
present place name unknown

Humfrey, Cornelius[47]
Antifederalist
S-11/ S-12
town unknown
present place name unknown

Husted, Ebenezer[48]
Federalist

A-12(d)
Washington
now in Stanford

Kent, James
Federalist
"A Country Federalist"
Poughkeepsie
prob. now in Poughkeepsie (c.)

LIVINGSTON, GILBERT[49]
Antifederalist
RaCon(yes)/ A-12/ [Surr]
Poughkeepsie
still in Poughkeepsie (t.)

Patterson, Matthew
Antifederalist
A-11/ A-12/ Comm
Frederickstown
now in Kent
Putnam Co.

PLATT, ZEPHANIAH
Antifederalist
RaCon(yes)/ [CoJdg]
Poughkeepsie
still in Poughkeepsie (t.)

Power, Nicholas[50]
Federalist
printer
Poughkeepsie
prob. now in Poughkeepsie (c.)

[46]Father of JAMES M. of New York County. Hugh Hughes authored six serialized essays published in the *New-York Journal*, under the pseudonym "A Countryman." (DeWitt Clinton of New York County also wrote under this pseudonym.) "Expositor" I, printed in three installments, and "Expositor" II were also written by Hughes and published in the *New-York Journal*. Hughes's "Interrogator," an attack upon *The Federalist* No. 15, was never published. In early April 1788 he was living in Dutchess County and planning to move to a farm in Yonkers (Westchester County) owned by JOHN LAMB whose children he had been tutoring.

[47]In the eleventh session, Humfrey voted the Antifederalist position on all three motions. He also appears with MORRIS GRAHAM and LEWIS DUBOIS on the spurious Antifederalist ticket of 4 March (see note 44 above). Though definitely Antifederalists, neither Graham nor Humfrey appear in a long list of "active Antifederalists," compiled by Theophilus Parsons, Jr., "The Old Conviction versus The New Realities: New York Antifederalist Leaders and the Radical Whig Tradition" (Ph.D. diss., Columbia University, 1974), Appendix.

[48]Probably Major Ebenezer Husted, Jr., son of Ebenezer, Sr., whose will is dated 1785. The son lived on a farm, later known as the Juckett Farm.

[49]Grandson of Gilbert, the youngest son of the first manor lord, and the family's sole Antifederalist in the ratification debate.

[50]Official printer of the Journal of the state ratifying convention, he published a Federalist newspaper, *The Country Journal, and the Poughkeepsie Advertiser* (continued in 1789 as *The Poughkeepsie Journal*), from 1785 until 1806, with various partners after 1796.

Sands, Robert
Federalist
RaCon(d)
Rhinebeck
still in Rhinebeck

SMITH, MELANCTON[51]
Antifederalist
RaCon(yes)
(North Ward, N.Y.C.)
See New York County

SWARTWOUT, JACOBUS[52]
Antifederalist
RaCon(no)/ S-11*/ S-12
Fishkill
now in Wappinger

Tallman, Isaac I.
Federalist
RaCon(d)/ A-12(d)
Pawling
still in Pawling

Tappen, Peter
Antifederalist
Comm
Poughkeepsie
now in Poughkeepsie (c.)

THOMPSON, EZRA[53]
Antifederalist
RaCon(nv)

Washington
now in Stanford

Tillotson, Thomas
Federalist
A-11/A-12(d)
Rhinebeck
still in Rhinebeck

Van Wyck, Isaac
Federalist
A-12(d)
Fishkill
still in Fishkill

Wiltse, Martin
Federalist
RaCon(d)
Fishkill
now in Beacon (c.)

Kings (now also Brooklyn boro.)[54]

Doughty, Charles[55]
Antifederalist
A-11/ RaCon(d)/ A-12(d)/ Comm
Brooklyn
now in Cadman Plaza area, near Fulton Ferry

---

[51]Listed on the Antifederalist tickets in Dutchess County and New York City, he won on the former and lost on the latter. Before the Revolution he moved from Queens County to Dutchess, settling in Poughkeepsie. In 1784 he moved to New York City.

[52]Swartwout was the only candidate nominated on both the Antifederalist ticket and a spurious Antifederalist ticket proposed by Federalists.

[53]Became ill and left the convention early.

[54]An original county, it is now one of the five boroughs of the city of New York and, like the other boroughs, a vestigal county for certain purposes. Hence, its city designation is Brooklyn borough, while its state designation remains Kings County. In 1788 it was in the southern Senate district.

[55]A prominent Kings County lawyer, not to be confused with the Charles Doughty who occupied the Kingsland House (still standing) in Queens County.

Giles, Aquila[56]
Federalist
A-12
Flatbush
still in Flatbush, near Erasmus
    Hall

LEFFERTS, PETER[57]
Federalist
RaCon(yes)
Flatbush
still in Flatbush, now Botanic
    Garden area

Vanderbilt, John[58]
Federalist
S-11/ S-12/ [Appt(88)]
Flatbush
still in Flatbush

VANDEVOORT, PETER
Federalist
RaCon(yes)/ A-12/ [Sher]
Brooklyn
prob. now in Bedford-
    Stuyvesant

Wyckoff, Cornelius[59]
Antifederalist

A-11/ RaCon(d)/ A-12(d)
town unknown
present area unknown

Wyckoff, Hendrick[60]
Antifederalist
Comm
Flatbush
present area unknown

Montgomery[61]

Arndt, Abraham[62]
Federalist
A-11/ RaCon(d)
Canajoharie
now in Fort Plain (v.)

Cooper, William[63]
Federalist

[56]Giles was then living in Melrose Hall, off the corner of Flatbush Avenue and what is now Winthrop Street, near Erasmus Hall Academy which he and many others (including ALEXANDER HAMILTON and AARON BURR) helped to establish.

[57]Lefferts Homestead was then located on Flatbush Avenue, near what is now the Botanic Garden. The home was later moved across Flatbush Avenue into Prospect Park. (See "A Guide to Historic Sites . . ." in this collection.)

[58]Of the many John Vanderbilts, this is probably Judge Vanderbilt who lived on Flatbush Avenue and led the drive to establish Erasmus Hall Academy.

[59]None of the many Cornelius Wyckoffs have been located in Kings County or nearby during this period.

[60]This Wyckoff could have been any one of several Hendricks: H.I, b. 1768, politically active, and living at a Bowling Green address in Manhattan; H.II, b. 1743 in Flatbush; and H.III, b. 1733, living on Wyckoff Lane (now Wyona Street), not far from the Wyckoff-Bennett House (now a private residence off Kings Highway in Sheepshead Bay).

[61]Established in 1772 from Albany County, its 1788 boundaries included all the western lands then claimed by New York; however its most settled areas in 1788 were limited to the present-day counties of Fulton, Herkimer, Montgomery, Otsego, and western Schoharie. In 1788 it was in the western Senate district.

[62]Canajoharie, later Minden, now Fort Plain.

[63]In 1787 William Cooper laid out the frontier hamlet of Coopers-Town, one of the first interior settlements of the Susquehanna Valley. In 1790 he brought his family, including his infant son James Fenimore, from Burlington, New Jersey. Addressed by the titles "Judge" and "Squire," he was later portrayed as "Marmaduke Temple" in his son's novel *The Pioneers*.

leading partisan
Otsego
now in Cooperstown (v.)
Otsego Co.

Crane, Josiah
Federalist
RaCon(d)
Palatine
still in Palatine

Fonda, Jellis[64]
affiliation unknown
S-11*/ S-12
Caughnawaga
now in Fonda (v.)

FREY, JOHN
Antifederalist
RaCon(no)/ A-11/ A-12/
   Comm
Palatine
still in Palatine

HARPER, WILLIAM[65]
Antifederalist
RaCon(no)/ A-12/ Comm
Mohawk
now in Florida

Livingston, James[66]
Federalist
A-11/ RaCon(d)

Caughnawaga
now in Johnstown (c.)
Fulton Co.

Paris, Isaac[67]
affiliation unknown
A-11/ [Surr]
Canajoharie
now in Fort Plain (v.)

Schuyler, Peter[68]
Federalist
S-11/ S-12/ RaCon(d)/
   [Appt(87)]
Canajoharie
now in Danube
Herkimer Co.

STARING, HENRY
Antifederalist
RaCon(no)/ A-12
German Flatts
now in Schuyler
Herkimer Co.

Van Horne, Abraham
Federalist
RaCon(d)
Canajoharie
now in Fort Plain (v.)

Van Vechten, Abraham
Federalist
RaCon(d)
Canajoharie
present place name unknown

VEEDER, VOLKERT
Antifederalist
RaCon(no)/ A-11/ A-12/
   Comm

[64]Elected to, but not present at, the eleventh session. In 1788 he was living either on his farm or on his new home site, both now located in the village of Fonda. He died in 1791 before construction was completed on his new home.

[65]The town of Mohawk was then south of the Mohawk River.

[66]The state civil list is incorrect in listing John Livingston as the assemblyman from Montgomery County. It is James who appears in the Assembly Journal.

[67]No voting record or other indication of party affiliation.

[68]Nephew of PHILIP SCHUYLER.

Caughnawaga
now in Mohawk

WINN, JOHN[69]
Antifederalist
RaCon(no)/ A-11/ A-12
Canajoharie
present place name unknown

YATES, CHRISTOPHER P.[70]
Antifederalist
RaCon(nv)/ A-12/ Comm/
    [CoClk]
Canajoharie
still in Canajoharie

New York (now also Manhattan
    boro.)[71]

Bancker, Evert[72]
Federalist
A-11
North Ward
Above Wall St., betw.
    Broadway & William St.

Bayard, Nicholas[73]
Antifederalist
A-11/ A-12(d)
Out Ward
now Lower East Side

Brooks, David[74]
Federalist
A-11
ward unknown
present area unknown

Burr, Aaron
Antifederalist
A-12(d)
South Ward
Above the Battery, inside
    Beaver & Broad sts.

Childs, Francis[75]
Federalist
printer
ward unknown
present area unknown

---

[69]Elected to the convention on the Antifederalist ticket, he had voted the Federalist position in the eleventh session on motions 1 and 2 and cast no vote for motion 3.

[70]Though he did not vote on the final ratification motion, he voted the Antifederalist position on preceding motions at the convention.

[71]An original county, its 1788 boundaries were confined to Manhattan Island. In 1788 the most densely settled areas were in what is today Downtown (or Lower) Manhattan and the Lower East Side. (For ward boundaries, see introduction, section on "Albany and New York City Wards: An Historical Note.") In 1788 it was in the southern Senate district.

[72]Father of ABRAHAM B. of Ulster County and uncle of ABRAHAM of Richmond County.

[73]Bayard was a long-time alderman and political leader for the Out Ward.

[74]There were several New Yorkers with the name David Brooks. According to one authority, probabilities favor Major David, assistant clothier general (1780–82) and lawyer. See Jackson Turner Main, *Political Parties before the Constitution* (Chapel Hill, N.C., 1973), 419.

[75]Published *The Daily Advertiser*, from 1 March 1785 through 1796, the first newspaper established as a daily in New York City. Childs took notes at the state ratifying convention and subsequently published the most complete account of convention debates in a pamphlet entitled *Debates and Proceedings of the Convention of the State of New-York.* . . . His printing shop was at 190 Water Street and he may have lived nearby.

Clinton, DeWitt[76]
Antifederalist
"A Countryman"
ward unknown
present area unknown

Clinton, George[77]
Antifederalist
RaCon(d)/ [Gov/Appt(87,88)/
    Rev (87,88)]
East Ward
East of William St., betw. Old
    & Burling slips

Denning, William
Antifederalist
RaCon(d)/ A-12(d)
East Ward
East of William St., betw. Old
    & Burling slips

DUANE, JAMES[78]
Federalist

RaCon(yes)/ S-11*/ S-12
North Ward
Above Wall St., betw.
    Broadway & William St.

Duer, William[79]
Federalist
"Philo-Publius"
West Ward
Broadway area, below
    Chambers St.

Gelston, David[80]
Antifederalist
S-12(d)/ [Surr]
East Ward
East of William St., betw. Old
    & Burling slips

Gilbert, William W.[81]
Federalist
A-12
West Ward
Broadway area, below
    Chambers St.

Greenleaf, Thomas[82]
Antifederalist

[76]Son of JAMES and nephew of GEORGE, DeWitt was born and raised at his father's home in Ulster County. Graduated from Columbia College, he authored five serialized essays under the pseudonym "A Countryman." (HUGH HUGHES of Dutchess County also wrote under this pseudonym.) DeWitt was a spectator and correspondent at the state ratifying convention.

[77]George Clinton was the first governor of New York State (1777–95 and 1801–04) and the principal leader of Antifederalists in the state. Listed as a convention delegate on the Antifederalist tickets in Ulster County and New York City, he won on the former and lost on the latter. (See Ulster County entry.)

[78]Mayor of New York City (1784–89), Duane also owned Albany County land, organized into the town of Duanesburgh in 1765, now Duanesburg in Schenectady County. In September 1787 William North married Duane's eldest daughter and, sometime in 1788,

removed to Duanesburgh with his bride to manage his father-in-law's landholdings.

[79]Secretary of the Board of Treasury under the Confederation Congress in 1788.

[80]Gelston/Ghelston. Born in Bridgehampton in the Suffolk County town of Southampton, he removed to New York City in 1786.

[81]Gilbert was a long-time alderman and political leader for the West Ward.

[82]Manager (1785–87) and then publisher (1787–98) of the *New-York Journal*, he was the lone newspaper publisher with clear Antifederalist leanings. During the ratification debate, the newspaper was published as a daily under the title *The New-York Journal, and Daily Patriotic Register* (19 November

printer
East Ward
East of William St., betw. Old
& Burling slips

HAMILTON, ALEXANDER[83]
Federalist
RaCon(yes)/ FedCon/
Cong(88)/ "Publius"
East Ward
East of William St., betw. Old
& Burling slips

HARISON, RICHARD
Federalist
RaCon(yes)/ A-11/ A-12
West Ward
Broadway area, below
Chambers St.

HARRISSON, JOHN[84]
preference unknown
printer
East Ward
East of William St., betw. Old
& Burling slips

HOBART, JOHN SLOSS
Federalist

1787–26 July 1788). During this period,
the Thursday edition, *The New-York
Journal, and Weekly Register*, carried
Antifederalist essays and other items to
the upstate and Long Island counties.

[83]A son-in-law of PHILIP SCHUYLER
of Albany County, Hamilton was a leading proponent of the proposed Constitution, coauthor (with JOHN JAY and
James Madison) of *The Federalist*, and a
principal organizer of the Federalists in
New York City.

[84]Published the city's only weekly at
this time, *The Impartial Gazetteer, and
Saturday Evening's Post* (renamed *The
New-York Weekly Museum* on 20 September 1788), from 17 May 1788 through
1804, initially joined by STEPHEN PURDY,
JR.

RaCon(yes)/ [SCt/ Rev]
North Ward
Above Wall St., betw.
Broadway & William St.

Hoffman, Nicholas
Federalist
A-12
Dock Ward
Below Wall St., betw. Broad &
William sts.

Hughes, James M.[85]
Antifederalist
Comm
North Ward
Above Wall St., betw.
Broadway & William St.

JAY, JOHN[86]
Federalist
RaCon(yes)/ "Publius"/ "A
Citizen of New York"
East Ward
East of William St., betw. Old
& Burling slips

Jones, Samuel[87]
Antifederalist
RaCon(d)/ Comm
Montgomerie Ward
East of William St., betw.
Burling & New slips

[85]Son of HUGH HUGHES of Dutchess
County.

[86]Secretary for Foreign Affairs un-
der the Confederation Congress in 1788.
Coauthor of *The Federalist* with
ALEXANDER HAMILTON and James
Madison.

[87]Listed on the Antifederalist tickets
in Queens County and New York City,
he won on the former and lost on the
latter. Unlike other candidates listed in
two counties, he maintained an active
residence in each county. (See Queens
County entry.)

King, Rufus[88]
Federalist
leading partisan
prob. East Ward
East of William St., betw. Old
   & Burling slips

Lamb, John[89]
Antifederalist
RaCon(d)/ Comm(Chairman)
East Ward
East of William St., betw. Old
   & Burling slips

Laurence, John[90]
Federalist
S-11*/ S-12
East Ward
East of William St., betw. Old
   & Burling slips

Lawrence, John[91]
Antifederalist
RaCon(d)
East Ward
East of William St., betw. Old
   & Burling slips

Livingston, Brockholst[92]
Federalist
A-12
West Ward
Broadway area, below
   Chambers St.

LIVINGSTON, ROBERT R.[93]
Federalist
RaCon(yes)/ [Chanc/ Rev]
West Ward
Broadway area, below
   Chambers St.

---

[88]A Massachusetts native, he was one of that state's delegates to the Confederation Congress and to the Constitutional Convention in 1787, as well as a member of the Massachusetts Convention of 1788. On 6 February the Massachusetts Convention voted to ratify the Constitution, and shortly thereafter King left for New York City to be with his wife, probably staying at the home of his father-in-law John Alsop. At the end of May, the Kings went to Boston, where Rufus relayed news of the New Hampshire Convention to ALEXANDER HAMILTON at the New York Convention. Later, the Kings returned to New York City where they settled until retiring after 1805 to a home on Long Island.

[89]Lamb was then serving as customs collector for the Port of New York.

[90]Laurence/Lawrence, the former spelling appearing in reference to his congressional service. Not to be confused with JOHN LAWRENCE, the New York City Antifederalist. Laurence is probably the attorney at 13 Wall Street.

[91]Of the many John Lawrences this is probably Jonathan, a Water Street merchant, who, like MELANCTON SMITH, had moved from Queens County to Dutchess County and then to New York City, maintaining business dealings with Smith and other Dutchess County Antifederalists.

[92]Born Henry Brockholst Livingston, he chose not to use his first name. A member of the "upper manor line," he was the son of William (brother of the third manor lord, first governor of New Jersey, and a Constitutional Convention delegate).

[93]Known as "the Chancellor," owing to his lengthy service (1777–1801) as chancellor of the powerful state court of chancery, he was the eldest son of Judge Robert R., head of the Clermont estate, then located in Columbia and Dutchess counties. In 1775 he inherited the Clermont estate, known as the "lower manor," though the original grant carried no manorial privileges. After ratification, he switched his support to Governor CLINTON.

Loudon, John[94]
Federalist
printer
East Ward
East of William St., betw. Old
& Burling slips

Loudon, Samuel[95]
Federalist
printer
ward unknown
present area unknown

LOW, NICHOLAS[96]
Federalist
RaCon(yes)/ A-11/ A-12
Montgomerie Ward
East of William St., betw.
Burling & New slips

Ludlow, Gabriel
Antifederalist
A-12(d)
Dock Ward
Below Wall St., betw. Broad &
William sts.

McKesson, John[97]
Antifederalist
Clerk(A-11/ A-12)/
Secretary(RaCon)/ Comm
South Ward
Above the Battery, inside
Beaver & Broad sts.

McKnight, Charles
Federalist
"Examiner"
North Ward
Above Wall St., betw.
Broadway & William St.

M'Lean, Archibald[98]
Federalist
printer
East Ward
East of William St., betw. Old
& Burling slips

M'Lean, John[99]
Federalist

[94]Joined his father SAMUEL in publishing *The New-York Packet* in 1785 and remained with the firm until his death in September 1789. His father's printing shop was at 5 Water Street. The firm of Samuel and John Loudon was state printer (1785–89).

[95]Began publishing the *New-York Packet* in New York City in 1776. The next year he reestablished the newspaper at the VAN WYCK House in Fishkill, returning after the Revolution to New York City where he continued publishing the newspaper until 1792. He also published Noah Webster's *The American Magazine.* . . .

[96]City directories for 1787 and 1789 place Low at 216 Water Street (Montgomerie Ward) and 24 Water Street (probably East Ward), respectively.

[97]As clerk of the state Assembly (1777–93), McKesson was appointed secretary of the convention along with ABRAHAM B. BANCKER of Ulster County, then clerk of the state Senate. In 1788 he was also clerk of the state supreme court and of the courts of nisi prius, oyer and terminer.

[98]On 2 July 1788 Archibald M'Lean joined his brother JOHN in publishing *The Independent Journal: or, the General Advertiser* (*The New-York Daily Gazette* from 29 December 1788) which he continued to publish after John's death until 1798. The M'Leans were the first to publish *The Federalist* in book form.

[99]Published the *Independent Journal* (later the *New-York Daily Gazette*) from 1783 until his death in 1789, initially with CHARLES R. WEBSTER and then with ARCHIBALD M'LEAN. The M'Leans also published the *Norfolk and Portsmouth Journal* (1786–89), a Virginia newspaper. John conducted the Norfolk paper; ARCHIBALD ran the New York paper.

printer
Out Ward
now Lower East Side

Macomb, Alexander
Federalist
A-12
West Ward
Broadway area, below
    Chambers St.

Malcom, William
Antifederalist
RaCon(d)
Montgomerie Ward
East of William St., betw.
    Burling & New slips

MORRIS, RICHARD[100]
Federalist
RaCon(nv)/ [SCt/ Rev]
North Ward
Above Wall St., betw.
    Broadway & William St.

Morton, William[101]
preference unknown
printer
East Ward
East of William St., betw. Old
    & Burling slips

Niven, Daniel[102]
Federalist
A-11
West Ward
Broadway area, below
    Chambers St.

Purdy, Stephen, Jr.[103]
preference unknown
printer
ward unknown
present area unknown

Randall, Thomas[104]
Federalist
Comm(Chairman)
South Ward
Above the Battery, inside
    Beaver & Broad sts.

ROOSEVELT, ISAAC
Federalist
RaCon(yes)/ S-12*
Montgomerie Ward
East of William St., betw.
    Burling & New slips

Russell, John[105]
preference unknown
printer
Out Ward
now Lower East Side

---

[100]Younger brother of LEWIS and half-brother of GOUVERNEUR, Richard was chief justice of the state supreme court from 1779 (after JOHN JAY retired) until 1790. At the convention, he did not vote on the final ratification motion, though he voted the Federalist position on preceding motions.

[101]Published *The New-York Morning Post, and Daily Advertiser* (a bipartisan newspaper in the ratification debate), from 1783 until 1792, initially with Samuel Horner. The *Morning Post* (begun in 1782 as the *New-York Evening Post*) was the only Loyalist newspaper to survive the Revolution.

[102]Party designation based solely on votes cast in the eleventh session. In all likelihood, this Niven was a lumber merchant on Cortlandt Street in 1788, probably located in the West Ward.

[103]Joined JOHN HARRISSON (1788–91) in publishing the *Impartial Gazetteer* (later, the *New-York Weekly Museum*). Their printing shop was at 3 Peck Slip, and Purdy may have lived nearby.

[104]In all likelihood, this Randall was living on Whitehall Street in 1788, probably located in the South Ward.

[105]Published *The New-York Museum*, a short-lived newspaper of 1788.

Rutgers, Henry
Antifederalist
A-12(d)
Out Ward
now Lower East Side

Sands, Comfort
Federalist
A-11/ A-12
East Ward
East of William St., betw. Old
& Burling slips

Smith, Melancton[106]
Antifederalist
RaCon(d)/ Cong (87)/
    A-12(d)/ Comm/
    "A Plebeian"
North Ward
Above Wall St., betw.
    Broadway & William St.

Stoughton, Thomas
Antifederalist
A-12(d)
Dock Ward
Below Wall St., betw. Broad &
    William sts.

Stoutenburgh, Isaac[107]
Antifederalist
RaCon(d)/ A-12(d)/ [Forf]
West Ward
Broadway area, below
    Chambers St.

Tillinghast, Charles[108]
Antifederalist
Comm(Secretary)
Out Ward
now Lower East Side

Varick, Richard[109]
Federalist
A-11(Speaker)
East Ward
East of William St., betw. Old
    & Burling slips

Verplanck, Gulian
Federalist
A-11/ A-12
East Ward
East of William St., betw. Old
    & Burling slips

Watts, John, Jr.
Federalist
A-12
West Ward
Broadway area, below
    Chambers St.

Webb, Samuel Blachley[110]
Federalist

[106]In 1787 he attended Congress in both February and September. In 1788 he was listed on Antifederalist tickets in Dutchess County and New York City, winning on the former and losing on the latter. (See Dutchess County entry.)

[107]According to Alfred F. Young, Stoutenburgh became a member of the small Federal-Republic Society in New York City of which CHARLES TILLINGHAST was secretary and JOHN LAMB was chairman. See *The Democratic Republicans of New York: The Origins, 1763–1797* (Chapel Hill, N.C., 1967), 50n.

[108]Son-in-law of JOHN LAMB, the Antifederalist committee chairman.

[109]Varick was recorder (chief legal officer) for the city of New York, 1784–89, and mayor, 1789–1801. He also served as state attorney general for a few months in 1789, resigning in September to become mayor.

[110]Webb was an active correspondent and observer, though he was not politically active in party organizations. Like PHILIP SCHUYLER of Albany County, Webb was a Federalist who visited Poughkeepsie during the state ratifying convention. His published letters and other writings appear in W. C. Ford, ed., *Correspondence and Journals of Samuel Blachley Webb*, 3 vols. (New York, 1893–1894); and James W. Webb, ed., *Reminiscences of General Samuel B. Webb* (New York, 1882).

leading partisan
prob. West Ward
Broadway area, below
    Chambers St.

Webster, Noah[111]
Federalist
"A Citizen of America"/
    "America"/ "Giles
    Hickory"/ magazine editor
ward unknown
present area unknown

Willett, Marinus[112]
Antifederalist
RaCon(d)/ A-12(d)/ Comm
East Ward
East of William St., betw. Old
    & Burling slips

Orange[113]

Carpenter, John
Antifederalist

A-12
New Cornwall
now in Cornwall

Clark, Jeremiah[114]
Antifederalist
A-11/ A-12
New Cornwall
now in Cornwall-on-
    Hudson (v.)

Coe, John D.
Federalist
A-12(d)
Haverstraw
now New City, Clarkstown
Rockland Co.

Gale, Coe
Antifederalist
Comm
Goshen
now in Goshen (v.)

HARING, JOHN[115]
Antifederalist
RaCon(no)/ Cong(87)/ S-11/
    S-12/ [CoJdg]

---

[111]A Connecticut native, he lived briefly in Philadelphia where in October 1787 he wrote a pamphlet in support of the Constitution, entitled *An Examination into the Leading Principles of the Federal Constitution. . . . By A Citizen of America.* He removed to New York City and edited *The American Magazine . . .*, the city's first monthly magazine (December 1787–November 1788). In his *American Magazine*, Webster used the pseudonym "Giles Hickory" for several important articles against the need for a bill of rights. He also published a long attack on "The Dissent of the Minority of the Pennsylvania Convention" under the pseudonym "America" in the New York *Daily Advertiser.*

[112]In 1788 Willett was alderman for the East Ward. He was sheriff of New York County, 1784–87 and 1791–95; Robert Boyd was sheriff from 29 September 1787 to 29 September 1791.

[113]An original county, its boundaries in 1788 include all of present-day Rockland County and most of present-day Orange County. In 1788 it was in the middle Senate district.

[114]Lived in the Canterbury area of New Cornwall, now located in the village of Cornwall, renamed Cornwall-on-Hudson in 1978.

[115]In 1787 he attended Congress in September, but not in February. In 1788 he voted the Federalist position in the state Senate on motions 1 and 3, but was clearly an Antifederalist. He served as county judge until 12 March 1788, at which time WILLIAM THOMPSON assumed that office. In 1794 Haring removed to Bergen County, New Jersey; and a decade later, he returned to Tappan, by then in Rockland County. Hence, this may have been the John Haring who appears as a New Jersey legislator in 1795–96 and a New York assemblyman in 1806. See Wilfred B. Talman, *How Things Began in Rockland County and Places Nearby* (Rockland County Historical Society, 1977), 30–33.

Orangetown
now Tappan, Orangetown
Rockland Co.

Hathorn, John
Antifederalist
S-11/ S-12/ Comm/
  [Appt(87)/ Forf]
Warwick
still in Warwick

Hopkins, Reuben
Antifederalist
Comm
Goshen
still in Goshen

Marvin, Seth
Federalist
A-12(d)
New Cornwall
now in Blooming Grove

Moffatt, Thomas
Antifederalist
Comm
New Cornwall
now in Blooming Grove

Post, James[116]
Federalist
A-12(d)
Warwick
still in Warwick

Pye, David
Federalist
A-12(d)
Haverstraw

now West Nyack, Clarkstown
Rockland Co.

Taulman, Peter
Antifederalist
A-11/ A-12(d)/ Comm
Orangetown
now in Piermont (v.)
Rockland Co.

Thompson, William[117]
affiliation uncertain
A-11/ [CoJdg]
Goshen
still in Goshen

Wisner, Henry, Jr.[118]
Antifederalist
A-11/ A-12
Wallkill
still in Wallkill
then Ulster, now Orange Co.

WISNER, HENRY, SR.
Antifederalist
RaCon(no)
Goshen
still in Goshen

WOOD, JOHN
Antifederalist
RaCon(no)
Goshen
now in Goshen (v.)

[116]In the Assembly elections of 1788, James Post and PETER TAULMAN each received 128 votes, tying for fourth place. As a result, neither could serve, thereby depriving Orange County of its fourth Assembly seat that year.

[117]Not voting on motions 1 and 2, Thompson voted the Federalist position on motion 3. On 12 March 1788, he replaced JOHN HARING as county judge.

[118]Henry, Jr., was the son of HENRY, SR., a prominent figure in provincial and state politics. Henry, Jr., represented Orange County in the Assembly; however, all evidence suggests that he was then living in the Phillipsburgh area of Wallkill, a town now in Orange, but then in Ulster County.

WOODHULL, JESSE[119]
Antifederalist
RaCon(yes)
New Cornwall
now in Blooming Grove

Queens[120]

CARMAN, STEPHEN[121]
Antifederalist
RaCon(yes)/ A-11/ A-12/
Comm
South Hempstead
now in Hempstead
Nassau Co.

Cornwell, Whitehead[122]
Antifederalist
A-11/ A-12
South Hempstead
now Far Rockaway,
Hempstead
Nassau Co.

JONES, SAMUEL[123]
Antifederalist
RaCon(yes)/ A-11/ A-12
Oyster Bay
still in Oyster Bay
Nassau Co.

LAWRENCE, NATHANIEL[124]
Antifederalist
RaCon(yes)
South Hempstead
now in Hempstead
Nassau Co.

Ledyard, Isaac[125]
Federalist
RaCon(d)
Newtown
now in Middle Village area
Queens borough

Lewis, Francis, Jr.[126]
Federalist

[119]Woodhull is depicted as a yeoman farmer and citizen politician by Michel-Guillaume Jean de Crèvecoeur, *Eighteenth-Century Travels in Pennsylvania and New York*, trans. and ed. Percy G. Adams (Lexington, Ky., 1961), 18–25.

[120]An original county, its boundaries in 1788 include present-day Queens County (now also a borough) and Nassau County. In 1788 it was part of the southern Senate district.

[121]Colonial Hempstead was divided into North and South Hempstead in 1784. In 1796 South Hempstead became Hempstead, while North Hempstead has retained its name.

[122]Cornwell/Cornell, the latter spelling appearing only in the state civil list. No voting record on key eleventh session motions. In 1788 he was listed on the Antifederalist ticket for the Assembly.

[123]Jones represented Queens County in the convention and the Assembly. An adroit lawyer, he was a leader of the Antifederalists in both bodies, though he later became a Federalist. (See New York County entry.)

[124]Nathaniel was the son of Captain James and the fifth generation of the so-called Thomas Lawrence line. The state civil list places Nathaniel Lawrence in South Hempstead; however, he may have resided, or just previously resided, in New York City, where the 1789 city directory lists a Nathaniel Lawrence as a Burling Slip lawyer.

[125]Ledyard lived in New York City and associated with ALEXANDER HAMILTON. He acquired the confiscated Van Dine estate in Newtown sometime before or during 1794, when he erected a mansion there, to which he removed with his family in 1795; however, it is not known whether he had any other connections to Queens County at the time of the ratification debate.

[126]Son of Francis, Sr., signer of the Declaration of Independence.

A-11/ RaCon(d)/ A-12(d)
Flushing
now Whitestone area
Queens borough

Onderdonck, Hendrick
Federalist
RaCon(d)
North Hempstead
now Roslyn, North Hempstead
Nassau Co.

SCHENCK, JOHN
Antifederalist
RaCon(yes)/ A-12
North Hempstead
now Manhasset, North
    Hempstead
Nassau Co.

Seaman, Nathaniel
Federalist
A-12(d)
South Hempstead
now in Hempstead
Nassau Co.

Townsend, Prior[127]
Federalist
RaCon(d)/ A-12(d)
Oyster Bay
still in Oyster Bay
Nassau Co.

Townsend, Samuel
Federalist
S-11*/ S-12
Oyster Bay

[127]According to Henry Onderdonk,
the candidate is Prior Townsend of Oyster Bay. (See *Queens in Olden Times* [Ja-
maica, N.Y., 1865], 71.) However,
Alfred F. Young discusses the candidacy
of James Townshend in *The Democratic
Republicans of New York*, 163.

still in Oyster Bay
Nassau Co.

Richmond (now also Staten
    Island boro.)[128]

BANCKER, ABRAHAM[129]
Federalist
RaCon(yes)/ A-12/ [Sher]
Castleton
prob. now Richmond Terrace,
    near Sailors' Snug Harbor

Dongan, John C.[130]
Antifederalist
A-11/ A-12
Castleton
prob. now Richmond Terrace,
    in Port Richmond

Micheau, Paul[131]
Federalist
S-12*/ [CoJdg]

[128]An original county, it is now Staten Island borough (officially renamed
in 1975) and Richmond County. In 1788
it was part of the southern Senate district.
[129]Not to be confused with his cousin
ABRAHAM B. of Ulster County. Abraham was the son of EVERT's brother
Adrian who was surrogate of Richmond
County (1787–92). Abraham and his
fellow Richmond County delegate
GOZEN RYERSS are generally regarded
as Federalists. Perhaps in error, they
were listed on the ticket as "sentiments
unknown," in the *New-York Journal*, 5
June 1788.
[130]In the eleventh session, he voted
the Federalist position on motion 3, but
did not vote on motions 1 and 2. However, an out-of-state newspaper referred to Dongan as "A pigmy antifederal frigid reptile, of Staten-Island" (*The
New-Jersey Journal, and Political Intelligencer*, 9 January 1788).
[131]Listed on the Federalist ticket for
the Senate.

Westfield
now Arthur Kill Road, in
   Greenridge

RYERSS, GOZEN[132]
Federalist
RaCon(yes)
Northfield
perhaps now in Port
   Richmond

Winant, Peter[133]
Federalist
A-11
Southfield
now Arthur Kill Road, near
   Richmondtown

Suffolk[134]

Cooper, Caleb
Antifederalist
Comm
Southampton
still in Southampton

Floyd, William[135]
Antifederalist
S-11/ [Appt(87)]

Brookhaven
now Mastic Beach,
   Brookhaven

Gardiner, Nathaniel[136]
Federalist
A-12/ RaCon(d)
East Hampton
now in East Hampton (v.)

HAVENS, JONATHAN N.
Antifederalist
RaCon(yes)/ A-11/ A-12/
   Comm
Shelter Island
still Shelter Island

HEDGES, DAVID[137]
Antifederalist
RaCon(nv)/ A-11/ A-12/
   Comm
East Hampton
now Sagaponack, East
   Hampton

Hunting, Benjamin[138]
Federalist
RaCon(d)
Southampton
now in Southampton (v.)

[132]See ABRAHAM BANCKER, note 129. Ryerss is said to have weighed so much that he had to occupy two seats at the convention.

[133]Party designation based solely on votes cast in the eleventh session.

[134]An original county, its boundaries have changed little since 1788 when it was part of the southern Senate district.

[135]Though Floyd voted the Federalist position on motions 1 and 2 in the eleventh session, he was considered a popular moderate by Assembly Antifederalists who in January 1788 sought unsuccessfully to have him replace the more partisan ALEXANDER HAMILTON in Congress. Floyd later was elected to the first federal Congress where he voted the Antifederalist position.

[136]Son of Colonel Abraham, who was the brother of John, fifth Proprietor of Gardiner's Island. Nathaniel Gardiner was defeated on the Federalist convention ticket and elected on the rival Assembly ticket. He was probably considered a viable candidate by both parties; however, based on two letters from "St. Patrick" (JONATHAN N. HAVENS) to JOHN SMITH of 5 and 7 April 1788, it seems likely that Gardiner's stance on the Constitution was Federalist.

[137]According to Linda Grant DePauw, it is likely that he left the convention early. See *The Eleventh Pillar*, 247.

[138]Hunting/Huntting. Colonel Benjamin, father of Benjamin of Sag Harbor.

L'Hommedieu, Ezra[139]
Federalist
S-11/ S-12*/ RaCon(d)/
  Cong (88)/ [CoClk]
Southold
still in Southold

Osborn, Daniel[140]
Federalist
A-11
prob. East Hampton
prob. still in East Hampton

SCUDDER, HENRY
Antifederalist
RaCon(yes)/ A-12/ Comm
Northport (v.), Huntington
still in Northport (v.)

Smith, Epenetus[141]
Antifederalist
Comm
Smithtown
now in Village of the
  Branch (v.)

Smith, George[142]
Federalist
RaCon(d)
Smithtown
now in Nissequogue (v.)

SMITH, JOHN[143]
Antifederalist
RaCon(yes)/ A-11/ A-12/
  Comm
Brookhaven
now Mastic Beach,
  Brookhaven

Strong, Selah
Federalist
RaCon(d)/ [CoJdg]
Brookhaven
now Setauket, Brookhaven

[139]L'Hommedieu was listed on the Federalist convention ticket and on both Federalist and Antifederalist tickets for the twelfth session of the Senate. He was clearly a Federalist and, like Antifederalist WILLIAM FLOYD, a moderate held in high regard by his colleagues.

[140]Party designation based solely on votes cast in the eleventh session. There were various Daniel Osborns in East Hampton around this time, and he may have been one of them. However, he is obviously not the one (b. 1774) whose house still stands.

[141]Epenetus (b. 1724), grandson of the town's founder, along with his son (Epenetus II, b. 1769) owned and operated a tavern still standing in what is now Village of the Branch, an historic district and incorporated village in the town of Smithtown.

[142]Probably George (1749–1822), son of Job and a member of the Richard Smith line of Smithtown. Born in Smithtown, George served in General Washington's spy ring with SELAH STRONG, SAMUEL TOWNSEND, and others. In 1780 George and his brother Woodhull inherited their family house, now in the village of Nissequogue, but it is unlikely that George lived there for any length of time thereafter. He is recorded in Connecticut for part of the Revolution; and then, by the births of his children, in Huntington (1784), Mechanicstown in Dutchess County (1788–90), and later in New York City. During the first half of 1788, he may have been in Smithtown, Huntington, or Dutchess County; however, he is placed in his home community, now the hamlet of St. James in the village of Nissequogue in the town of Smithtown.

[143]Son of Judge William, third lord of the Manor of St. George, John Smith long courted and finally wed a member of the wealthy FLOYD family. Under these fortuitous circumstances, his father left the manor estate to John's son. The manor house is now located in Mastic Beach, though the property extends into the hamlet called Shirley.

TREDWELL, THOMAS
Antifederalist
RaCon(no)/ S-11/ S-12/
    Comm/ [Surr]
Smithtown
now Fort Salonga, Smithtown

Wickes, Thomas
Antifederalist
Comm
Huntington
now Centerport, Huntington

Ulster[144]

Bailey, Patrick[145]
Antifederalist
Comm
prob. New Windsor
prob. still in New Windsor
now in Orange Co.

Bancker, Abraham B.[146]
Antifederalist
Clerk(S-11/ S-12)/
    Secretary(RaCon)

Kingston (t.)
now in Kingston (c.)

Bruyn, Jacobus S.
Federalist
RaCon(d)
Kingston (t.)
now in Kingston (c.)

Bruyn, James[147]
Antifederalist
A-11
Rochester
still in Rochester

Bruyn, Johannes
Federalist
RaCon(d)
Shawangunk
still in Shawangunk

CANTINE, JOHN
Antifederalist
RaCon(no)/ A-11/ A-12
Marbletown
still in Marbletown

CLARK, EBENEZER
Antifederalist
RaCon(no)/ A-12
New Windsor
still New Windsor
now in Orange Co.

CLINTON, GEORGE[148]
Antifederalist

---

[144]An original county, its 1788 boundaries include all of present-day Sullivan County, most of present-day Ulster County, and parts of present-day Delaware and Orange counties. In 1788 it was in the middle Senate district.

[145]Probably lived in New Windsor, he certainly lived in one of the border towns then in Ulster County and added to Orange County in 1798. These towns are Montgomery, Newburgh, New Windsor, and Wallkill.

[146]Not to be confused with his cousin ABRAHAM, a convention delegate from Richmond County. Abraham B. [Boelen] Bancker was the son of EVERT of New York County. Born in New York City, Abraham B. eventually settled in Kingston where he first became Senate clerk (1784–1801). As Senate clerk in 1788, he was appointed convention secretary with JOHN MCKESSON of New York City.

[147]Party designation based solely on votes cast in the eleventh session. His cousins, JACOBUS S. and JOHANNES, were Federalists.

[148]Born and raised in the Little Britain area of New Windsor, he served as the clerk of Ulster County throughout much of his adult life (1760–1812). Though he represented Ulster County in the convention, he was then living in New York City. As convention presi-

RaCon(nv)/ [CoClk]
(East Ward, N.Y.C.)
See New York County

CLINTON, JAMES[149]
Antifederalist
RaCon(no)/ A-11/ S-12*
New Windsor
still in New Windsor
now in Orange Co.

De Witt, Charles[150]
no affiliation
A-11
Kingston (t.)
now in Rosendale

Hardenbergh, Johannis G.[151]
Antifederalist
A-12
Rochester
still in Rochester

Jensen, Cornelius T.[152]
Federalist

RaCon(d)
Shawangunk
still in Shawangunk

Parks, Arthur[153]
affiliation uncertain
S-11
Montgomery
still in Montgomery
now in Orange Co.

SCHOONMAKER, CORNELIUS C.
Antifederalist
RaCon(no)/ A-11/ A-12/
    Comm
Shawangunk
still in Shawangunk

Smith, Nathan
Antifederalist
A-11/ A-12/ Comm
New Windsor
prob. still in New Windsor
now in Orange Co.

Snyder, Johannes[154]
Antifederalist
Comm
Kingston (t.)
now in Saugerties

Tappen, Christopher[155]
Antifederalist

---

dent, he could not vote on the final ratification motion; however, he earlier voted the Antifederalist position on key motions in the committee of the whole when HENRY OOTHOUDT of Albany County was presiding.

[149]Elder brother of GEORGE and father of DEWITT, James lived in the Little Britain area of the town of New Windsor, where his later home (built 1798) still stands.

[150]Died on 27 April 1787 before the Constitutional Convention met.

[151]Hardenbergh/Hardenburgh, the former being the standard spelling, though the latter appears on both the Antifederalist ticket and the state civil list. Johannes G. was the grandson of Johannes, a patentee of the Great Hardenbergh Patent.

[152]Jensen/Jansen. Known locally by the latter spelling, though the former appears on the Federalist ticket.

[153]Though Parks voted the Antifederalist position in the eleventh session, he has not been found in subsequent lists of active Antifederalists. See Theophilus Parsons, Jr., "The Old Conviction versus The New Realities," Appendix.

[154]PETER VAN GAASBEEK suspected that Snyder was a Federalist spy, although there is no evidence to confirm this suspicion.

[155]Tappen/Tappan, the latter spelling appearing only on the Antifederalist ticket. His sister Cornelia was the wife of GOVERNOR GEORGE CLINTON, and the two stayed at Christopher's house, then on North Front Street, when they were in Kingston.

A-12
Kingston (t.)
now in Kingston (c.)

Van Gaasbeek, Peter[156]
Antifederalist
leading partisan
Kingston (t.)
now in Kingston (c.)

WYNKOOP, DIRCK
Antifederalist
RaCon(no)/ Comm/ [CoJdg]
Kingston
now in Hurley

Washington and Clinton[157]

BAKER, ALBERT
Antifederalist
RaCon(no)/ A-11/ Comm
Kingsbury
now in Hudson Falls (v.)

[156]Variously recorded as a "renegade," first for challenging an early Antifederalist convention ticket framed in Kingston, then for becoming a Federalist in 1789, subsequently for organizing the first Federalist machine in Ulster County (and perhaps in the state), and finally for supporting AARON BURR's gubernatorial bids in 1792 and 1795. See Alfred F. Young, *The Democratic Republicans of New York*, 278, 285. Also see Steven R. Boyd, *The Politics of Opposition: Antifederalists and the Acceptance of the Constitution* (Millwood, N.Y., 1979), 76.

[157]Washington County was established in 1772 from Albany County. Its bounds in 1788 included all of present-day Warren County and most of present-day Washington County. The state's fourteenth county, Clinton, formed 4 March 1788 from Washington County, was represented with Washington County in the twelfth session of the legislature and the state ratifying convention. In 1788 these two counties were in the eastern Senate district.

HOPKINS, DAVID
Antifederalist
RaCon(no)/ S-11/ S-12/
  Comm/ [Appt(88)]
Hebron
still in Hebron

McCracken, Joseph
Antifederalist
A-12
Salem
still in Salem

PARKER, ICHABOD
Antifederalist
RaCon(no)
Granville
still in Granville

Russell, Ebenezer[158]
Antifederalist
S-11/ Comm/ [Appt(87)/
  CoJdg]
Salem
still in Salem

Savage, Edward[159]
Antifederalist
A-11/ A-12/(S-12*)/ [Surr]
Salem
still in Salem

Tearse, Peter B.[160]
Antifederalist

[158]Russell's Senate seat (the sixth up for election in 1788) was vacant in the twelfth session. See EDWARD SAVAGE, note 159. Russell replaced ALEXANDER WEBSTER as county judge on 17 March 1788.

[159]The state civil list incorrectly places Savage in the twelfth session of both the Assembly and Senate. He may have run successfully for both seats, but he only served in the Assembly.

[160]Tearse/Tierce, the latter spelling appearing only in the state civil list.

A-11/ A-12
Argyle
now in Fort Edward (v.)

Webster, Alexander[161]
Antifederalist
A-11/ A-12/ Comm/ [CoJdg]
Hebron
still in Hebron

WILLIAMS, JOHN
Antifederalist
RaCon(no)/ S-11/ S-12/
    Comm
Salem
now in Salem (v.)

Westchester[162]

CRANE, THADDEUS
Federalist
RaCon(yes)/ A-12
North Salem
still in North Salem

Drake, Samuel[163]
Antifederalist
A-11/ Comm
Mount Pleasant
now in Ossining (v.)

Gilbert, Abijah
Antifederalist

A-11/ RaCon(d)/ A-12(d)/
    Comm
Salem
now South Salem, Lewisboro

HATFIELD, RICHARD
Federalist
RaCon(yes)/ [CoClk]
White Plains
now White Plains (c.)

Horton, Jonathan
Federalist
A-12
Westchester (t.)
perhaps now City Island
Bronx borough

LIVINGSTON, PHILIP R.[164]
Federalist
RaCon(yes)/ A-12
Westchester (t.)
now Throg's Neck area
Bronx borough

Lockwood, Ebenezer
Antifederalist
A-11/ RaCon(d)/ A-12(d)
Poundridge
still in Poundridge

Morris, Gouverneur[165]
Federalist

[161]Webster served as county judge until 17 March 1788, at which time EBENEZER RUSSELL assumed that office.

[162]An original county, its 1788 boundaries include all of present-day Westchester County and the Bronx, now a county and borough. In 1788 it was in the southern Senate district.

[163]At this time Drake was living in the hamlet of Sparta in the town of Mount Pleasant where he owned a mill and a tavern on property acquired from the confiscated Philipsburg estate. Sparta became part of the village of Ossining in 1906.

[164]Not to be confused with his uncle Philip, a signer of the Declaration of Independence. Philip R. (known as "Gentleman Phil") was the son of Peter Van Brugh of New York City, who was the brother of the third manor lord.

[165]Half-brother of RICHARD and LEWIS, he moved to Pennsylvania in 1779 to seek his political fortune. He was a Pennsylvania delegate to the Constitutional Convention, traveled to Virginia later in 1787, returned briefly to Morrisania in 1788, and then went off to Europe for a decade of diplomatic service.

leading partisan
Morrisania
now Morrisania area
Bronx borough

MORRIS, LEWIS[166]
Federalist
RaCon(yes)/ S-11/ S-12
Morrisania
now Morrisania area
Bronx borough

Pell, Philip, Jr.[167]
Antifederalist
Comm/ [Surr]
Pelham
now in Pelham (v.)

Rockwell, Nathan
Federalist
A-12

Salem
now South Salem, Lewisboro

SARLS, LOTT W.
Federalist
RaCon(yes)
Bedford
still in Bedford

Seaman, Walter
Federalist
A-12
Bedford
still in Bedford

Strang, Joseph[168]
Antifederalist
A-11/ RaCon(d)/ A-12(d)/
    Comm
Yorktown
now Yorktown Heights,
    Yorktown

Thomas, Thomas[169]
Antifederalist
A-11/ RaCon(d)/ A-12(d)/
    Comm/ [Sher]
Harrison
now Harrison (t-v.)

Tompkins, Jonathan G.[170]
Antifederalist

[166]Elder brother of RICHARD and half-brother of GOUVERNEUR, Lewis was the third and last lord of the manor of Morrisania and a signer of the Declaration of Independence. The short-lived town of Morrisania (1788–91) may have been created at the request of Lewis for a combination of reasons, including the protection of his manor interests and his belief that Morrisania might be an eligible site for the new federal capital. With respect to the latter, there is record of a 1790 memorial by Lewis Morris to President Washington in which the special advantages of the town are enumerated. See J. Thomas Scharf, *History of Westchester County, New York*, 2 vols. (Philadelphia, 1886), II:823.

[167]Son of Philip III, the two men were living in a farmhouse built in 1750 by the father on property adjacent to the remaining manor house lands (owned by Thomas Pell). Those lands had been much reduced after a period of many subdivisions both within the family and to outside groups (including the Huguenots).

[168]Strang/Strong, the latter being a misspelling of the former.

[169]On 22 March 1788, Thomas replaced Philip Pell III, father of PHILIP PELL, JR., as sheriff. Thomas lived in The Purchase section of Harrison on what is now the State University of New York (SUNY), College at Purchase. In 1975, to prevent the secession of Purchase, the town of Harrison combined its villages to form the coterminous town-village of Harrison, a distinct form of local government.

[170]Scarsdale is now also a coterminous town-village.

A-11/ RaCon(d)/ A-12(d)/
Comm
Scarsdale
now Scarsdale (t-v.)

VAN CORTLANDT, PHILIP[171]
Federalist
RaCon(yes)/ A-12/ [Forf]
Cortlandt
now in Croton-on-Hudson (v.)

Van Cortlandt, Pierre[172]
Federalist
[LtGov]
Cortlandt
still in Cortlandt

[171]Son of Lieutenant Governor
PIERRE VAN CORTLANDT, and elder
brother of Pierre, Jr., Philip left GOV-
ERNOR GEORGE CLINTON's ranks to support the Constitution, returning to the
Republican fold in the early 1790s. In
1788 he was occupying the manor house
where he had been raised. That manor
house is still standing and is known as
the Van Cortlandt Manor in Croton-on-
Hudson.

[172]Upon inheriting Cortlandt Manor,
he moved there from New York in 1749
with his wife and infant son PHILIP. In
1788 he was living in a second manor
house on lands adjacent to those of his
son Philip. Pierre served as lieutenant
governor under GOVERNOR GEORGE
CLINTON from 1777 to 1795.

A Preliminary Inventory of the Homes of New York Federalists and Antifederalists

compiled by
STEPHEN L. SCHECHTER
Russell Sage College

Ｎone of the public buildings that were part of the ratification debate in New York still stand. The City Hall where the Confederation Congress met in New York City was subsequently enlarged, renamed Federal Hall, and later demolished. The third courthouse where the state ratifying convention met in Poughkeepsie was destroyed by fire in 1806. Also gone are most of the public meeting places (and all of the more well-known taverns) where political leaders met. However, many of the homes of Federalist and Antifederalist leaders still stand, and these surviving sites are inventoried here.

Of the 255 Federalists and Antifederalists listed in the biographical gazetteer, the homes of 70 (or about 27 percent) have survived. These findings, gathered as part of the research for the biographical gazetteer, form the basis for the preliminary inventory of surviving sites.

Most of the entries in this inventory are to the one surviving home occupied and, in all likelihood, owned by one of these men. The exceptions include: (1) two Albany County men, Francis Nicoll and Richard Sill, who consecutively occupied one house; (2) three men, each of whom owned and occupied two homes still standing (Philip Schuyler of Albany County, John Frey of Mont-gomery County, and Ebenezer Lockwood of Westchester County); (3) one man, Samuel Drake of Westchester County, who owned but probably did not live in a tavern which still stands, in contrast to Epenetus Smith of Suffolk County, whose tavern was also his family home; (4) one entry for William Cooper of Otsego County, indicating various sites at Cooperstown associated with him; and (5) one entry for Johannis G. Hardenbergh of Ulster County, whose room interiors supply the backdrop for the "Hardenbergh Rooms" at the Henry Francis DuPont Winterthur Museum in Winterthur, Delaware. With these exceptions, the total number of sites, struc-tures, and collections is seventy-five.

To facilitate cross-references, the inventory is organized in the same way as the biographical gazetteer; namely, alphabetically by the names of the counties of 1788 and, within each county, alphabetically by the occupant's last name. The first element of each entry is the occupant's name. The second element, when known, is reserved for the name and construction date of the house. The third element is the present ownership and status of the house; and the final element is its present location.

Most of the entries are to homes occupied by politicians while they were involved in the debates of 1787–88. However, all sur-viving homes are included, so long as the homes and politicians were closely associated. One reason is the difficulty in pinpointing dates of occupancy; another is the danger of dismissing earlier or later occupancies that may be of relevance. Among the most com-mon examples of earlier and later occupancies are: (1) homes in which politicians were raised, such as the Van Gaasbeek's house (now known as the Senate House) in Kingston and the Smith fam-ily's Manor of St. George in Suffolk County; (2) homes of early construction to which politicians later retired, such as the John Jay Homestead in Westchester County and the [Rufus] King Manor in Queens County; and (3) homes of later construction and oc-cupancy, most notably the first home that Alexander Hamilton ever owned, now known as the Hamilton Grange in Manhattan, not completed until 1802. About twenty instances of earlier or later occupancy are identified, and these are noted in the inven-tory; however, others may also exist. Most of the known instances of later occupancy are apparent from the dates of construction indicated in the second element of the entry. Instances of earlier and later occupancies that are not apparent are indicated by foot-note reference.

As concerns present usage, most of the structures still stand-ing are now private residences (forty-four), of which a small num-ber are located in historic districts. Another six are private busi-nesses and institutional headquarters. One of these, Hendrick Onderdonck's Queens County home, is now a restaurant. Six structures are closed, with only two now under restoration for subsequent reopening as historic sites (the Bethlehem House in Albany County and the James Clinton House now in Orange County).

Of the structures still standing, nineteen are historic sites or historical museums open to the public. For these sites, the occu-pant's name appears in CAPITALS AND SMALL CAPITALS, as does the occupant's name for other sites that can be viewed from the outside, either because they are private residences located in an historic district or because they are historic sites currently closed and unoccupied. All sites open to or viewable by the public are described in the guide to historic sites that follows this inventory.

Preliminary Inventory

Albany

Peter Gansevoort, Jr.
"The Old Yellow House"
  (1787)
private residence
Gansevoort, Saratoga Co.

JOHN KNICKERBACKER, JR.
Knickerbacker Mansion (1772)
Knickerbocker Society
closed and unrestored
(no plans for restoration)
Schaghticoke, Rensselaer Co.

FRANCIS NICOLL
Bethlehem House (1736)
owned by private realtor
closed for restoration
(planned for public use)
Bethlehem, Albany Co.

PHILIP SCHUYLER
Schuyler Mansion (1764)
state historic site in
The Pastures area
South End, City of Albany

PHILIP SCHUYLER
Schuyler House (1777)
national historic site in
Saratoga National Historic
  Park
Schuylerville, Saratoga Co.

RICHARD SILL
(See Nicoll entry)

Dirck Swart
private residence
Stillwater, Saratoga Co.

ABRAHAM TEN BROECK
Ten Broeck Mansion (1798)

Albany County Historical
  Association
historic site in Arbor Hill area
Downtown, City of Albany

ANTHONY TEN EYCK
Ten Eyck House (ca. 1775)
private residence in
Schodack Landing District
Schodack, Rensselaer Co.

DIRCK VAN INGEN
Van Ingen House (1790)
private residence in
Stockade District
Schenectady, Schenectady Co.

ISAAC VROOMAN
Vrooman House (1754)
private residence in
Stockade District
Schenectady, Schenectady Co.

Peter Vrooman
private residence
Schoharie, Schoharie Co.

Columbia

John Bay
private residence
Claverack, Columbia Co.

John Livingston
"Oak Hill" (by 1796)
private residence
Livingston, Columbia Co.

ROBERT R. LIVINGSTON
Clermont (1778–81)
state historic park
Germantown, Columbia Co.

William H. Ludlow
private residence

now under restoration
Claverack, Columbia Co.

PETER SILVESTER
Silvester House (1797)
private residence in
Kinderhook Village District
Kinderhook, Columbia Co.

PETER VAN NESS[1]
Van Ness House (1797)
later known as "Lindenwald,"
or Martin Van Buren Home
Kinderhook, Columbia Co.

PETER VAN SCHAACK
Van Schaack House (1785)
private residence in
Kinderhook Village District
Kinderhook, Columbia Co.

Dutchess

Isaac Bloom
Bloom House (ca. 1798)
private residence
Pleasant Valley, Dutchess Co.

Ebenezer Cary[2]
private residence in
Gardiner Hollow area
Beekman, Dutchess Co.

John De Witt, Jr.
private residence in
Frost Mills area
Clinton, Dutchess Co.

Morris Graham
Graham House (ca. 1772)

private residence
Pine Plains, Dutchess Co.

Jacob Griffin
"Rendez-vous" (ca. 1750s)
private residence
Fishkill, Dutchess Co.

Gilbert Livingston[3]
"The Pynes" (1764)
private residence
Tivoli, Dutchess Co.

Zephaniah Platt
Platt Home (ca. 1735)
American Legion Post
Poughkeepsie, Dutchess Co.

Robert Sands
psychiatric patient home
Rhinebeck, Dutchess Co.

Jacobus Swartwout
Later Swartwout House
  (ca. 1798)
private residence
Wappinger, Dutchess Co.

ISAAC VAN WYCK
Van Wyck Homestead (1732,
  bef. 1756)
Fishkill Historical Society
historical homestead museum
Fishkill, Dutchess Co.

Kings (now also Brooklyn
  boro.)

PETER LEFFERTS
Lefferts Homestead (1783)
city owned historic site

---

[1]Built in 1797 by Van Ness who lived
here until 1803. However, this house is
remembered for and restored to the
later occupancy of Martin Van Buren,
eighth U.S. president.
[2]Cary's occupancy is probable, not
certain.

[3]Built in 1764 for a Gilbert Livingston, probably this Gilbert. Not known
is whether Gilbert ever lived in this
house.

now in Prospect Park
Flatbush, Brooklyn

Montgomery

WILLIAM COOPER[4]
various sites in the village
and at The Farmers' Museum
Cooperstown, Otsego Co.

Jellis Fonda
private residence
Fonda, Montgomery Co.

John Frey
"Fort Frey" (ca. 1750)
private residence
Palatine, Montgomery Co.

John Frey
Second Frey House (1806)
private residence
Palatine, Montgomery Co.

Isaac Paris
D.A.R. Chapter House
Fort Plain, Montgomery Co.

Peter Schuyler
private residence
Danube, Herkimer Co.

Christopher P. Yates
private residence
Canajoharie, Montgomery Co.

[4]None of Cooper's houses survives.
However, there are surviving structures
of the period in the village, a recreated
rural community at The Farmers' Museum, and Cooper collections at the
headquarters of the New York State
Historical Association.

New York (now also Manhattan boro.)

AARON BURR[5]
Morris-Jumel Mansion
    (ca. 1765, 1810)
city owned historic site in
Jumel Terrace District
Washington Heights,
    Manhattan

ALEXANDER HAMILTON[6]
"Hamilton Grange" (1802)
national memorial in
Hamilton Heights District
Upper West Side, Manhattan

John Jay
(See Westchester County)

Rufus King
(See Queens County)

Robert R. Livingston
(See Columbia County)

Orange

John D. Coe
private residence
New City, Rockland Co.

Coe Gale
boutique and residence
Goshen, Orange Co.

John Hathorn
private residence
Warwick, Orange Co.

[5]Occupied by Burr for only six
months in 1833 during his equally short-
lived marriage to Eliza Jumel.
[6]Built in 1802 by Hamilton who lived
here until his death in 1804.

David Pye
private residence
West Nyack, Rockland Co.

Peter Taulman
private residence
Piermont, Rockland Co.

Henry Wisner, Sr.
private residence
Goshen, Orange Co.

John Wood
private residence
Goshen, Orange Co.

Jesse Woodhull
private residence
Blooming Grove, Orange Co.

Queens

Stephen Carman
private residence
Hempstead, Nassau Co.

RUFUS KING[7]
King Manor (1730, 1750)
city owned historic site
Jamaica, Queens

HENDRICK ONDERDONCK[8]
Onderdonck House (1740, 1750)
George Washington Manor Restaurant
Roslyn, Nassau Co.

Nathaniel Seaman
private residence
Hempstead, Nassau Co.

SAMUEL TOWNSEND
Raynham Hall (ca. 1740)
town owned historic site
Oyster Bay, Nassau Co.

Richmond (now also Staten Island boro.)

No surviving homes of ratification leaders

Suffolk

WILLIAM FLOYD
William Floyd Estate (1724, 1930)
national historic site
Mastic Beach, Suffolk Co.

David Hedges
private residence
Sagaponack, Suffolk Co.

Benjamin Hunting
Hunting-Foster House (1708)
private residence
Southampton, Suffolk Co.

Ezra L'Hommedieu
private residence
Southold, Suffolk Co.

EPENETUS SMITH
Epenetus Smith Tavern (bef. 1750)
Smithtown Historical Society
historical tavern museum
Smithtown, Suffolk Co.

George Smith[9]
Job Smith House (bef. 1719)

[7]King retired here sometime after he purchased the property in 1805.

[8]Two houses built ten years apart (1740, 1750) were later joined and then altered to form the present structure. Not known is whether the joining of the two houses was undertaken during Onderdonck's occupancy or later.

[9]Smith was raised here, and he and his brother Woodhull inherited the property in 1780. However, records suggest that Woodhull, not George, lived here after 1780.

private residence in
the hamlet of St. James
Nissequogue, Suffolk Co.

JOHN SMITH[10]
Manor of St. George (1693,
    1803)
trustee-maintained historic site
Mastic Beach, Suffolk Co.

Thomas Tredwell
private residence
Fort Salonga, Suffolk Co.

Ulster

Johannes Bruyn[11]
"Brykill Estate"
private residence
Shawangunk, Ulster Co.

John Cantine
private residence
Marbletown, Ulster Co.

JAMES CLINTON
James Clinton Historic House
    (1798)
Orange County Historical
    Society
closed for restoration
(scheduled to open in 1986)
New Windsor, Orange Co.

JOHANNIS G. HARDENBERGH[12]
"Hardenbergh Rooms" in the
Winterthur Museum
Delaware

Cornelius T. Jensen
private residence
Shawangunk, Ulster Co.

Arthur Parks
private residence
Montgomery, Orange Co.

Cornelius C. Schoonmaker
Schoonmaker House
    (1716–21)
private residence
Shawangunk, Ulster Co.

PETER VAN GAASBEEK[13]
Senate House (after 1730)
state historic site in
Kingston Stockade District
City of Kingston, Ulster Co.

Washington and Clinton

David Hopkins
Hopkins House (1790)
private residence
Hebron, Washington Co.

Edward Savage
Savage House (1794)
private residence
Salem, Washington Co.

Westchester

Thaddeus Crane
private residence
North Salem, Westchester Co.

SAMUEL DRAKE[14]
"Jug Tavern" (ca. 1758)

[10]Smith was raised here but never inherited the manor.
[11]Bruyn's occupancy is probable, not
certain.
[12]The original interiors from Hardenbergh's house form a backdrop for
two "Hardenbergh Rooms" furnished
with New York State pieces in the Queen
Anne style.

[13]Van Gaasbeek was raised in the
original structure later rebuilt after the
fire of 1777. In 1788 he inherited the
property by marriage and lived here until his death in 1791.
[14]This structure may have been
owned by Drake who operated a tavern
here or in the immediate vicinity.

owned by the town of
   Ossining
closed yet partially restored
(no plans for full restoration)
Ossining, Westchester Co.

JOHN JAY[15]
John Jay Homestead (1787)
also known as "Bedford
   House"
now state historic site
Katonah, Westchester Co.

Ebenezer Lockwood
Pre-Revolutionary House
commercial nursery
Poundridge, Westchester Co.

Ebenezer Lockwood[16]
Post-Revolutionary House
church property
Poundridge, Westchester Co.

Jonathan G. Tompkins
private residence
Scarsdale, Westchester Co.

PHILIP VAN CORTLANDT
Van Cortlandt Manor
   (by 1750)
Sleepy Hollow Restorations
historical manor museum
Croton-on-Hudson,
   Westchester Co.

PIERRE VAN CORTLANDT
Van Cortlandt Upper Manor
   House
also known as "Peekskill
   Manor"
owned by town of Cortlandt
closed and unrestored
(no plans for restoration)
Cortlandt, Westchester Co.

[15]Built in 1787 by Jay who periodi-
cally visited the homestead until retiring
here in 1801.
   [16]Evidence suggests that Lockwood's
second home may still be standing and
now serving as a church parsonage.

A Guide to Historic Sites of the Ratification Debate in New York

STEPHEN L. SCHECHTER
Russell Sage College

For those interested in how the Federalists and Antifederalists lived, New York offers a rich variety of materials to explore. There are, of course, the many forms of written material, fully described in the essays by Gaspare J. Saladino and Jack VanDerhoof found in section III. But there are also historic sites and museum collections wherein one can acquire not only a sense of the way of life in 1787–88, but also an independent basis for interpreting the ratification debate.

In this guide, those previously inventoried homes open to the public are highlighted and the reader is alerted to other well-known historic sites, districts, and museum collections. Taken together, these places are intended to provide a representative view of both the urban and rural life of political leaders in those regions of the state that were part of the ratification debate.

New York City

Little remains of the urban life that existed during the years 1787–88 in Lower Manhattan south of Chambers Street. None of the townhouses and countinghouses of Federalists and Antifederalists have survived. Also gone are the printing shops and public meeting places that were so prominent during the ratification debate. As is so common to Lower Manhattan generally, there are various out-of-the-way places that can be explored for a secondhand look back to this period, including two reminiscent structures of 1790s construction in the South Street Seaport area. But St. Paul's Chapel is the only downtown structure even remotely connected with the ratification debate that has survived the fires and development of the ensuing years.

The present Federal Hall, now a national memorial administered by the national park service, is two steps removed from the old City Hall, where the Confederation Congress met. In late September 1788 Pierre L'Enfant was commissioned by the City Council to remodel the old City Hall to meet the needs of the new federal government. The product of L'Enfant's work was the first Federal Hall, completed early in 1789 and immortalized by Peter Lacour's engraving done at the time of George Washington's inauguration on 30 April 1789. That building has long since been demolished, and in its place stands the present hall—a nineteenth-century structure of different style, construction, and materials. The original Fraunces Tavern also no longer stands. In its place is a twentieth-century building of the same name, owned by the Sons of the Revolution in the State of New York, and dubbed a *"highly conjectural* construction."[1] Whatever one's view of the exteriors, the real value of Federal Hall and Fraunces Tavern is on the inside, where the former maintains models and exhibits of earlier city and federal halls, and the latter provides an upstairs museum of tavern life in the eighteenth century.

No longer standing are the country homes that dotted the Out Ward in what is today the Lower East Side. Also gone are the homes and hills of the area known as the "village hills," and still referred to as the Villages. Perhaps the most famous of these homes was Richmond Hill, on a hill of the same name, located in what is now the Charlton-King-Vandam district; however, neither home nor hill now stands. This house was the residence of Vice President John Adams and then of Aaron Burr during the 1790s. One of the most vivid accounts of Richmond Hill (house and hill) is that of Adams's wife Abigail. Writing to an English acquaintance in 1790, she stated:

---

[1]Norval White and Elliot Willensky, *AIA Guide to New York City*, revised edition, for the New York Chapter, American Institute of Architects (New York, 1978), 11.

. . . I have a situation here, which, for natural beauty, may vie with the most delicious spot I ever saw. It is a mile and half distant from the city of New-York. The house stands upon an eminence; at an agreeable distance, flows the noble Hudson bearing upon her bosom the fruitful productions of the adjacent country. On my right hand are fields beautifully variegated with grass and grain to a great extent, like the valley of Honiton in Devonshire. Upon my left, the city opens to view, intercepted here and there, by a rising ground, and an ancient oak. In front, beyond the Hudson, the Jersey shores present the exuberance of a rich well cultivated soil. The venerable oaks, and broken ground, covered with wild shrubs, which surround me, give a natural beauty to the spot which is truly enchanting. A lovely variety of birds serenade me morning and evening, rejoicing in their liberty and security. . . .[2]

The surviving homes of Federalists and Antifederalists are located well outside the downtown area. Closest is the HAMILTON GRANGE NATIONAL MEMORIAL, moved from its original site to 287 Convent Avenue, between W. 141st and W. 142nd Streets, in the Hamilton Heights District on the Upper West Side. Considered his "sweet project," Hamilton began work on this country home in 1798. Completed in 1802, he lived there until his death two years later. Today, the restoration of one floor is complete. (Some of Hamilton's furniture can also be seen in the Museum of the City of New York, located on Fifth Avenue at 103rd Street; other pieces are stored in Federal Hall.) Of a different calibre is the MORRIS-JUMEL MANSION, located at W. 160th Street and Edgecombe Avenue in the Jumel Terrace District of Washington Heights. Built by Roger Morris in 1765 as a summer residence, then used as a tavern until 1810 when Stephen Jumel remodeled it, Aaron Burr lived here for only six months in 1833. Reflecting the various periods of its early occupants, from colonial through empire, the mansion is a jewel in the area but not very informative for students of the political history of the 1780s. Like other city-owned historic sites, the mansion is on public park property and administered by a private association.

Farther north are three sites that present a representative view of the different strata of late eighteenth-century life. How-

---

[2]To Thomas Brand-Hollis, 6 September 1790, John Disney, ed., *Memoirs of Thomas Brand-Hollis, Esq., F.R.S. and S.A.* (London, Eng., 1808), 40.

ever, none of the occupants were leaders in the ratification debate. The Dyckman House, rebuilt around 1783, is typical of the small farmhouses of Upper Manhattan. Located on Broadway at W. 204th Street, it is now maintained as a city-owned historic site. In the Bronx, then part of Westchester County, is the middle-class Valentine-Varian House, 3266 Bainbridge Avenue between Van Cortlandt Avenue East and E. 208th Street, owned by the Bronx Historical Society. And in Van Cortlandt Park, between W. 242nd and W. 246th Streets, is the Van Cortlandt Mansion. Now a city-owned historic site, the mansion was occupied in 1788 by Frederick, a relative of the upper Van Cortlandt line of Philip and Pierre, whose manor houses still stand (see Lower Hudson region below).

Like the Bronx, Staten Island has no surviving homes of the ratification leaders. Abraham Bancker probably lived on Richmond Terrace, not far from the Neville House of that period (now a private residence). In 1795 Gozen Ryerss built a home in Northfield (now Port Richmond), later turned into a hotel where Aaron Burr spent his last days. And Peter Winant lived two census enumerations west of the Voorlezer House, which is now located in Richmondtown Restoration, a city-owned historic area administered by the Staten Island Historical Society.

LEFFERTS HOMESTEAD in Brooklyn is the only surviving home in New York City occupied by a political leader at the time of the ratification debate. Built by Peter, Sr., in 1783, it was moved in the early 1900s from its original location at 563 Flatbush Avenue to Prospect Park (at Flatbush Avenue and Empire Boulevard), where it is now operated as a city-owned historic site. Neither of the Wyckoffs involved in the ratification debate were associated with the Pieter Claessen Wyckoff House in Flatlands, though Hendrick may have lived near or been associated with the Wyckoff-Bennett House, now a private residence in Sheepshead Bay. Finally, in Jamaica, Queens, there is the KING MANOR, to which Rufus King retired after purchasing the house in 1805. A city-owned historic site, the manor is now located in King Park on Jamaica Avenue between 150th and 153rd Streets. Though furnished from various periods, the original construction is mid-eighteenth century, and the library contains King's books.

Long Island

As one travels farther out on Long Island, the picture steadily improves. Three surviving homes are open to the public and located on the North Shore (two in Nassau County and one in Suffolk County). Two more homes are historic sites in Mastic Beach on the South Shore.

Proceeding from east to west, the first home is that of Hendrick Onderdonck, now the GEORGE WASHINGTON MANOR RESTAURANT, located at 1305 Old Northern Boulevard in the North Shore community of Roslyn, Nassau County. Originally, the site contained two houses (one built in 1740, the other in 1750), later combined and altered. Also standing is a grist mill (1714), now owned by Nassau County. Though the date when the two houses were joined is unknown, Hendrick Onderdonck lived here at the time of the ratification debate.

The second home in Nassau County is RAYNHAM HALL, now owned by the North Shore town of Oyster Bay and maintained as an historic site, located at 20 W. Main Street. The house was owned by Samuel Townsend, who purchased the property in 1738, enlarged the original farmhouse around 1740, and remained there until his death in 1790. The front portion of the present structure is of Townsend's time; the back portion is of the 1860s.

Also on the North Shore, but in Suffolk County, is the EPENETUS SMITH TAVERN, built before 1750. The tavern was owned and operated by Epenetus and his son Epenetus II at the time of the ratification debate. It is now owned by the Smithtown Historical Society and maintained as an educational museum of eighteenth-century taverns and their role in society. Open to school classes and small groups by appointment, the tavern is located at 211 Middle Country Road (Rte. 25), Village of the Branch (Smithtown). Inquiries should be addressed to: Smithtown Historical Society, P. O. Box 69, Smithtown, NY 11787 (tel.: 516-265-6768).

The principal South Shore sites are the country estate of William Floyd and the Smith family's Manor of St. George, both located in Mastic Beach, Suffolk County. The WILLIAM FLOYD ESTATE, occupied by the Floyd family from 1724 to 1976, is now a national historic site and a unit of Fire Island National Seashore. William Floyd was born on the estate in 1738 and lived there until 1803 when he moved to the town of Western in Oneida County. In 1755 his parents died of typhoid fever, and William, the eldest son, assumed responsibility for the estate and his eight younger siblings. The estate, located at 20 Washington Avenue, is a preservation of changes since Floyd's occupancy, not a restoration to his occupancy.

The MANOR OF ST. GEORGE is now operated as a private museum by its trustees, George C. and George H. Furman. John Smith was raised here, perhaps living at the manor during the ratification debate; but the smaller wing (now the kitchen) of the present structure is the only part that remains from his time. In 1788 the manor was owned by John's father Judge William Smith who bequeathed the manor to John's son, owing to John's marriage into the wealthy Floyd family. The manor is now located off the William Floyd Parkway, one mile south of the Smith Point Bridge. Inquiries should be addressed to: Manor of St. George, P. O. Box 349, Patchogue, NY 11772.

Brief mention might be made here of Long Island sites that might be mistakenly associated with ratification leaders. In Queens County, the Kingsland House in Flushing was owned by a different Charles Doughty than the Charles of Brooklyn; the Queens County Farm Museum in Bellerose, formerly known as the Cornell House, was not occupied by either Samuel Cornell or Whitehead Cornwell; and the Vander-Ende Onderdonck House in Ridgewood was not occupied by Hendrick Onderdonck.

Old Bethpage Village in Nassau County is a special case. The Schenck House was moved to the village from Manhasset where it had been owned and occupied in 1788 by Minne Schenck, a close cousin of John Schenck who might well have frequented the house. However, the Lawrence House was moved to the village from Flushing, and neither the house nor the owner was closely related to the Antifederalist convention delegate Nathaniel Lawrence (a fifth generation of the so-called Thomas Lawrence line).

Lower Hudson Valley

In the late 1780s, the Lower Hudson region encompassed various settlement patterns. Manor estates occupied much of the western half of Westchester County in a widening band, beginning with the Fordham and Morrisania manors (in what is now northern Bronx County) and proceeding up the Hudson River Valley to include the Philipsburgh Manor (whose confiscated Loyalist lands had been recently sold), the Pelham Manor (whose lands had been greatly subdivided by the Pells), and the Van Cortlandt Manor of upper Westchester County. Farther north were the settlements of the Philipse's Highland patent, the southernmost of several large land patents, then in Dutchess County, now in Putnam County.

Outside of the band of manor and patent lands, New Englanders had developed communities hugging the Connecticut border and Long Island Sound.

On the west side of the Hudson, the southernmost lands (now in Rockland County) were dominated by Dutch and other homestead settlements in the old Tappan patent and a few river settlements (notably at present-day Nyack and Piermont) wherever breaks in the Palisades allowed. Farther north lay the settlements of Orange County formed out of three great patents—the Minisink in the west (including part of the town of Wallkill); the Wawayanda in the middle (including the towns of Goshen, Warwick, and Chester); and the long-extinguished Evans patent in the east (including the inland border town of Montgomery and the river settlements north of the Highlands, from Cornwall, to New Windsor, and on to Newburgh in the old German patent).

Proceeding up the Hudson River Valley from the Bronx, the first site in Westchester County is St. Paul's Church and Parish Hall in Mount Vernon. Among its pewholders and vestrymen in 1787 were the Pells, Van Cortlandts, Roosevelts, and Drakes. During the late 1780s, the church was used during the week as a court of oyer and terminer where Aaron Burr and others practiced law. Now a national historic site, the church and parish hall are located at 897 South Columbus Avenue. The parish hall is the site of the first Bill of Rights Museum in the national park system.

Northward into central Westchester County, the landscape begins to assume a different character. Traveling the Post Road from Philipsburgh in Yonkers to Mount Pleasant in 1794, Englishman William Strickland made these observations:

> From Philipsburgh to a tavern [probably Samuel Drake's] near Mount Pleasant church where we breakfasted, the road leads through a country hardly to be surpassed in beauty by any in the world. On our left the river, here called the Tapaan Sea, and not less than four miles in breadth, is generally in sight. . . . On our right hand, is in general a cultivated country, swelling into gentle and various inequalities, the knolls coverd with wood, with various patches of copse and wood scatterd over the country, and the whole gradually sloping down to the edge of the water. The country strikingly resembles the best parts of Hertfordshire, and would be still more like it, were the fields only divided by well planted hedges instead of the vile railing which every where so greatly disfigures it, and

here wood being still plentiful the railing is of the worst description, what they call worm fencing, which is not easy to describe either by words or the pencil.[3]

Later that morning, Strickland arrived at the Mount Pleasant tavern, probably Drake's tavern; now the JUG TAVERN (closed and unrestored) or a nearby site, on Rte. 9 near the Arcadian Shopping Center in the village of Ossining. He wrote:

> We had seen little yet to give us a favourable idea of the comforts of travelling in this country, and the external appearance of the tavern at Mountpleasant added nothing to it; we put up our horses in a shed, much like that at a Blacksmith's shop in a country village, and expected no better appartment for ourselves in which to eat our homely meal which we desired to be prepared while we took a walk to survey the neighbourhood; our surprise however on our return was of a very agreable nature when we saw in a neat room on a table cloth white as snow preparations made for breakfast which consisted of tea and bread and butter; honey; sweetmeats and marmalades of various kinds, of quinces and wild fruits of the country; beefsteaks; mutton chops; pickles of several sorts; milk and cheesecakes; such a scene gladdened our hearts, we praised American fare and enjoyed a meal so well suited to our stomachs, after a long ride in a frosty morning.[4]

Farther up the Hudson in the upper Westchester County village of Croton-on-Hudson is VAN CORTLANDT MANOR. Built by 1750 and restored to the post-Revolutionary period, the manor is superbly maintained as an historical museum by Sleepy Hollow Restorations. Inherited by Pierre Van Cortlandt in 1749, it was occupied by his son Philip during the ratification debate. The Van Cortlandt Manor is located on Rte. 9A, Croton Point Avenue, and is the subject of a book published by Sleepy Hollow Restorations headquartered at 10 White Plains Road, Tarrytown, NY 10591. In the late 1780s Pierre was living in the Upper Van Cortlandt (Peekskill) Manor, located on what is now Oregon Road in the town of Cortlandt. That structure was recently given as a gift to the town to be used for public purposes, but is now closed for lack of restoration funds.

[3]William Strickland, *Journal of a Tour in the United States of America, 1794–1795* (New York, 1971), 91.
[4]*Ibid.*, 93–94.

East of the Van Cortlant Manor is another well-maintained site, the JOHN JAY HOMESTEAD, built in 1787 and later known as the Bedford House. Located on what is now Jay Street (Rte. 22) in Katonah (town of Bedford), the homestead is maintained as a state historic site and will undoubtedly figure prominently in the state's commemoration of the bicentennial of the Constitution. Although Jay did not settle here until his retirement in 1801, he supervised the building of the home in 1787, frequently visited it during the ensuing years, and lived out a lengthy retirement here from 1801 to his death in 1829. The present house, partially restored to the federal period, includes the original four-room house of 1787, an enlargement made by Jay in 1800, and subsequent additions (in 1818 by Jay, and in 1904 and 1924). Not far from the homestead is the Bedford Court House, also built in 1787 and located on what is now Rte. 22. Though restored to a later period, the courthouse is maintained as an historical museum and provides a sense of court life in the late eighteenth and early nineteenth centuries when Bedford and White Plains were both county seats, with county court sessions alternating each year between the two.

Of the inventoried homes still standing in Putnam, Rockland, and Orange counties, none are now maintained as historic sites open to the public. In the northern Orange County town of New Windsor, the JAMES CLINTON HISTORIC HOUSE is presently being restored by the Orange County Historical Society and should be open to the public in 1986. The house was not built until 1798 by James, elder brother of George and father of DeWitt, and only the foundation of the early house remains. Nonetheless, restoration should afford a sense of the importance of the Clinton family and New Windsor in the late eighteenth century when the town was a center for inland commerce. For additional information, write to the Orange County Historical Society, Arden, NY 10910.

Mid-Hudson Region

Journeying north into the Mid-Hudson counties of Ulster and Dutchess, the most complete view of the urban life of this region in the eighteenth century is found in the Stockade District of the city of Kingston, in Ulster County. Bounded by Clinton Avenue and Pearl, Green, and North Front streets, the district contains several structures constructed or rebuilt in the eighteenth century. Of particular interest is the SENATE HOUSE, so named because it stands on the site of the building in which the first New York State Senate met for approximately four weeks (9 September–15 October 1777), before the British troops set the village afire. In fact, the original Senate House, partially destroyed and rebuilt, is most closely associated with Abraham Van Gaasbeek and his son Peter. Abraham moved into the original house sometime after his marriage to Sarah Ten Broeck in 1751, and Peter was undoubtedly raised here. In 1776 Sarah died and Peter joined the American secret service, thereby leaving the old house nearly vacant. This probably occasioned the renting of the house to the Senate. Sometime after the 1777 fire, Abraham probably rebuilt the house and resumed occupancy until his death in 1794. He bequeathed the house to his niece Sarah Du Pont who promptly married Peter, and the two lived there until Peter's death three years later. This house is now a state historic site located off Clinton Avenue in the northeast corner of the Stockade District. To visit the Senate House, one must first go to the museum building, situated to the southwest, wherein some of Peter's papers are housed.

Two other structures in the Stockade might be mistakenly linked to ratification leaders. The first is the Cornelius Tappen House, now owned by the Albany Savings Bank on Crown Street. Cornelius was the brother of Christopher and brother-in-law of Governor George Clinton, but his house played little part in the lives of those two leaders. When Governor Clinton visited Kingston, he stayed at Christopher's house, located at what is now the corner of North Front and Wall streets. However, that house was demolished in the early 1900s. The second, now the Hoffman House Restaurant at North and Green streets, was owned by an Anthony Hoffman, but not the state senator of the 1780s.

The name of another Ulster County man, Johannis G. Hardenbergh, is associated with a different kind of legacy. The interiors of two rooms in his Rochester home were saved from destruction and removed to the Winterthur Museum. Those interiors now form the backdrop for the museum's HARDENBERGH ROOMS—a bedroom and a sitting room furnished with New York State pieces in the Queen Anne style. The museum is located in Winterthur, Delaware, five miles north of Wilmington on Rte. 52.

Across the river in Dutchess County, none of the buildings associated with the state ratifying convention in Poughkeepsie still stand. The courthouse where the convention met was the county's third one, built in 1785-86 and lost by fire in 1806. Gone also are the Federalist and Antifederalist meeting places, known respectively as Hendrickson's Inn (later the Nelson House) and Poole's Inn. There are several homes of eighteenth-century construction still standing in Poughkeepsie, but their history is associated more with the Revolution than the Constitution. One, known as the Clinton House, had long been assumed to be Governor George Clinton's headquarters, until research proved otherwise.

Outside the city of Poughkeepsie are various surviving homes of Dutchess County ratification leaders; however, most are now private residences and only one is an historic site open to the public. This is the VAN WYCK HOMESTEAD, located on Rte. 9, one mile south of the Fishkill business section. Now owned by the Fishkill Historical Society, the homestead has two sections—the original structure (1732) and the main building (before 1756); both built by Isaac Van Wyck's grandfather Cornelius. Isaac was the head of the household by 1788. Today, the kitchen has been restored to the late eighteenth century; however, the remaining rooms of the house are essentially unfurnished. For additional information, write to the Fishkill Historical Society, P. O. Box 133, Fishkill, NY 12524.

The Twenty Mile Historic District is traversed by River Road between the Hudson River and Rte. 9 from Staatsburg north to Germantown in Columbia County. Driving this strip of River Road is worthwhile for a sense of eighteenth-century siting; however, the homes are not readily visible from the road and, in any case, most are of a nineteenth-century character. The clearest vista of this historic district is available from the river and can be most simply obtained by driving east across the Kingston-Rhinecliff Bridge. For the more adventurous, there are cruises departing from 1 Rondout Creek, Kingston, near the Hudson River Maritime Center. For more information, contact Hudson River Cruises in Kingston.

Upper Hudson Region

The Upper Hudson Valley is among the richest in historic sites, parks, and districts, representing a variety of late eighteenth-century life styles. Its southern reaches include Clermont Manor and several historic districts in the river communities and inland villages that flourished after the Revolution. The Schuyler Mansion in the city of Albany represents one of the clearest examples of town life in the late eighteenth century, while the Schuyler House in Saratoga County presents an equally sharp image of an eighteenth-century country estate.

Proceeding north through the Twenty Mile District, one enters CLERMONT STATE HISTORIC PARK, located off Rte. 9G in Germantown, now in Columbia County. The original mansion was built about 1730 by Robert of Clermont, Chancellor Robert R. Livingston's grandfather, and burned by the British in 1777, two years after Robert R. inherited the estate. Within a few years, the mansion was rebuilt, incorporating the remnants of the earlier building in its walls. Over the next decade, the chancellor, who had been raised in New York City, divided his time between the new Clermont house (which he shared with his mother) and his New York City residence on the Bowling Green. Finally, in 1794, he completed another and still grander mansion, also known as Clermont (or Arryl), near the second mansion. It was in this third house, destroyed by fire in 1909, that the chancellor held sessions of court and followed his Jeffersonian-like scientific pursuits. The second mansion still stands, but with several nineteenth-century additions. Nonetheless, its siting, exhibits, and tours provide a sense of late eighteenth-century life.

From Clermont, one continues north on Rte. 9G to the Columbia County city of Hudson, the southernmost of several river communities and inland villages that flourished after the the Revolution and that retain features of their development in the late eighteenth century. In the city of Hudson, Lower Warren Street affords a look back to the growth of that city as a planned New England community. Going east on Rte. 23B, Claverack provides some excellent views of late eighteenth-century development, including Columbia County's first courthouse (1786) and the homes of JOHN BAY, WILLIAM LUDLOW, and others attracted by the prospects of a new county seat. All are located on Rte. 23B in Claverack and are identified on the Penfield Map of 1799, parts of which have been reprinted by the Claverack and Columbia County historical societies. From Claverack, one travels north on Rte. 9H to the town of Kinderhook and the LINDENWALD HOUSE, built by Peter Van Ness in 1797 and now a national historic site restored to the later occupancy of Martin Van Buren. From this site, one proceeds to Hudson Street and thence on to its intersection with Rte. 9 at the village square in the Kinderhook Village Historic District. Just south of the village square, on Rte. 9 (Broad

Street) are the VAN SCHAACK HOMES—Peter's (built in 1785 and later remodeled in the Victorian style) and his brother David's (built in 1774 and retaining much of its original Georgian style). Both are now private residences. From Broad Street, one explores the village streets and then continues northward on Rte. 26A to Stuyvesant Landing and, from there, north on Rte. 9J to the Schodack Landing Historic District in Rensselaer County. Located on Rte. 9J in this district are several homes of eighteenth-century construction, including the TEN EYCK HOUSE (ca. 1775).

North of Schodack Landing, one crosses the Hudson River and proceeds north to the city of Albany, stopping along the way to see the NICOLL-SILL HOUSE (1736), located in the southeastern section of the town of Bethlehem on Vanderzee Road off Rte. 144 and presently closed and undergoing restoration. In the city of Albany, the SCHUYLER MANSION (1764) presents a happy coincidence of late eighteenth-century architectural and political history. Now maintained as a state historic site, the mansion is restored to Philip Schuyler's occupancy and reflects much of his position, activities, and connections (most notably to his son-in-law Alexander Hamilton). The mansion is now located on Clinton and Catherine streets (the former named for the family that supplied Schuyler's nemesis). Below the mansion, and to the northeast, lies The Pastures preservation district, containing row houses of early nineteenth-century construction.

Several other Albany structures deserve mention. The first is the TEN BROECK MANSION, known as Arbor Hill, and located on what is now Ten Broeck Place in the city's Arbor Hill section. Built by Abraham Ten Broeck in 1798, the mansion has been restored to a later period and contains only a few items of Abraham or his occupancy. The second is Cherry Hill, built in 1787 by Henry K. Van Rensselaer's brother Philip. Located on what is now South Pearl Street, Cherry Hill is the only surviving historic site of the Van Rensselaer family. Gone but not entirely lost is the mansion of Stephen Van Rensselaer, "The Great Patroon." Built in 1765, the mansion was located on a Tivoli Street site over which the RCA dog now sits. In 1893 the mansion was moved to Williams College, Williamstown, Massachusetts, where it remained until it was demolished in the 1970s. Stones from the original structure are said to have been saved and are awaiting reassemblage.

North of Albany, in Saratoga County, is the SCHUYLER HOUSE, now a national historic site in Saratoga National Historic

Park. A carefully restored example of a late eighteenth-century country home, this historic site nicely complements Schuyler's Albany mansion. The Saratoga house was built by Philip Schuyler in 1777 to replace an earlier house that had been burned by the British. In 1787 Schuyler gave the house to his son John Bradstreet Schuyler who remained there until his death in 1795. At that time, the house reverted back to Philip and was retained by him until 1804 when he gave it to his grandson. The present house, restored to the 1787–1804 period, is located in Schuylerville, eight miles north of the Saratoga Battlefield.

Central New York

The adoption of the Constitution was a major factor in opening up the lands west of the Hudson River Valley. In the years immediately following the adoption of the Constitution, the river valleys of central and western New York became well-traveled routes in the first westward expansion of the new republic. Returning to the Mohawk River Valley in 1791, Elkanah Watson wrote of the emigrants "swarming into these fertile regions in shoals, like the ancient Israelites, seeking the land of promise."[5] However, in 1790 there were only about 7,500 residents in central and western New York, and the principal settlements were largely confined to the areas of present-day Utica and Rome in Oneida County and Cooperstown in Otsego County.

In 1788 there were only two areas of western settlement represented in the state legislature and the state ratifying convention. And both were a part of the late colonial period of expansion. The first was the eastern section of the Mohawk Valley, from Schenectady west through the present-day counties of Montgomery, Fulton, and Herkimer. The westernmost convention candidates were Peter Schuyler (defeated) and Henry Staring, both from that part of Montgomery County now in Herkimer County just east of Utica. The second area was the Schoharie Valley, located just west of the Hudson River Valley; an area settled before the Revolution and represented by Peter Vrooman at the convention.

Throughout much of the late eighteenth century, the urban center of the Mohawk Valley was Schenectady, a city that still

[5]*History of the Rise, Progress, and Existing Conditions of the Western Canals in the State of New-York, from September 1788, to the Completion of the Middle Section of the Grand Canal, in 1819* . . . (Albany, 1820), 31.

retains its westward orientation toward the Mohawk River. In 1788 the center of Schenectady was still essentially contained within the old stockaded area of the town bounded by State Street, Ferry Street, and, on its remaining sides, the Mohawk River. Today, the Stockade Historic District is enlarged to include the area bounded by State Street, Erie Boulevard, and the Mohawk River. Within this district are several late eighteenth-century homes, including those of DIRCK VAN INGEN (1790) on North Church Street and ISAAC VROOMAN (1754) on Front Street. These homes, like others in the district, are now private residences; however, this is an ideal area for a walking tour from which much can be gleaned about this frontier urban settlement. For additional information, contact the Schenectady County Historical Society, 32 Washington Avenue, Schenectady, NY 12305.

West of Schenectady, little remains of the frontier life of the political leaders involved in the ratification debate. There are several surviving homes of Federalist and Antifederalist leaders, but these are now occupied as private residences. Most of the historic sites open to the public are either earlier forts or later villages; however, two roundabout avenues can be followed. First are the homes now maintained as historic sites, restored or otherwise, and tied to a slightly earlier period. These include: Guy Park State Historic Site (1773), altered over the years, located on West Main Street, Amsterdam, Montgomery County; Johnson Hall State Historic Site (1763), dominated by the earlier occupancy of Sir William Johnson, located on Hall Avenue, Johnstown, Fulton County; Fort Johnson (ca. 1755), an earlier home of Sir William and well maintained by the Montgomery County Historical Society, located west of Amsterdam on Rte. 5; and Herkimer Home State Historic Site (1760), comparable to the foregoing homes by virtue of the aspirations of its original occupant General Nicholas Herkimer, located on Rte. 169, just south of Little Falls, Herkimer County.

Also of interest are three sites at COOPERSTOWN, Otsego County. In the village, the only surviving structure dating back to the 1780s is a smithy, now housing a commercial art gallery, located on Pioneer Street. Out of the village, on Rte. 80 (Lake Road), the Fenimore House, now the headquarters of the New York State Historical Association, contains Cooper memorabilia. Across Lake Road is The Farmers' Museum, an outdoor museum, composed of authentic buildings from the region, arranged to depict a pre-industrial nineteenth-century village crossroads. From here, one can compare the original smithy (1786) in the village with later structures at the museum; and throughout the area, one can still see signs of original siting and lakefront locations.

Conclusion

By way of review, it might be useful here to highlight those historic sites of prime importance in each region. In New York City, any list of such sites would include the Hamilton Grange, the only home Alexander Hamilton ever owned; the Lefferts Homestead, the only surviving home in the city occupied by a ratification leader during the ratification debate; and Federal Hall and Fraunces Tavern, because of their value as namesakes and for the special exhibits they contain. On Long Island, the most significant sites would include the William Floyd Estate and the Manor of St. George, owing to the prestige of their occupants, and Raynham Hall and the Epenetus Smith Tavern, by virtue of their focus on the period.

In the Lower Hudson region, the John Jay Homestead and Van Cortlandt Manor are of great importance; the former perhaps more for its occupant, the latter perhaps more for its restoration to the period. Farther up the Hudson, the James Clinton Historic House in New Windsor promises to provide a much needed view of the late eighteenth-century role of that region. In the Mid-Hudson region, the Senate House in Kingston and the Van Wyck Homestead in Fishkill are of prime significance for the views they provide of that region's urban and rural life, respectively. Still farther up the Hudson, Clermont Manor is valuable more for its connection to Chancellor Robert R. Livingston than for its focus on Livingston's period. Elsewhere in the Upper Hudson region, the Schuyler Mansion in Albany and the Schuyler House in Saratoga County are of great consequence, both for the role of their occupant and the period to which they have been restored. Farther west along the Mohawk, the Schenectady Stockade affords the clearest view of that region in the late eighteenth century.

A Chronology of Constitutional Events during the American Revolutionary Era, 1774–1792

1774

5 September– 26 October	First Continental Congress meets in Philadelphia.

1775

10 May	Second Continental Congress convenes.
16 May	Massachusetts asks Congress for advice on reorganizing its government.
9 June	Congress advises Massachusetts to honor its Charter of 1691, but to hold new elections. By July Massachusetts has resumed government without a royally appointed governor.
18 October	New Hampshire's delegates in Congress ask for advice on reorganizing its government.
3 November	Congress advises New Hampshire to "call a full and free representation of the people" to form a new government.

1776

5 January	New Hampshire legislature adopts new state constitution.

9 January	Thomas Paine's *Common Sense* published.
26 March	South Carolina legislature adopts provisional constitution.
May	Rhode Island removes name of Crown from all government documents. Its Charter of 1663 stays in effect.
1 May	Massachusetts General Court gives up the Charter of 1691 and removes the Crown's name from appointments.
10, 15 May	Congress advises colonies to form new governments and to suppress the authority of the Crown.
7 June	Richard Henry Lee of Virginia offers a resolution in Congress calling for independence and the preparation of a form of government.
11 June	Congress appoints a committee to draft a declaration of independence.
12 June	Congress appoints a committee to prepare a plan of confederation.
12 June	Virginia legislature adopts a declaration of rights.
29 June	Virginia legislature adopts a constitution.
2 July	Congress votes for independence.
2 July	New Jersey legislature adopts a constitution.
4 July	Declaration of Independence adopted.
12 July	Committee presents Congress with draft Articles of Confederation.
21 September	Delaware Convention adopts a constitution and declaration of rights.
28 September	Pennsylvania Convention adopts a constitution and declaration of rights.
October	Connecticut declares its Charter of 1662 to be in effect.
8 November	Maryland Convention adopts a constitution and declaration of rights.
14 December	North Carolina legislature adopts constitution and a declaration of rights on 17 December.

1777

4 February	Georgia legislature adopts constitution.
20 April	New York legislature adopts constitution.

| June 1777–
February 1778 | Massachusetts General Court drafts constitution for adoption by people voting in towns. |
| 15 November | Congress adopts Articles of Confederation and sends them to the states for ratification. |

1778

| March | People in towns in Massachusetts vote to reject proposed constitution. |
| 5 March | A new constitution enacted by South Carolina General Assembly on 5 March and signed into law by state's president on 19 March. |

1779

| 1 September 1779–
2 March 1780 | Massachusetts Convention prepares constitution and declaration of rights for consideration of towns. |

1780

16 June	Massachusetts Convention declares constitution to have been accepted by two-thirds of the voters.
25 October	Massachusetts Constitution goes into effect.
8–22 November	Hartford Convention.

1781

2 January	Virginia cedes its western lands to U.S.
3 February	Congress submits Impost of 1781 to states for approval.
1 March	Articles of Confederation takes effect with signature of Maryland delegates.
19 October	British surrender at Yorktown.

1782

| 1 November | Rhode Island rejects Impost of 1781. |
| 30 November | Preliminary Treaty of Peace. |

1783

| 18 April | Congress proposes Impost of 1783 and asks for supplementary revenues. Congress also proposes an amendment to apportion expenses according to population, including three-fifths of slaves. |

2 July	British Orders-in-Council restricting U.S. trade with West Indies.
3 September	Treaty of Peace signed in Paris ending Revolutionary War.

1784

14 January	Congress ratifies Treaty of Peace.
23 April	Congress adopts Ordinance for the Government of the Western Territory.
30 April	Congress proposes grant of temporary power to regulate commerce.

1785

20 May	Congress adopts Ordinance for the Sale of Western Lands.

1786

21 January	Virginia legislature chooses delegates to meet with delegates from other states to consider commercial problems (Annapolis Convention).
August–January 1787	Shays's Rebellion in Massachusetts.
11–14 September	Delegates from New York, New Jersey, Pennsylvania, Delaware, and Virginia meet at Annapolis Convention and adopt a report calling for a convention in Philadelphia in May 1787 to revise Articles of Confederation. Report sent to Congress and the states.
20 September	Congress receives Annapolis Convention report.
23 November–10 February 1787	New Jersey, Virginia, Pennsylvania, North Carolina, New Hampshire, Delaware, and Georgia appoint delegates to convention in Philadelphia.

1787

21 February	Congress calls for a convention to meet in Philadelphia on the second Monday in May to revise Articles of Confederation.

3 March–17 May	Massachusetts, New York, South Carolina, Maryland, and Connecticut elect delegates to convention in Philadelphia.
14 March, 5 May, 16 June	Rhode Island refuses to elect delegates to convention in Philadelphia.
25 May	A quorum is present in the Constitutional Convention for the first time.
29 May	Edmund Randolph introduces Virginia Resolutions which are debated by the Constitutional Convention.
15 June	William Paterson introduces the "New Jersey Amendments" as an alternative to the Virginia Plan.
19 June	Constitutional Convention rejects the New Jersey Amendments as an alternative to the Virginia Plan.
13 July	Congress adopts Ordinance for the Government of the Territory Northwest of the River Ohio (Northwest Ordinance).
6 August	Committee of Detail submits a draft constitution to the Constitutional Convention.
12 September	Committee of Style submits report to the Constitutional Convention.
12–15 September	Constitutional Convention considers Committee of Style report and rejects proposals to adopt a bill of rights.
17 September	Convention delegates sign Constitution and Constitutional Convention adjourns.
20 September	Constitution is read in Congress and 26 September is assigned for its consideration.
26–28 September	Congress debates Constitution and sends it to the states for their consideration without approbation or amendment.
28–29 September	Pennsylvania becomes the first state to call a state convention to consider Constitution.
6 October	James Wilson becomes first member of Constitutional Convention publicly to defend Constitution in Philadelphia speech.
27 October	First essay of The Federalist by "Publius" published in New York City.
3 November	Elbridge Gerry's objections to the Constitution published.
6 November	Pennsylvania elects delegates to state convention.
12 November	Connecticut elects delegates to state convention.

16 November	Richard Henry Lee's proposed amendments to the Constitution published but receive little attention until subsequent publications on 6 and 20 December.
19 November– 7 January 1788	Massachusetts elects delegates to state convention.
20 November– 15 December	Pennsylvania Convention.
21, 22 November	George Mason's objections to the Constitution published.
26 November	Delaware elects delegates to state convention.
27 November– 1 December	New Jersey elects delegates to state convention.
3–7 December	Delaware Convention.
4–5 December	Georgia elects delegates to state convention.
7 December	Delaware Convention votes unanimously to ratify Constitution becoming the first state to ratify.
11–20 December	New Jersey Convention.
12 December	Pennsylvania Convention ratifies Constitution, 46–23.
18 December	"Dissent of the Minority of the Pennsylvania Convention" published in Philadelphia, the first "official" Antifederalist analysis of the Constitution.
18 December	New Jersey Convention ratifies Constitution unanimously.
25 December– 5 January 1788	Georgia Convention.
27 December	Edmund Randolph's objections to the Constitution published.
31 December	Georgia Convention ratifies Constitution unanimously.
31 December– 12 February 1788	New Hampshire elects delegates to state convention.

1788

3–9 January	Connecticut Convention.
9 January	Connecticut Convention ratifies Constitution, 128–40.
9 January– 7 February	Massachusetts Convention.

6 February	Massachusetts Convention ratifies Constitution, 187–168, and proposes amendments.
13–22 February	New Hampshire Convention meets and adjourns without voting on Constitution.
3–31 March	Virginia elects delegates to state convention.
24 March	Rhode Island referendum on Constitution boycotted by Federalists; Constitution rejected 2,711–239.
28–29 March	North Carolina elects delegates to state convention.
7 April	Maryland elects delegates to state convention.
11–12 April	South Carolina elects delegates to state convention.
21–29 April	Maryland Convention.
26 April	Maryland Convention ratifies Constitution, 63–11.
29 April–3 May	New York elects delegates to state convention.
12–24 May	South Carolina Convention.
23 May	South Carolina Convention ratifies Constitution, 149–73, and proposes amendments.
2–27 June	Virginia Convention.
17 June–26 July	New York Convention.
18–21 June	New Hampshire Convention, second session.
21 June	New Hampshire Convention ratifies Constitution, 57–40, and proposes amendments. New Hampshire is the ninth state to ratify, satisfying requirements for ratification of the Constitution.
25 June	Virginia Convention ratifies Constitution, 89–79, and proposes amendments.
2 July	New Hampshire ratification read in Congress, which appoints committee to prepare an act for putting Constitution into operation.
21 July–4 August	North Carolina Convention.
26 July	New York Convention ratifies Constitution, 30–27, proposes amendments, and adopts a circular letter calling for a second constitutional convention.
2 August	North Carolina Convention declines to ratify Constitution, 180–80, and proposes amendments.
13 September	Congress adopts act setting dates for election of the President of United States and meeting of the first U.S. Congress under the Constitution.
30 November	North Carolina calls second convention.

1789

21–22 August	North Carolina elects delegates to second convention.
26 September	U.S. Congress proposes twelve amendments to the Constitution to be sent to the states for ratification.
16–23 November	Second North Carolina Convention.
21 November	Second North Carolina Convention ratifies Constitution, 194–77, and proposes amendments.

1790

17 January	Rhode Island calls convention.
8 February	Rhode Island elects delegates to state convention.
27 February	New York ratifies proposed amendments to Constitution.
1–6 March	Rhode Island Convention meets and adjourns without voting on Constitution.
24–29 May	Rhode Island Convention, second session.
29 May	Rhode Island Convention ratifies Constitution, 34–32, and proposes amendments.

1791

15 December	First ten amendments to Constitution ratified by the eleventh state, Virginia, satisfying requirement for ratification of amendments to Constitution.

1792

1 March	Secretary of State Thomas Jefferson notifies the states that the first ten amendments to the Constitution had been ratified (two proposed amendments, concerning apportionment and the size of the House of Representatives and restricting Congress' power to set its own salaries, are not ratified by the states).

A Chronology of New York Events, 1777–1788

1777

20 April	New York legislature adopts state constitution.
June	George Clinton elected first governor.

1778

6 February	Legislature adopts Articles of Confederation.

1780

25–26 September	Legislature appoints delegates to Hartford Convention.
8–22 November	Hartford Convention.

1781

19 March	Legislature adopts Impost of 1781.

1782

21 July	Legislature instructs congressional delegates to move for a constitutional convention.

1783

15 March	Legislature repeals its adoption of the Impost of 1781.
25 November	British evacuate New York City.

1785

4 April	Legislature adopts grant of commercial power to Congress.
9 April	Legislature adopts amendment to Articles of Confederation changing method of apportioning expenses of government.

1786

14 March	Legislature receives Virginia's call for Annapolis Convention.
18 April	Paper money act takes effect.
4 May	Legislature conditionally adopts Impost of 1783.
5 May	Legislature appoints delegates to Annapolis Convention.
11–14 September	Annapolis Convention.

1787

13 January	Legislature receives report of Annapolis Convention.
15 February	Assembly rejects alteration in state's approval of Impost of 1783.
20 February	Legislature instructs congressional delegates to move for a constitutional convention.
21 February	Melancton Smith and Egbert Benson move in Congress that a constitutional convention be called (rejected).
23 February	Legislature receives congressional resolution of 21 February calling Constitutional Convention.
6 March	Legislature appoints delegates to Constitutional Convention.
25 May	Robert Yates and Alexander Hamilton first attend Constitutional Convention.
2 June	John Lansing, Jr., first attends Constitutional Convention.
16 June	John Lansing, Jr., speech in Constitutional Convention.
18 June	Alexander Hamilton speech in Constitutional Convention.

10 July	Yates and Lansing leave Constitutional Convention.
21 July	Alexander Hamilton attacks George Clinton in *Daily Advertiser*
17 September	Alexander Hamilton signs Constitution for New York.
21 September	Constitution first published in New York (*Daily Advertiser*).
24 September	First original commentary on Constitution published in New York (*Daily Advertiser*).
27 September	First of seven "Cato" essays published.
29 September	First of three "Curtius" essays published.
1 October	First of two "Caesar" essays published.
3 October	Publication of first commentary on Constitution in inland newspaper (Poughkeepsie *Country Journal*).
18 October	First of sixteen "Brutus" essays published.
27 October	First of eighty-four essays by "Publius," The Federalist, published.
30 October	First of four "Philo-Publius" (William Duer) essays published.
1 November	First of six "Cincinnatus" (Arthur Lee) essays published.
2 November	First of seven "Americanus" (John Stevens, Jr.) essays published.
c. 2–8 November	"Federal Farmer" Letters published.
15 November	*New-York Journal* becomes a daily newspaper.
21 November	First of six "A Countryman" (Hugh Hughes) essays published.
6 December	First of four "A Countryman" (DeWitt Clinton) essays published.
11 December	First of five "Examiner" (Charles McKnight) essays published.
21 December	Yates-Lansing letter to Governor Clinton.

1788

11 January	Governor Clinton addresses legislature and delivers Constitution, resolution of Congress of 28 September, and Yates-Lansing letter.

14 January	First publication of Yates-Lansing letter to governor.
31 January	Assembly calls state convention to consider Constitution.
1 February	Senate concurs with Assembly's call of state convention.
7 February	Constitution burned at Montgomery, Ulster County.
22 March	Publication of first volume of *The Federalist*.
15 April	Publication of "A Citizen of New-York" (John Jay).
17 April	Publication of "A Plebeian" (Melancton Smith).
29 April–3 May	Elections of delegates to state convention.
27 May	County supervisors authorized to open ballot boxes and count ballots.
28 May	Publication of second volume of *The Federalist*.
14 June	Governor Clinton leaves New York City for convention.
17 June–26 July	Convention.
17 June	George Clinton elected president of Convention.
18 June	Convention reads Constitution.
19 June	Henry Oothoudt elected chairman of committee of the whole.
24 June	News of New Hampshire's ratification of Constitution arrives in Poughkeepsie.
2 July	News of Virginia's ratification of Constitution arrives in Poughkeepsie.
7 July	Convention finishes discussion of Constitution, and John Lansing presents a bill of rights to be prefixed to Constitution.
10 July	John Lansing presents plan of ratification with conditional amendments.
11 July	John Jay proposes unconditional ratification of Constitution.
17 July	Melancton Smith and Zephaniah Platt propose limited-term ratification of Constitution.
19 July	Melancton Smith withdraws motion for limited-term ratification.
23 July	Convention's committee of the whole votes to ratify Constitution without conditional amendments (31 to 29).

25 July	Convention rejects John Lansing's motion for limited-term ratification.
25 July	Committee of the whole agrees to Form of Ratification.
26 July	Convention ratifies Constitution (30 to 27) and unanimously approves Circular Letter to the states calling for a second constitutional convention.

Index

Contributors

MARTIN DIAMOND was Professor of Political Science at Northern Illinois University (1971–77). Just before his death in 1977, he accepted the Thomas and Dorothy Leavey Chair in Foundations of American Freedom at Georgetown University. A leading authority on the Constitution and its framing, his books include *The Founding of the Democratic Republic* and *The Revolution of Sober Expectations*.

DANIEL J. ELAZAR is Professor of Political Science at Temple University, where he also directs the Center for the Study of Federalism. A leading authority on American federalism, his writings on the subject include *American Federalism: A View From the States*, now in its third edition, and *The American Partnership: Intergovernmental Cooperation in the Nineteenth-Century United States*.

JOHN P. KAMINSKI and GASPARE J. SALADINO are co-editors of *The Documentary History of the Ratification of the Constitution*. RICHARD LEFFLER serves as associate editor. This multi-volume collection is co-sponsored by the National Historical Publications and Records Commission, the National Endowment for the Humanities, and the University of Wisconsin, Madison, where the project is housed. With six volumes published to date, *The Documentary History* is the definitive source for the debate over the ratification of the Constitution.

STEPHEN L. SCHECHTER is Associate Professor of Political Science and History at Russell Sage College, where he also directs the Upper Hudson program. He is the editor of various publications, including *Teaching About American Federal Democracy* and *Local History in the Classroom*.

JACK VANDERHOOF is Professor of History at Russell Sage College. He has lectured widely on the subject of history and fiction. His publications include *A Bibliography of Novels Related to American Frontier and Colonial History*, cited by the American Library Association as an outstanding reference work.

Designed by William Kasdorf

Typeset in Baskerville
on a Penta-driven APS-μ5
by Impressions, Inc.,
P.O. Box 3304, Madison, Wisconsin 53704,
from text originally input on
Xerox and IBM PC diskettes

Printed on 55# Sebago Natural
and perfect bound in 80# Curtis Linen Eggshell cover

ON THE COVER:

This illustration appeared in the Charleston *City Gazette* on 11 August 1788 as a preface to the report of New York's ratification of the Constitution. The *City Gazette* first used a similar illustration with eight pillars on 28 May 1788 in its report of the ratification of the Constitution by South Carolina on 23 May. On 16 July the illustration, showing nine pillars, accompanied the report of Virginia's ratification, and on 22 July another pillar was added for New Hampshire.

In the late eighteenth century, the thirteen original states were traditionally listed in geographical order from north to south. This practice, followed in Congress in recording votes and signing official documents, was used in this illustration. The state columns start with New Hampshire on the left and end with Georgia on the right. The two missing columns are therefore easily identifiable as Rhode Island and North Carolina.